Advance praise for
TRUE REFUGE

"Tara Brach writes and teaches with an open and loving heart. She reminds us that we each have the capacity to connect to ourselves and others in a deep and lasting way. The techniques she offers for establishing a practice are both simple and profound, and accessible to all."
—Sharon Salzberg, author of *Lovingkindness* and *Real Happiness*

"This profound and timely book is rich with practical help coming from Tara's long professional experience and her heartfelt openness about her own pains and losses. Based on a deep understanding of the body and mind, and illuminated by contemplative wisdom, *True Refuge* will help you find the sanctuary inside that brings strength, peace, and healing."
—Rick Hanson, Ph.D., author of *Buddha's Brain: The Practical Neuroscience of Happiness, Love, and Wisdom*

"Tara Brach's accessible invitation to learn how to find refuge and solace in the interior sanctuary—our sacred spiritual center—and rely on it through thick and thin, is a marvelous contribution to the applied Buddhism and mindfulness movement currently bringing revolutionary transformation to our agitated time and place."
—Lama Surya Das, author of *Awakening the Buddha Within: Tibetan Wisdom for the Western World* and founder of the Dzogchen Center and Dzogchen Retreats

"The truth that compassion—warm-hearted, wise attention—is the fundamental ground out of which healing, reconciliation, and new growth happens is the leitmotif of this book. Tara's voice, so gentle it might be singing, is the medium that makes that message ring clear. To read the book is to feel consoled."
—Sylvia Boorstein, author of *Happiness Is an Inside Job: Practicing for a Joyful Life*

"A powerful and seminal book. Tara Brach is one of the great teachers of our time. In *True Refuge* she gives a priceless gift lighting the path to emotional healing while opening us up to a deeper connection to life. Read it carefully, bring it into your heart and you will discover a freedom you may not have thought existed before."

—Elisha Goldstein, Ph.D., author of *The Now Effect* and co-author of *A Mindfulness-Based Stress Reduction Workbook*

"This is a beautifully written book that directly taps into the beating heart of wisdom and compassion. It offers useful, pragmatic advice on how to deepen one's mindfulness practice and have greater self-compassion when faced with suffering. A wonderful follow-up to *Radical Acceptance*, this is a must-read for anyone who wants to develop greater insight and open-heartedness in their life."

—Kristin Neff, Ph.D., author of *Self-Compassion*

"There is something very special about this exquisitely written book— its clarity, beauty, simplicity and humanity practically *sing* to you. Inspiring and uplifting to read, it also has eminently practical, implementable, step-by-step guidance to practice and live by. While turning the pages, I thought of a half dozen people who could really use this book as a friendly, loving reference point—myself included!"

—Belleruth Naparstek, author of *Invisible Heroes* and creator of the Health Journeys guided imagery audio series

"Tara Brach's new book is aptly named. *True Refuge* is not only a book *about* the three great classical refuges of Buddhism, but it is a book that *is itself* a refuge. Tara does not shrink from sharing her own suffering, doubt, and confusion, and the very personal nature of this book makes its highly practical teachings go in so much deeper. This book is a rich mine of wisdom: I will read it over and over again."

—Stephen Cope, author of *The Great Work of Your Life: A Guide for the Journey to Your True Calling*

"This excellent book on finding refuge—which is protection from fear and negative emotions—is a wise, timely, and practical guide. Tara Brach's writing is lucid, with well-chosen examples and stories. Most important, she has given us a book that is accessible, insightful, and practical. Tara shows us how each of us can cultivate an awakened heart, which is a gift for us all."

—Tsoknyi Rinpoche, author of *Open Heart, Open Mind*

"Meditation has been important to me and meaningful to the teams I've coached. People often ask me for good books on the topic. I can now recommend *True Refuge*—it's just the ticket for people looking for technical information about the compassionate path."

—Phil Jackson, former NBA coach of the World Champion Chicago Bulls and Los Angeles Lakers

"Tara Brach has eloquently written the ultimate guidebook, filled with engaging stories and deep wisdom. In this world of change and instability, *True Refuge* reveals that the safe haven we are looking for is right inside the human heart, and it shows us how to get there. This book is a real treasure!"

—James Baraz, co-founding teacher, Spirit Rock Meditation Center, author of *Awakening Joy: 10 Steps That Will Put You on the Road to Real Happiness*

"This book is a rare gift. It speaks to the tender heart in us all when things go wrong in our lives. In a natural and deeply personal way, Tara Brach accompanies the reader into 'presence,' a warm embrace of who we are and the life we're given. She offers tools and gentle guidance for living safely and peacefully even in the midst of challenging circumstances. At once inspiring, humble, and wise, this book uniquely captures the ineffable, healing essence of mindfulness meditation practice.

—Christopher K. Germer, Ph.D., clinical instructor, Harvard Medical School, and author of *The Mindful Path to Self-Compassion*

ALSO BY TARA BRACH, PH.D.

Radical Acceptance

TRUE REFUGE

TRUE REFUGE

Finding Peace and Freedom
in Your Own Awakened Heart

TARA BRACH, Ph.D.

BANTAM BOOKS
NEW YORK

The names, identifying characteristics, and other details of the clients, students, and other case studies presented in this book have been changed to protect the privacy and preserve the confidences of those individuals and their families.

Published in the United States by Bantam Books, an imprint of
The Random House Publishing Group, a division of Random House, Inc., New York.

BANTAM BOOKS and the rooster colophon are registered trademarks of Random House, Inc.

Library of Congress Cataloging-in-Publication Data

Brach, Tara.
True refuge : finding peace and freedom in your own awakened heart / Tara Brach.
p.   cm.
ISBN 978-0-553-80762-2
eBook ISBN 978-0-345-53862-8
I. Buddhism—Psychology.   2. Emotions—Religious aspects—Buddhism.   I. Title.
BQ4570.P76B68 2012
294.3'444—dc23   2012016158

Printed in the United States of America on acid-free paper

www.bantamdell.com

8 9

Book design by Karin Batten

To Jonathan, whose heart is a loving,
safe refuge, and good humor,
one of this life's great delights

CONTENTS

Part III: The Gateway of Love

Part IV: The Gateway of Awareness

GUIDED REFLECTIONS AND MEDITATIONS

I wish I could show you
When you are lonely or in darkness,
The astonishing light
Of your own Being!

HAFIZ *(as translated by Daniel Ladinsky)*

⊷

LOVING LIFE
NO MATTER WHAT

My earliest memories of being happy are of playing in the ocean. When our family began going to Cape Cod in the summer, the low piney woods, high dunes, and wide sweep of white sand felt like a true home. We spent hours at the beach, diving into the waves, bodysurfing, practicing somersaults underwater. Summer after summer, our house filled with friends and family—and later, with spouses and new children. It was a shared heaven. The smell of the air, the open sky, the ever-inviting sea made room for everything in my life—including whatever difficulties I was carrying in my heart.

Then came the morning not so long ago when two carloads of friends and family members took off for the beach without me. From the girl who had to be pulled from the water at suppertime, I'd become a woman who was no longer able to walk on sand or swim in the ocean. After two decades of mysteriously declining health, I'd finally gotten a diagnosis: I had a genetic disease with no cure, and the primary treatment was painkillers. As I sat on the deck of our summer house and watched the cars pull out of the driveway, I felt ripped apart by grief and loneliness. In the midst of my tears, I was aware of a single longing. "Please, please, may I find a way to peace, *may I love life no matter what.*"

This book came out of my own search for a place of peace, connectedness, and inner freedom, even in the face of life's greatest challenges. I call this place "true refuge" because it does not depend on anything outside ourselves—a certain situation, a person, a cure, even a particular mood or emotion. The yearning for such refuge is universal. It is what lies beneath all our wants and fears. We long to know we can handle what's coming. We want to trust ourselves, to trust this life. We want to live from the fullness of who we are.

My search for refuge led me deeper into the spiritual teachings and Buddhist meditation practices that were so central to my life. I am a clinical psychologist and had been teaching meditation for over thirty years. I am also the founder and senior teacher at the Insight Meditation Center in Washington, D.C. My inner work and work with others gave rise to my first book, *Radical Acceptance*, and I also started training psychologists and laypeople on how to bring meditation into emotional healing. At the time of my diagnosis, as the insecurity of this existence shook my inner world, the teachings that had always guided me became more embodied and alive.

In the Buddhist tradition in which I teach, the Pali word "dukkha" is used to describe the emotional pain that runs through our lives. While it is often translated as "suffering," dukkha encompasses all our experiences of stress, dissatisfaction, anxiety, sorrow, frustration, and basic unease in living. The word "dukkha" originally referred to a cart with a damaged wheel. When we are suffering, we are out of balance, jolting uncomfortably along the road of our life. We feel broken or "off," disconnected from a sense of belonging. Sometimes this shows up as mild restlessness or discontent; at other times, as the acute pain of grief or grip of fear. But if we listen deeply, we will detect beneath the surface of all that troubles us an underlying sense that we are alone and unsafe, that something is wrong with our life.

In *Radical Acceptance*, I wrote about the deep and pervasive suffering of shame, the pain of believing that "something is wrong *with me*." I am now addressing dukkha in a broader sense. Since that book was published, I've encountered major loss—the death of my father, the physical and mental decline of dear ones, and the challenges of my own chronic illness. Many of my students have also had their lives overturned. Some have been uprooted from their jobs; they worry about having enough to live on, and are hungry for meaningful work. Others are estranged from family and friends and long for connection. Many more are grappling with aging, sickness, and the inevitability of death. For them, "something is wrong with me" has become entangled with the pain of struggling against life itself.

The Buddha taught that this experience of insecurity, isolation, and basic "wrongness" is unavoidable. We humans, he said, are conditioned to feel separate and at odds with our changing and out-of-control life. And from this core feeling unfolds the whole array of our disruptive emotions—fear, anger, shame, grief, jealousy—all of our limiting stories, and the reactive behaviors that add to our pain.

But the Buddha also offered a radical promise, one that Buddhism shares with many wisdom traditions: We can find true refuge within our own hearts and minds—right here, right now, in the midst of our moment-to-moment lives. We find true refuge whenever we recognize the silent space of awareness behind all our busy doing and striving. We find refuge whenever our hearts open with tenderness and love. We find refuge whenever we connect with the innate clarity and intelligence of our true nature.

In *True Refuge*, I use the word "presence" to try to capture the immediacy and aliveness of this intrinsic awareness. Presence is hard to describe, because it's an embodied experience, not a concept. For me, when I sense the silent, inner wakefulness that is here, I come home to a sense of wholeness. I'm at home in my body and heart, at home in the earth and with all beings. Presence creates a boundless sanctuary where there's room for everything in my life—even the illness that keeps me from surfing the waves.

This book is filled with stories of people discovering presence in the midst of crisis and confusion. It also explores some of the greatest challenges I myself have faced over these past decades. I hope some of these stories connect to the heart of your own situation. Through them, we'll explore the forces that draw us away from presence, and why we so often pursue false refuges. I also suggest many different practices—some ancient, some new, some specifically supported by modern neuroscience— that have reliably opened me and many others to presence. These include one of the most practical, in-the-trenches mindfulness meditations I've worked with in years. Called RAIN (an acronym for the four steps of the process), it helps you address many difficult emotions on the spot and can be personalized to almost any situation.

True Refuge is organized around three fundamental gateways to refuge that are found in every stream of Buddhism as well as within many other traditions: truth (of the present moment), love, and awareness. As you will see, each of these gateways opens us directly to healing and spiritual freedom. They are the keys to overcoming very common difficulties such as obsessive thinking, limiting beliefs, and traumatic fear, and to tapping into self-compassion and intimacy in relationships. They are also the key to finding peace and happiness, to being at home in our lives.

That day on Cape Cod I didn't know if I could ever be happy living with a future of pain and physical limitation. While I was crying, Cheylah, one of our standard poodles, sat down beside me and began nudging me with concern. Her presence was comforting; it reconnected me to the here and now. After I'd stroked her for a while, we got up for a walk. She took the lead as we meandered along an easy path overlooking the bay. In the aftermath of grieving, I was silent and open. My heart held everything—the soreness of my knees, the expanse of sparkling water, Cheylah, my unknown future, the sound of gulls. Nothing was missing, nothing was wrong. These moments of true refuge foreshadowed one of the great gifts of the Buddhist path—that we can be "happy for no reason." We can love life just as it is.

If you are drawn to this book, you are already awakening on a path of true refuge. Perhaps you've been at war with yourself and want to be more kind. You may be struggling with an addiction and long to free your life from compulsion and shame. You may be facing loss—of a job, of someone you love, of your health in body and mind—and wonder if your heart will ever be whole again. You may be grieving the enormity of suffering in our world and searching for a way to be part of the healing. *No matter how challenging the situation, there is always a way to take refuge in a healing and liberating presence.*

Writing this book has been a journey of discovery, as I learned every day from my own experiences and from those around me. My prayer is that these teachings and practices will offer you company and confidence as we walk the spiritual path together.

TRUE
REFUGE

PART I

OUR SEARCH
FOR REFUGE

ONE

WINDS OF HOMECOMING

Ah, not to be cut off,
not through the slightest partition
shut out from the law of the stars.
The inner—what is it?
if not intensified sky,
hurled through with birds and deep
with the winds of homecoming.

RAINER MARIA RILKE

At the end of a daylong meditation workshop, Pam, a woman in her late sixties, drew me aside. She and her husband, Jerry, were at the end of an ordeal that had begun three years earlier. Now near death from lymphoma, Jerry had asked Pam to be his primary caregiver, the person guiding and supporting him in his passing. "Tara," she implored, "I really need some help."

Pam was desperate to do anything she could for her husband. "I wanted so much to save him," she told me. "I looked into ayurvedic medicine, acupuncture, Chinese herbs, every alternative treatment I could find, tracked every test result . . . We were going to beat this thing." She sat back wearily in her chair, shoulders slumped. "And now I'm keeping in touch with everyone, giving updates . . . coordinating hospice care. If he's not napping I try to make him comfortable, read to him . . ."

I responded gently, "It sounds like you've been trying really hard to take good care of Jerry . . . and it's been *very busy.*" At these words, she gave me a smile of recognition. "Hmm, busy. That sounds crazy, doesn't it?" She paused. "As far back as I can remember I've really been busy . . . But now . . . well, I just can't sit back and let him go without a fight."

Pam was silent for a few moments and then she looked at me anxiously. "He could die any day now, Tara . . . Isn't there some Buddhist practice or ritual that I should learn? Is there something I should be reading? What about *The Tibetan Book of the Dead*? How can I help him with this . . . with dying?"

Before answering, I asked her to listen inwardly, and to let me know what she was feeling. "I love him so much and I'm terrified that I'm going to let him down." She began weeping. After some time, she spoke again. "All my life I've been afraid of falling short, I guess I've always been on overdrive trying to do a better job. Now I'm afraid I'm going to fail at the thing that matters most. He'll die and I'll feel *really* alone, because I failed him."

"Pam," I said, "you've already done so much . . . but the time for all that kind of activity is over. At this point, you don't have to make anything happen, you don't need to *do* anything." I waited a moment and then added, "Just *be* with him. Let him know your love through the fullness of your presence."

At this difficult time I was calling on a simple teaching that is central to my work with my meditation students and therapy clients: It is through realizing loving presence as our very essence, through *being* that presence, that we discover true freedom. In the face of inevitable loss, this timeless presence brings healing and peace to our own hearts and to the hearts of others.

Pam nodded. She and Jerry were Catholic, she told me, and the mindfulness practices they'd learned in my weekly class had helped them experience their faith more deeply. But Pam was now overwhelmed by Jerry's dramatic turn for the worse: "I know the hospice aides are doing everything they can to help, but I just feel like this shouldn't be happening—so much exhaustion, so much pain. No one should have to go through something like this; it's just plain wrong." For Pam, as for so many people, sickness felt unfair, an enemy to be resisted. She was face-to-face with *dukkha*, the suffering in life.

"In those most difficult moments," I suggested, "you might pause and recognize what you are feeling—the fear or anger or grief—and then inwardly whisper the phrase 'I consent.'" I'd recently heard this phrase from Father Thomas Keating, and thought that as a Catholic, Pam might find it particularly valuable. Saying "I consent," or as I more frequently teach, "yes," relaxes our armoring against the present moment and allows us to meet life's challenges with a more open heart.

Pam was nodding her head, but she had an intent, worried look. "I want to do this, Tara, but when I'm most upset, my mind speeds up. I start talking to myself . . . I talk to him . . . How will I *remember* to pause?" It was a good question, one that I'm frequently asked. "You probably will forget, at least some of the time," I responded, "and that's totally natural. All you can do is have the intention to pause, the intention to feel what is going on and 'let be.'" Pam's face softened with understanding. "That I can do. I can intend, with all my heart, to be there for Jerry."

OUR CRY FOR HELP

"All religions and spiritual traditions begin with the cry 'Help!'," wrote nineteenth-century American psychologist and philosopher William James. In my counseling sessions and meetings with meditation students, the cries for help I hear come in many forms. "How do I handle this clutching fear?" "This sense of failure, of unworthiness?" "This anguish of loss?"

As Pam was finding, no matter how hard we try to control life, we have no sway over the bedrock realities of change, loss, and mortality. Insecurity is inherent in this impermanent world. And so we pray for refuge: "Help! I want to feel protected and safe . . . loved and at peace. I want to belong to something larger than just myself. I want to feel at home in my life."

Yet if we look honestly at our lives, it's clear that we don't often respond wisely to our own deep prayer. Rather than seeking true refuge, we turn toward what I call *false refuges*. They are false because while they may provide a temporary sense of comfort or security, they create more suffering in the long run. We might, like Pam, have a fear of failure and take refuge in staying busy, in striving to perform well, or in taking care of others. Or we might feel unlovable and take refuge in pursuing wealth or success. Maybe we fear being criticized, and take refuge in avoiding risks and always pleasing others. Or we feel anxious or empty and take refuge in alcohol, overeating, or surfing the Web. Instead of consenting and opening to what we are actually feeling, our turn toward false refuges is a way of avoiding emotional pain. But this only takes us further from real comfort, further from home.

As long as we pursue false refuges, suffering will pursue us. How many of us sleep fitfully, waking up in the middle of the night full of anxiety or dread? Or struggle to get through the day, too tense or restless to savor what's going on right now? Instead of bringing us satisfaction or banishing our fear, our false refuges fuel a fundamental self-doubt. Pam had dedicated herself wholeheartedly to Jerry's care. Yet nothing she did seemed like enough. Her anxious efforts to "do it right" reinforced her sense of inadequacy, of not being at home with who she was and what she could offer to Jerry.

Often it is not until we are jolted by crisis—a betrayal of the heart, the death of a loved one, our own impending death—that we see clearly: Our false refuges don't work. They can't save us from what we most fear, the pain of loss and separation. A crisis has the power to shatter our illusions, to reveal that in this impermanent world, there really is no ground to stand on, nothing we can hold on to. At these times, when our lives seem to be falling apart, the call for help can become fully conscious. This call is the heart's longing for a refuge that is vast enough to embrace our most profound experience of suffering.

COMING HOME TO LOVING PRESENCE

A month after my conversation with Pam, she called to let me know that Jerry had died. Then she told me what had happened the evening after our talk. When she arrived back at their apartment, she had invited Jerry to join her in silent prayer. "When we were done," she told me, "we shared our prayers. I let him know how much I wanted him to feel my love." Pam was quiet for a moment, then her voice choked up. "He had been praying for the same . . . in reverse. We just hugged and cried."

Even in those final weeks, Pam acknowledged, she had struggled with the urge to be busy, to find ways to feel useful. One afternoon, Jerry began talking about having only a short time left, and about not being afraid of death. She bent over, gave him a kiss, and said quickly, "Oh dear, today's been a good day, you seemed to have more energy. Let me make you some herbal tea." He fell silent, and the quietness shook her. "It became so clear to me in those moments that anything other than listening to what was really going on—anything other than being fully present—actually separated us. I hadn't wanted us to admit to what was happening out loud; that just made it too real. So I avoided reality by suggesting a cup of tea. But my attempt to steer away from the truth took me away from him, and that was heartbreaking."

While Pam boiled water for tea, she prayed, asking that her heart be fully present with Jerry. This prayer guided her in the days that followed. "Over those last few weeks I had to keep letting go of all my ideas of how his dying should be and what else I should be doing, and just remind myself to say 'I consent.' At first I was mechanically repeating the words, but after a few days I felt as if my heart actually started consenting." She described how she would pause when she was gripped by strong feelings and check inside to see what was going on. When her gut tightened with clutches of fear and feelings of helplessness, she'd stay with those feelings, consenting to the depth of her vulnerability. When the restless urge to "do something" arose, she'd notice that and be still, letting it come and go. And as the great waves of grief rolled through, she'd again say, "I consent," opening herself to the huge aching weight of loss.

This intimate presence with her inner experience allowed Pam to fully attend to Jerry. As she put it, "When all of me was truly consenting to the fear and pain, I knew how to take care of him. I sensed when to whisper words of encouragement or just listen, ways to reassure him with touch . . . how to sing to him, be quiet with him. How to *be* with him."

Before she ended the call, Pam shared with me what she considered to be the gift of her last days with Jerry, the answer to her prayers: "In the silence I could see past a sense of 'him' and 'me.' It became clear that we were a field of loving—total openness, warmth, light. He's gone, but that field of loving is always with me. My heart knows that I came home . . . truly I came home to love."

LEARNING TO TRUST THE WAVES

Pam's willingness to be present with her inner life, no matter how painful, made it possible for her to connect with the vastness of love. Her growing capacity for presence, for staying with the truth of her moment-to-moment experience, enabled her to find her way home even in the midst of great loss. Presence is the essence of true refuge.

A different kind of loss drew me to my first Buddhist mindfulness retreat. At the time, my son, Narayan, was four and I was on the verge of divorce. I had already benefited from Buddhist meditation, and I hoped that a period of intensive practice would help me navigate my anxiety and stress. After leaving Narayan with my parents in New Jersey, I drove through a winter snowstorm to the retreat center in Massachusetts. During that slow, icy drive, I had plenty of time to reflect on what most mattered to me. I didn't want a breakup that would bury the love I still shared with my husband; I didn't want us to turn into uncaring, even hostile, strangers. And I didn't want a breakup that would deprive Narayan of feeling secure and loved. My deep prayer was that through all that was happening, I'd find a way to stay connected with my heart.

Over the next five days, through hours of silent meditation, I cycled many times through periods of clarity and attentiveness, followed by stretches when I was swamped in sleepiness, plagued by physical discomfort, or lost in a wandering mind. Early one evening I became inundated by thoughts about the upcoming months: Should my husband and I hire lawyers or a mediator to handle the process of divorce? When should we move to separate residences? And, most important, how should I be there for our son during this painful transition? As each anxious thought surfaced, I wanted to really dig in and work everything out in my mind. Yet something in me knew I needed to stay with the unpleasant feelings in my body. A verse from Ryokan, an eighteenth-century Zen poet, came to mind: *To find the Buddhist law, drift east and west, come and go, entrusting yourself to the waves.*

The "Buddhist law" refers to the truth of how things really are. We can't understand the nature of reality until we let go of controlling our experience. There's no way to see clearly what is going on if on some level we are attempting to ignore or bypass the stormy weather. During the last few days of the retreat I tried to let go over and over, but felt repeatedly stymied by my well-worn strategy for feeling better—figuring things out. Now Ryokan's verse was rife with possibility: Perhaps I could *entrust* myself to the waves. Perhaps the only way to real peace was by opening to life just as it was. Otherwise, behind my efforts to manage things, I'd always sense a lurking threat, something right around the corner that was going to cause trouble.

I tried to open to the waves of feeling, but my old habits didn't give up easily. I'd contact some tightness in my chest, but flip right back into worrying about my son's new preschool, about carpooling, about how to find a babysitter with more flexible hours. Then I'd become hypercritical, harshly judging myself for "wasting" my retreat time. Gradually, I recognized that my heart was clenched tight, afraid to let the intensity of life wash through me. I needed help in "entrusting."

The teachers had been leading the whole group in a lovingkindness meditation each afternoon, and I decided to try weaving this practice into my sitting. The classical form of the meditation consists of sending loving prayers to ourselves and to widening circles of other beings. I began to offer kind wishes to myself: "May I be happy and at ease; may I be happy and at ease." At first, repeating the words felt like a superficial mental exercise, but soon something shifted. My heart meant it: I cared about my own life, and becoming conscious of that caring softened some of the tightness around my heart.

Now I could more easily give myself to the waves of fear and sorrow, and simply notice the drifting thoughts and physical sensations—squeezing and soreness—that were coming and going. Whenever the worries that had been snagging me appeared, I sensed that they too were waves, tenacious ones that pressed uncomfortably on my chest. By not resisting, by letting the waves wash through me, I began to relax. Rather than fighting the stormy surges, I rested in an ocean of awareness that embraced all the moving waves. I had arrived in a sanctuary that felt large enough to hold whatever was going on in my life.

NATURAL PRESENCE: WAKEFUL,
OPEN, AND TENDER

Presence is not some exotic state that we need to search for or manufacture. In the simplest terms, *it is the felt sense of wakefulness, openness, and tenderness that arises when we are fully here and now with our experience.* You've surely tasted presence, even if you didn't call it that. Perhaps you've felt it lying awake in bed and listening to crickets on a hot summer night. You might have sensed presence while walking alone in the woods. You might have arrived in full presence as you witnessed someone dying or being born.

Presence is the awareness that is intrinsic to our nature. It is immediate and embodied, perceived through our senses. If you look closely at any experience of presence, you'll find the three qualities I mentioned above:

Our *wakefulness* is the basic consciousness that is aware of what is happening, the intelligence that recognizes the changing flow of moment-by-moment experience—the sounds that are here around us, the sensations of our body, our thoughts. It is the "knowing" quality of awareness.

Our *openness* is the space of awareness in which life takes place. This awareness does not oppose our experience, or evaluate it in any way. Even when our feelings and thoughts are painfully stirred up, it simply recognizes what's happening and allows our emotional life to be as it is. Like the sky when weather systems come and go, the open space of awareness is unstained by the changing expressions of life moving through us. And yet awareness has a natural sensitivity and the capacity to express warmth. This responsiveness is what I call *tenderness.* Our tenderness allows us to respond with compassion, love, and awe to whatever arises, in all its beauty and sorrow.

We can refer to these as the three qualities of presence, but in fact they're inseparable. Think of a sunlit sky. There is no way to separate the light of the sky from the space it illuminates; there is no way to separate the warmth we feel from the space and light around us. Light, space, and warmth are all inextricable expressions of a whole.

Our longing to live fully—from our beingness—calls us home to this natural presence. Our realization of truth arises from the lucidity of presence. Love flows from the receptivity of presence. Aliveness and creativity flower when we inhabit the openness of presence. All that we cherish is already here, sourced in presence. Each time we cry out for help, our longing can remind us to turn toward our true refuge, toward the healing and freedom of natural presence.

COMING BACK TO PRESENCE

After my retreat, I returned home with the intention of taking refuge in presence whenever I was irritated, anxious, and tight. I was alert when the first flare-up occurred, a week after I got back. My ex-husband called to say he couldn't take care of Narayan that evening, leaving me scrambling to find a babysitter so I could see my therapy clients. "I'm the breadwinner, and I can't even count on him for *this!*" my mind sputtered. "Once again he's not doing his share, once again he's letting me down!" But when I was done for the day I took some time to pause and touch into the judgment and blame lingering in my body, and my righteous stance softened. I sat still as the blaming thoughts and swells of irritation came and went. Underneath the resentment was an anxious question: "How will I manage?" As I let the subterranean waves of anxiety move through me, I found a quiet inner space that had more breathing room—and more perspective. Of course I couldn't figure out how the future would play out. The only time I had was right now, and this moment was okay. From this space I could sense my ex-husband's stress about finding a new place to live, working out our schedules, and more deeply, adapting to a different future than he had imagined. This helped me feel more tolerant and kind.

At other times I was much more resistant to entrusting myself to the waves, especially when my ex and I disagreed on finances or on the particulars of our custody arrangement. Any kind of entrusting felt like a setup for getting taken advantage of. I found that I first needed to hold myself with compassion, really honoring my need to take care of myself. Then I could regard even my most angry, mean-spirited thoughts with forgiveness. Gradually my heart would unclench some and I'd allow my-self to simply feel the painful currents of anger and fear moving through me. Then, as I'd experienced at the retreat, I'd reconnect with a spacious presence that included whatever was happening, and it allowed me to regard my life with more wisdom. Resting in this presence, I could begin to more clearly distinguish my own healthy needs—for separating out our finances fairly, for having our own living spaces—from my anxious and distrustful impulses. I felt at home in myself when I stood up for what I needed, but not when I tried to exert a tightfisted control. And, as I discovered, the more my ex-husband sensed me trying to be respect-ful and flexible, the more he responded in kind.

Taking refuge in presence made it possible for me and my ex-husband to continue to be dear friends and to still consider each other family. But it wasn't easy. Both of us were dedicated to spiritual practice, so we en-tered the separation process naively, believing that we could navigate it in an honorable, mature way. Neither of us anticipated that when we were really stressed, we'd purposefully act in hurtful ways. Yet at times we did—we misled each other, we said things we regretted, we some-times exuded anger or disdain. What carried us through this emotion-ally painful season was a commitment to keep our son's best interests in the foreground, and not to give up on loving each other. The practice of taking refuge in presence allowed me to forgive both of us for our hu-manness and helped to keep our caring alive.

When we are suffering, our call of "Help!" can arise from a deep place within us. As Pam found at Jerry's side, and as I experienced at the end of my first marriage, our sincere longing awakens us. It guides us to the wholeness and freedom that can be found in the present moment. And yet, when we're in trouble, here and now is often the last place we want to be. What stops us from coming home to the true refuge of pres-ence? What stops us from choosing to be here? My name for this chal-lenge to presence is "the trance of small self," and we will explore it in the following chapter.

Guided Meditation: A Pause for Presence

A natural entry into presence is through your body. You can do this short meditation anytime you have a bit of quiet and privacy.

———— ✼ ————

Find a place to sit comfortably and close your eyes. Begin with three conscious breaths: Inhale long and deep, filling the lungs, then exhale slowly, sensing a letting go of any tensions in your body and mind.

Invite your awareness to fill your whole body. Can you imagine your physical form as a field of sensations? Can you feel the movement and quality of the sensations—tingling, vibrating, heat or cool, hard or soft, tight or flowing? Take a few moments to bring your full attention to this dance of sensations.

Now let your awareness open out into the space around you. Can you imagine receiving the symphony of sounds, letting it wash through you? Can you listen to the changing play of sounds, not just with your ears but with your whole awareness? Take a few moments to bring an open attention to listening to sounds.

Keeping your eyes closed, let your awareness receive the play of images and light at the eyelids. You might notice a flickering of light and dark or certain shapes, shadows or figures of light. Take a few moments to attend to seeing.

Feeling your breath and sensing the space around you, be receptive to any scents that might be in the air. Discover what it is like to smell and receive the odors present in the surrounding area.

Now let all your senses be wide open, your body and mind relaxed and receptive. Allow life to flow freely through you. Take as long as you'd like, listening to and feeling your moment-to-moment experience. Notice the changing flow of sensations, sounds, aliveness, and also the background of presence that is here. Let yourself appreciate this awake, inner space of presence. When you are finished, sense the possibility of bringing an alert, open awareness to whatever you are doing next.

———— ✼ ————

As you move through the day, pause periodically and briefly reawaken your senses, primarily by feeling bodily sensations and listening to sounds. With practice, you will become increasingly at home in natural presence.

TWO

LEAVING HOME: THE TRANCE OF SMALL SELF

Whatever came from being
is caught up in being, drunkenly
forgetting the way back.

RUMI

We are born with a beautiful open spirit, alive with innocence and resilience. But we bring this goodness into a difficult world.

Imagine that at the moment of birth we begin to develop a space suit to help us navigate our strange new environment. The purpose of this space suit is to protect us from violence and greed and to win nurturance from caretakers who, to varying degrees, are bound by their own self-absorption and insecurities. When our needs aren't met, our space suit creates the best defensive and proactive strategies it can. These include tensions in the body and emotions such as anger, anxiety, and shame; mental activity such as judging, obsessing, and fantasizing; and a whole array of behavioral tactics for going after whatever is missing—security, food, sex, love.

Our space suit is essential for survival, and some of its strategies do help us become productive, stable, and responsible adults. And yet the same space suit that protects us can also prevent us from moving spontaneously, joyfully, and freely through our lives.

This is when our space suit becomes our prison. Our sense of who we are becomes defined by the space suit's "doings," its strengths and weaknesses. We become identified with our skill in problem-solving or communicating; identified with our judgments and obsessions; identified with our anxiety and anger. "Identified" means that we think we *are* the space suit! It appears to us that we actually *are* the self who possesses the anxiety and anger; we *are* the self who judges; we *are* the self whom others admire; we *are* the self who is special or imperfect and alone.

When we become fused with the space suit, we begin living in what I call trance, and our sense of who we are is radically contracted. We have forgotten who is gazing through the space-suit mask; we have forgotten our vast heart and awareness. We have forgotten the mysterious presence that is always here, behind any passing emotion, thought, or action.

Living in trance is like being caught in a dream, and while we are in it we are cut off from our own moment-to-moment experience, disconnected from this living world. We have left home—our awareness and aliveness—and become unknowingly confined in a distorted fragment of reality.

We each have our own styles of leaving home—our space-suit strategies to cope with the pain of unmet needs. Yet waking up is a universal process. Slowly or quickly, we come to see that we've been living in a contracted and often painful reality. We want to reconnect with our innocence, our basic goodness. We want to know the truth of who we are. Our sincere longing turns us toward a path of true refuge.

This awakening began in my own life eight years before my first Buddhist retreat, and I'd like to share its beginnings with you. As you already know from chapter I, it certainly wasn't achieved all at once. Yet when the trance dissolves, even for a short time, we can see the potential for freedom and a path out of suffering.

THE PERFECTION PROJECT

For as long as I can remember I have yearned to know truth, to be aware and kind. When I discovered yoga in college, I was convinced I had found the fast track to becoming the person I wanted to be. Immediately after graduation, I entered an ashram—a dedicated yoga community—near Boston. I was sure that if I gave it my all, this path would lead to spiritual freedom.

Our community followed a rigorous regimen, rising before dawn for a cold shower, followed by several hours of yoga, meditation, chanting, and prayer. We also worked long hours running a yoga center, vegetarian restaurant, and retail store in Harvard Square. I was devoted and zealous, often getting up even earlier or staying up even later than my fellow yogis for additional spiritual practice.

My sincere spiritual longing was intertwined with a belief—one held by this and many similar spiritual and religious communities—that if we are to be happy and free, we must purify our egos of all selfishness, aggression, and insecurity. The highs of an athletic style of yoga and the sometimes rapturous feelings that emerged in meditation often reassured me that I was progressing. And yet at other times I'd become acutely aware of my "impurities," and throw myself at my spiritual practices with added vigor.

Such striving to be perfect is an outward sign of living in trance. My trance was fueled and sustained by the belief that I was a limited, not-okay self. Without being fully aware of it, I carried around many ideals about how a spiritual person should feel and look and behave. I also had ideals about how a "together" worldly person should be. I regularly scrutinized myself to see how I was doing compared to my current notion of that perfect self. Of course, I almost always fell short—right below the surface lurked my selfishness and mixed motives, my ambition and judgment. Looking back, I can see how the combination of genuine spiritual aspiration with unconscious perfectionism became so confusing and combustible. I can see how, as poet Danna Faulds puts it, "Perfection is not a prerequisite for anything but pain."

THE PERFECTION PROJECT COLLAPSES

The morning practices at the ashram energized me and freed me temporarily from the tension of a self-centered focus. I enjoyed the sweetness of meditating and chanting with my friends, and that camaraderie of breakfast and carpooling to work together. While this sense of well-being often lasted for hours, on one morning I had a distinctive crash.

At that time, I was director of our yoga center, and we were behind in promoting our major event of the year, which featured a number of well-known teachers. When the head of our local community arrived late to our weekly staff meeting, visibly upset, I asked him what was wrong.

"What's wrong?" he said in a barely controlled voice. "Just take a look at this." He thrust in front of me the flyer I had created for the event, and I immediately saw the typo in bold print—it was the wrong date. My heart sank, and I felt my face heat up with embarrassment. We had just printed three thousand of these flyers. I had screwed up big-time.

We talked about producing a new flyer, rescheduling the mailing, and pursuing other ways of getting the word out. Although my mind scrambled to solve the problem, the weight of failure sat like a big stone on my chest. At the end of our meeting I began an apology: "This was my responsibility," I said in a low monotone, "and I'm really sorry for messing up . . ." Then as I felt the others' eyes on me, I felt a flash of anger and the words tumbled out: "But, you know, this has been a huge amount of work and I've been totally on my own." I could feel my eyes burning, but I blinked back the tears. "It would have been nice if someone had been available to proofread . . . maybe this kind of thing wouldn't have happened."

For the rest of the week I was trapped in self-disgust. Hour after hour, my mind replayed every recent incident that highlighted my flaws. I saw myself lying to get out of a social obligation, exaggerating the size of my yoga classes to another teacher, gossiping with a friend to feel more like an insider. Instead of generosity and selfless service, my focus was on my own spiritual progress and striving to shine as a yoga teacher. Once again I found myself facing what I most disliked about myself: insecurity and self-centeredness. I felt disconnected from everyone around me, and stuck inside a self I didn't want to be.

As I struggled through those difficult days, it came to me that for as long as I could remember I had been trying to prove that I was okay, trying to reassure myself that I was making progress. I had a checklist of accomplishments—as a student and social activist, yogi and teacher. In all of these roles I'd tried to embody the definition of a "good person"— helpful, good listener, constructive confidant, "positive" in all situations. I was ardent about doing my yoga and meditations. Yet now, my sense of competency had been undone by a single mistake, my sense of being a good, spiritual person erased by a moment of angry reactivity.

Despite all of my self-improvement strategies, I was left face-to-face with the feeling of being a fundamentally flawed self.

SPACE-SUIT SELF IS SMALL SELF

When I teach about trance, students sometimes assume that any experience of self is bad or nonspiritual, that it is something they should try to eliminate or transcend. This certainly was my view in the ashram—my sense of self was inseparable from imperfection! Now I think of space-suit self as *a small self*, or, as it's more commonly known, "ego."

"Ego" usually comes with negative connotations, but in actuality, the small self (or ego) is a natural part of our conditioning and is essential for navigating life. In all humans, it arises from the sense of "I" and includes all the mental activities that promote and defend our functioning. It includes the fearful, protective self that some traditions refer to as the body of fear. It includes the wanting self that seeks to satisfy its needs for food and sex, security and respect.

Yet this small self is not our *true self*—it does not encompass the fullness of who we are. To put it another way, when we identify with a small self, we are perceiving ourselves as a cluster of ocean waves, not recognizing that we are made of ocean. When we realize our true self is ocean, the familiar pattern of waves—our fears and defensiveness, our wants and busyness—remains a part of us, but it does not define us.

Our mistaken identity is at the heart of the Buddha's teachings. He saw that we are all conditioned to hold on to pleasant or familiar experiences (which he called grasping or clinging), and to resist unpleasant experiences (which he called aversion). Both grasping and aversion narrow our sense of who we are—making us cling to an identity as a limited, individual, isolated existence.

This mistaken identity is sustained by the stories we tell ourselves. We believe that we are the voice in our head, we believe that we are the self-character in our story, and we believe that our view of the world "out there" is reality. You might have a crowded and stressful life, with more demands from work, family, and friends than you feel you can meet. Perhaps this summons up stories and feelings of how overwhelmed you are—of how you always have too much to do, how others expect too much from you, how you wish you had more free time but don't want to be irresponsible. Such stories easily lead to false refuges such as overwork, lying to protect your time, and overconsuming to numb anxiety. By continually replaying your stories, you strengthen your identification with a beleaguered, overly accommodating self. This becomes the dominant sense of who you are. You become trapped inside the space suit.

Or consider what happens if you believe that everyone is really out for their own welfare and that if you don't take advantage of a situation, someone else will. You might feel angry, even violated, whenever other people try to have their way. This might lead to false refuges such as controlling other people and focusing on accumulating power and possessions. By generating stories that sustain your worldview, your identity becomes consolidated as an aggressive, controlling self.

The more our stories are driven by fear, the more imprisoned we become in our confined sense of self. Not only does our mind believe, as I did, that "something is wrong with me," but our body is gripped by the emotions correlated with this belief—depression, shame, and even more fear. Then "something is wrong with me" is not just an idea we can easily release, it's a gut-level conviction. It *feels* real. When we've been hurt by someone, the belief that something is wrong with them also feels real. We are caught in a trance that divides us both from our inner life and from others.

Our identification with a small self is always generated and sustained outside the light of awareness. And it continues as long as we are unaware that our stories are simply stories (not reality), unaware of the raw feelings in our body, unaware of the fear or wanting that drives our behaviors. This is the nature of trance: It is incompatible with awareness and dissolves when we take refuge in presence.

AWAKENING FROM TRANCE

My week of self-aversion, triggered by a typo, began a lifelong process of recognizing and releasing my identification with a small self. Because my self-doubts seemed so "unspiritual," I didn't talk about them with any-one. At work I was all business. I withdrew from the casual banter and playfulness at group meals, and when I did try to be sociable, I felt like an impostor.

Several weeks later, the women in our ashram decided to form a sensitivity group where we could talk about personal challenges. I won-dered whether this might be an opportunity for me to get more real.

Our opening meeting took place one summer evening. For the first hour, as the other women talked about their stress at work, about chil-dren and health problems, I felt my anxiety build. Finally, when there was a pause in the conversation, my confession came pouring out. "I know I do a lot of yoga and teach a lot of classes, that it looks like I'm a helpful, caring person . . . That may be true in some ways, but it's also a front. What I'm covering up, what I don't want anyone to see, is how self-centered I am, how selfish and judgmental." After pausing and glancing around at the solemn faces, I took the real plunge. "This is hard to say, but . . . I don't trust that I'm a good person, and that makes it hard to really feel close with anyone."

I have no recollection of how the other women responded to my at-tempt at honesty. They might have felt empathetic or recognized similar feelings in themselves, but I was too caught up in my own shame to notice. I left the meeting as quickly as I could. Retreating to my room, I curled up in a fetal position on my futon and cried.

By naming my experience out loud to the group, I had stripped away a layer of the small self's protection. Feeling raw and exposed, I started mentally berating myself for having said anything. How could I face anyone the next day? I told myself I should get up right that moment and do some yoga. But instead I began trying to figure out what really had gone wrong, what was making me feel so badly about myself.

Suddenly I realized that this inner processing was yet more of the same. I was still trying to control things by figuring them out, by trying more practice, by trying to manage how others might see me. Recognizing these false refuges stopped me in my tracks—I didn't want to stay stuck.

An inner voice asked, "What would happen if, in this moment, I didn't try to do anything, to make anything different?" I immediately felt the visceral grip of fear and then a familiar sinking hole of shame—the very feelings I had been trying to avoid for as long as I could remember. But then the same inner voice whispered very quietly, a familiar refrain: "Just *let it be.*"

I stretched out on my back, took a few full breaths, and felt the weight of my body supported by the futon. Again and again my mind tried to escape into reviewing what I had said hours earlier, or rehearsing what else I could say to explain myself. Again and again the intention to "let it be" brought me back to the fear and shame I was experiencing. Sometime during the night, lying there alone in the darkness, these emotions gave way to grief. I was struck by how much of my life—my aliveness and loving—was lost when I was caught in feelings of unworthiness. I let myself open to that fully too, now sobbing deeply, until the grief gradually subsided.

I got up, sat on my cushion in front of my small meditation altar, and continued to pay attention. My mind quieted naturally and I became increasingly aware of my own inner experience—a silent presence that was suffused with tenderness. This presence was a space of being that included everything—waves of sadness, the feeling of my drying tears, the sounds of crickets, the humid summer night.

In this open space thoughts again bubbled up—the memory of being defensive at the staff meeting and my subsequent attempts to offer a real apology; then a flash-forward to me teaching the yoga class that I'd scheduled for the following morning, trying to project a positive, confident energy. This time, as these scenes came into view, I felt like I was witnessing a character in a play. The character was continually trying to protect herself, but in the process, she was disconnecting more and more from herself, from authenticity, from the potential sustenance of feeling connected to others. And in each scene, I saw her perpetually "doing" in order to feel better about herself, "doing" in order to avoid pain, "doing" in order to avoid failure.

As I sat there watching this play, I had, for the first time, a compelling sense that this character wasn't really "me." Her feelings and reactions were certainly familiar, but they were just ripples on the surface of what I really was. In the same way, everything happening at that moment—the thoughts, the sensations of sitting cross-legged, the tenderness, the tiredness—were part of my being but could not define me. My heart opened. How sad to have been living in such a confined world, how sad to have felt so driven and so alone!

TRANCE AND AWAKENING ARE BOTH NATURAL

When we are in trance and caught in an emotion like fear or shame or anger, our inner intelligence knows something is off-kilter. For a while, perhaps even decades, we may mistakenly think that "something is wrong with me" or "something is wrong with the world," that we need to fix our imperfections and somehow prevent ourselves from failing. Then either suddenly or gradually we recognize that *it is our mistaken perception of who we are that's causing the difficulty.* We see how we've been living inside the identity of a small, isolated, deficient self. At that moment of recognition, it's easy to pile on another delusion: "I'm flawed for being repeatedly caught in trance." And yet any awakening of awareness, of realizing and allowing "what is happening," begins to dissolve our narrowed identity and relax us into our natural wholeness.

That night by my altar, an old sense of self was falling away. Who was I, then? In those moments I sensed that the truth of what I was couldn't be contained in any idea or image of self. Rather, it was the space of presence itself—the silence, the wakeful openness—that felt like home. A feeling of gratitude and reverence filled me that has never entirely left.

As I've seen since, there are many paths to awakening, and most of them include training our attention, whether formally or informally. One friend took a painting class that taught her to see past the idea of "trees" or "clouds" into a mysterious world of changing forms, shades, shadows, and essence. As she described it, "Rather than being the observer noticing a particular kind of tree, there was simply this subjective intimacy of living textures, colors . . . I was part of a dance of aliveness." A parent I know told me how her awareness opened up after she took a course in talking with teens. As she listened to her daughter she consciously noticed and released her ideas of how her daughter should be, and simply took in the sounds of her voice, the look in her eyes, and what she sensed her daughter's heart was trying to communicate. Learning to listen without judgment also enlarged her sense of her own being: "I was no longer trapped in the critical parent . . . what a breath of fresh air!"

Most reliably, a regular meditation practice trains our attention to recognize the appearance of trance—our deeply familiar stories of failure or blame and the layers of fear, anger, or depression. In the chapter that follows, I'll show how we can practice coming back to presence again and again, and how the realization of who we are will continue to awaken in our consciousness. Over time, we will recognize trance more quickly when we get lost in it, and we will know that blaming ourselves—or others or the world—or striving for control or perfection is not the way out. Rather, the suffering of trance reminds us to come home into this moment and reconnect with the larger truth of what we are.

The experience of waking up to our true self can be hard to describe. As the Indian teacher Sri Nisargadatta says: "On realization you feel complete, fulfilled, free . . . and yet not always able to explain what happened . . . You can put it only in negative terms: 'Nothing is wrong with me any longer.'" When the veil of trance lifts, the pleasures and pains, the hopes and fears of our small, space-suit self still come and go, but they no longer define us. We no longer take things so personally, we no longer feel like "something is wrong with me." Instead we begin to trust the innocence and goodness of being that our trance had obscured. This turns out to be a tremendous relief and a taste of freedom.

Guided Meditation: Lovingkindness:
Being Kind to Yourself

The lovingkindness (*metta*, in Pali) meditation awakens us to our connectedness with all of life. Often the starting place is an offering of care
to our own being. This simple practice is a direct and powerful way to
awaken from trance. By regarding ourselves with kindness, we begin
to dissolve the identity of an isolated, deficient self. This creates the
grounds for including others in an unconditionally loving heart. (See
"Lovingkindness: Seeing Past the Mask," on page 223.)

---

*Sit comfortably and quietly, and relax any areas of the body that might be tense or tight.
Take some moments to feel the breath at the heart: breathing in, sense that you are receiving warmth and energy, breathing out, sense that you are letting go into openness.*

*Silently or in a whisper, begin offering yourself prayers of lovingkindness. To start,
choose four or five phrases that resonate for you. They might include:*

May I be filled with lovingkindness; may I be held in lovingkindness.
May I feel safe and at ease.
May I feel protected from inner and outer harm.
May I be happy.
May I accept myself just as I am.
May I touch deep, natural peace.
May I know the natural joy of being alive.
May I find true refuge within my own being.
May my heart and mind awaken; may I be free.

*As you repeat each phrase, open to whatever images and feelings arise with the
words. Approach the meditation as an experiment, sensing what words and images best
serve to soften and open your heart. You might explore placing your hand gently on top
of your heart to see if this deepens the experience of holding yourself with kindness.*

*Take as long as you like, offering yourself these phrases and reflecting on them. As
you end your meditation, sit quietly for a few moments and notice the feelings in your*

body and heart. *Is there a new sense of space and tenderness? Do you feel more at home in your own being?*

Throughout the day: *The more you remember to regard yourself with kindness, the more readily you will find a sense of connectedness and freedom from trance. You can practice anywhere, offering yourself the phrases of lovingkindness as you walk, drive, and conduct the tasks of daily life.*

If you become agitated or upset: *The prayers of lovingkindness can seem discordant and artificial if you are in the grip of fear, shame, or confusion. At times they may even highlight how undeserving and bad you feel about yourself. Without judgment, include this reactivity in the meditation: "May this too be held in lovingkindness." Then simply resume your meditation, accepting whatever thoughts or feelings arise.*

If the words seem mechanical: *Don't worry if you sometimes find yourself just reciting the phrases. Your heart has natural seasons of feeling open and closed. What most matters is your intention to awaken lovingkindness.*

—◆◆◆—

THREE

MEDITATION: THE PATH TO PRESENCE

Is there anything I can do to make myself enlightened?
As little as you can do to make the sun rise in the morning.
Then of what use are the spiritual exercises you prescribe?
To make sure you are not asleep when the sun begins to rise.

ANTHONY DE MELLO

Do you make regular visits to yourself?

RUMI

Jeff was convinced he had fallen out of love with his wife, Arlene, and that nothing could salvage their twenty-six-year marriage. He wanted relief from the oppressiveness of feeling continually judged and found wanting. Arlene, for her part, was hurt and angry because she felt Jeff avoided any real communication or emotional intimacy. As a last-ditch effort, she convinced him to attend a weekend workshop for couples sponsored by their church. Much to their surprise, they both left with a glimmer of hope for their future together. The message they took away was "Love is a decision." While we don't always feel loving, their guides at the workshop had insisted, love is here should we choose to awaken it.

Yet back at home, when their old styles of attacking and defending were triggered, deciding on love seemed like an ineffectual mental maneuver. Discouraged, Jeff sought me out for a counseling session. "I don't know how to get from point A to point B," he declared. "Like when we were together yesterday . . . my mind told me to decide on love, but that didn't make a difference . . . my heart was in lockdown. Arlene was blaming me for something, and all I wanted to do was get away from her!"

"Let's take another look at what happened yesterday," I suggested. I invited him to close his eyes, put himself back into the situation, and then let go of his notions of who was right or wrong. "Just let yourself experience what it is like in your body to feel blamed and want to get away." Jeff sat still, his face tightening in a grimace. "Keep allowing the feelings to be there," I said, "and find out what unfolds."

Gradually his face softened. "Now I'm feeling stuck and sad," he said. "We spend so much time caught in this. I withdraw, often without knowing it . . . that hurts her . . . she gets upset . . . then I very consciously want to get away. It's sad to be so trapped."

He looked up at me and I nodded with understanding. "What would it be like, Jeff, if instead of pulling away during this kind of encounter, you were able to let her know exactly what you were experiencing?" Then I added, "And if she too, without accusing you of anything, were able to report on her feelings?"

"We'd have to know what we were feeling!" he said with a small laugh. "We're usually too busy reacting."

"Exactly!" I responded. "You'd both have to be paying attention to what's going on inside you. And that runs counter to our conditioning. When we are emotionally stirred up, we're lost in our stories about what is happening, and caught in reflexive behaviors—like blaming the other person or finding a way to leave. That's why we need to train ourselves to pay attention, so that we are not at the mercy of our conditioning."

I went on to explain how the practice of meditation cultivates our capacity for presence, for directly contacting our real, moment-to-moment experience. This gives us more inner space and creativity in responding—rather than reacting—to our circumstances. When I suggested that he and Arlene might consider coming to my weekly meditation class, he readily agreed. They were both there the following Wednesday night, and a month later, they attended a weekend meditation retreat I was leading.

Some weeks after the retreat, the three of us spoke briefly after class.

Arlene said that thanks to their meditation practice, they were learning how to decide on love: "We have to *choose* presence with each other, over and over and over," she told me. "We have to choose presence when we're angry, presence when we aren't in the mood to listen, presence when we're alone and running the same old stories about how the other is wrong. Choosing presence is our way of opening our hearts." Jeff nodded his agreement. "I realized that it's not about getting from point A to point B," he said with a smile. "It's about bringing a full presence to point A, to the life of this moment, no matter what's going on. The rest unfolds from there."

Taking refuge in presence—choosing presence—requires training. When "point A" is unpleasant, the last thing we want to do is to stay and feel our experience. Rather than entrusting ourselves to the waves, we want to get away, to lash out, to numb ourselves, to do anything but touch what is real. Yet as Jeff and Arlene were realizing, false refuges keep us feeling small and defended. Only by deepening our attention and letting life be just as it is can we find real intimacy with ourselves and others. In more than thirty-five years of teaching meditation, I've seen it help countless people to reawaken love, relieve emotional anguish, and let go of addictive behaviors. For so many the commitment to practicing meditation has created the grounds for a deep and beautiful transformation of heart and spirit.

TRAINING YOUR MIND

When we're in the thick of lifelong patterns of insecurity or blame, it's hard to believe that change is possible. Until recently, scientific evidence seemed to confirm this skepticism. Neurologists thought that once we reached adulthood, the basic wiring of our brain was fixed; we were stuck with our core emotional patterning. If we were passive, anxious, and confused during our first decades of life, we were destined to continue that way. Now, with the help of brain imaging and other techniques, researchers have discovered the brain's inherent neuroplasticity: New neural pathways can be created and strengthened, and the brain and mind can continue to develop and change throughout life. So while we may get caught in very deep emotional ruts, we have the capacity to create fresh ways of responding to life.

Whatever you think or do regularly becomes a habit, a strongly conditioned pathway in the brain. The more you think about what can go wrong, the more your mind is primed to anticipate trouble. The more you lash out in anger, the more your body and mind are geared toward aggression. The more you think about how you might help others, the more your mind and heart are inclined to be generous. Just as weight lifting builds muscles, the way you direct your attention can strengthen anxiety, hostility, and addiction, or it can lead you to healing and awakening.

Imagine presence as a spring-fed forest pond—clear, still, and pure. Because we've spent so much time lost in the woods of our thoughts and emotions, we often have trouble finding this pond. But as we sit down to meditate again and again, we become familiar with the path through the woods. We can find the gap between the trees, we know the roots we've tripped over before, we trust that even if we get caught up in the brush and bramble, we'll find our way.

Regular meditation practice creates new pathways in our mind, ones that carry us home to the clarity, openness, and ease of presence. The Buddha taught many strategies for cultivating these pathways, but he considered the practice of mindfulness to be of central importance. *Mindfulness is the intentional process of paying attention, without judgment, to the unfolding of moment-by-moment experience.* If you get lost in worries about paying bills, mindfulness notices the worried thoughts and the accompanying feelings of anxiety. If you get lost in rehearsing what you'll tell another person, mindfulness notices the inner dialogue and the feelings of excitement or fear. Mindfulness recognizes and allows, without any resistance, all these sensations and feelings as they come and go. The most deeply grooved pathways in our mind are those that lead away from the present moment. By intentionally directing the mind to what is happening right now, mindfulness deconditions these pathways and awakens us to a fresh and intimate sense of being alive. Just as a clear pond reflects the sky, mindfulness allows us to see the truth of our experience.

The primary style of Buddhist meditation that I teach is called *vipassana,* meaning "to see clearly." In vipassana, the path to mindfulness begins with concentration—a one-pointed focusing of attention. It's difficult to be mindful of your experience if your mind is lost in a continuous stream of discursive thought. So first we collect and quiet the mind by directing attention to a sensory anchor. This might mean following the breath, or scanning the body for sensations, or listening to sounds, or silently repeating a phrase such as "May I be happy" or "May I be peaceful." With practice, whatever anchor you choose can become a reliable home base for your attention; like a good friend, it will help you reconnect with an inner sense of balance and well-being.

Psychiatrist and author Daniel Siegel offers a useful metaphor for understanding how our minds continuously move away from presence while we meditate. Imagine your awareness as a great wheel. At the hub of the wheel is presence, and from this hub, an infinite number of spokes extend out to the rim. Your attention is conditioned to leave presence, move out along the spokes, and affix itself to one part of the rim after another. Plans for dinner segue into a disturbing conversation, a self-judgment, a song on the radio, a backache, the feeling of fear. Or your attention gets lost in obsessive thinking, circling endlessly around stories and feelings about what is wrong. If you are not connected to the hub, if your attention is trapped out on the rim, you are cut off from your wholeness and living in trance.

Preselecting a home base or anchor, like the breath, allows you to notice when you've left presence and to find your way back to the hub more easily. I call this part of practice "coming back." Once you're back at the hub, the anchor also helps you to quiet and calm the mind. No matter how often your attention flies out to some fantasy or memory on the rim, you can gently return to the hub and ground yourself once again in presence.

As your attention becomes more settled, you will sense that the boundaries of the hub are softening and opening. This is the phase of practice that I call "being here." You continue to be in touch with your anchor, but at the same time you can recognize and allow the changing experiences on the rim—the sound of a dog barking, the pain in your knee, a thought about how long you'll continue to meditate. Rather than fixating on these experiences or pushing them away, you let them come and go freely. Of course the mind will still sometimes lose itself on the rim, and at these times, when you notice, you again gently return to the hub. It's natural for practice to flow between "coming back" and "being here."

The more you inhabit the alert stillness at the center of the wheel and include in mindfulness whatever is happening, the more the hub of presence becomes edgeless, warm, and bright. In the moments when there is no controlling of experience—when there is effortless mindfulness—you enter fully into presence. The hub, spokes, and rim are all floating in luminous open awareness.

Remembering What Matters

With so many styles of meditation or contemplative practice being taught today, students sometimes worry about choosing the "right one." But more than the particular form of practice or set of teachings, what makes the difference in terms of spiritual awakening is your quality of earnestness or *sincerity*. We become sincere when we connect with what most matters to our heart. In the Buddhist teachings, the conscious recognition of our heart's deepest longing is called wise aspiration. Yours might be for spiritual realization, for loving more fully, for knowing truth, for finding peace. Whatever its flavor, the awareness of what you care about energizes and guides your practice. As Zen master Suzuki Roshi taught, "The most important thing is remembering the most important thing."

It is helpful to start your meditation with a reflection on what matters to you. Some meditation students bring to mind an all-encompassing aspiration, while others focus on a particular intention for the sitting or the day. For instance, you might connect with your aspiration for loving fully or decide to embrace whatever difficult emotions arise during your practice. You might aspire to the truth—to really see what is happening and what is real—or you might have the particular intention to recognize and let go of thoughts. When you begin by asking your heart what matters, you are already on the path to presence.

Cultivating a Wise Attitude

If you currently meditate, take a moment to reflect on your overall attitude toward your practice. Do you think you should be practicing more and having better results? Do you feel like it's too hard, and resign your-self to not doing a good job? Do you put in the time but feel like your efforts are halfhearted? Are you eager to practice? Curious about what unfolds? Relaxed about your progress?

A healthful attitude is one that sincerely cares about presence, yet does not judge what unfolds. Rather, we regard whatever happens with an interested, relaxed, and friendly attention. Making meditation part of a self-improvement project can actually undermine your practice. Most people have an internal template for the kind of meditative experience they consider "good" (quiet, open, clear, loving, and so on) and then judge themselves when their mind wanders or when difficult emotions arise. Truly, there is no "right" meditation, and striving to get it right reinforces the sense of an imperfect, striving self. On the other hand, resigning yourself to a halfhearted effort reinforces the sense of a disen-gaged, disconnected self.

When Buddhist teacher Thich Nhat Hanh was invited to the San Francisco Zen Center in the 1970s, the students asked him what they could do to improve their practice. He had entered a monastery at age sixteen, was an ordained monk, and had endured the horrors of the war in Vietnam. I imagine they expected some rigorous prescription for deepening their spiritual life. Thich Nhat Hanh's response: "You guys get up too early for one thing, you should get up a little later. And your practice is too grim. I have just two instructions for you this week. One is to breathe, and one is to smile."

This is such good advice. Approach your practice (and your life) with an earnest yet relaxed heart. You can make a dedicated effort with-out tension and striving. Whether you are new to practice or an experi-enced meditator, keep alert for judgment. Whenever it arises, give permission for your experience to be whatever it is. Judging is a habit, and when you remember to release it, you will reconnect with the inner ease and sincerity that naturally carry you to presence and freedom.

Creating Time and Space to Practice

The hallmark of our culture is that most of us speed through the day, fitting whatever we can into already full schedules. Even when we're not plugged into our cell phones and computer screens, or rushing from obligation to obligation, our minds are still cooking away. Creating some time and space to be with our inner life is counter to the currents of the world around us.

New meditation students often mention the value of learning to focus and settle the mind, but they also name something more basic. As one person put it recently, "Just having those moments to be quiet is a gift to my soul." It *is* a gift to the soul. Stepping out of the busyness, stopping our endless pursuit of getting somewhere else, is perhaps the most beautiful offering we can make to our spirit. And yet it is so simple. We are learning, as Rumi says, to make regular visits to ourselves.

Look for ways to create a rhythm of practice. Many contemplative traditions recommend setting a regular time of day to meditate—usually early in the morning, because the mind is calmer on waking than it is later in the day. However, the best time for you is the time you can realistically commit to on a regular basis. Some people choose to do two short meditations, one at the beginning of the day and one at the end.

How long should you practice? Between fifteen and forty-five minutes works for many people. If you are new to meditation, fifteen minutes may seem like an eternity, but that impression will change as your practice develops. If you meditate each day, you will experience noticeable benefits (less reactivity, more calm) and you will probably choose to increase your practice time. Whatever the length, it's best to decide *before* beginning and have a clock or timer nearby. Then, rather than getting entangled in thoughts about when to stop, you can fully give yourself to the meditation.

If possible, dedicate a space exclusively to your daily meditation. Choose a relatively protected and quiet place where you can leave your cushion (or chair) so that it is always there to return to. You may want to create an altar with a candle, inspiring photos, statues, flowers, stones, shells—whatever arouses your sense of beauty, wonder, and the sacred. This is certainly not necessary, but it can help create a mood and remind you of what you love.

Sustaining Your Practice

Sustaining a regular practice can be challenging. During the twelve years I lived in the ashram, I had others to practice with each day. With that kind of support, creating the time for daily meditation became a given in my life. It wasn't as easy after I left. Within a year I gave birth to my son, Narayan, and found myself with a new infant and an increasingly erratic schedule.

One morning I woke up feeling particularly ornery, and after I snapped at Narayan's father for forgetting something at the supermarket, he recommended that I take some time to meditate. I handed the baby over, plunked down in front of my little altar, and immediately dissolved into tears. I missed the rhythm of my practice. I missed making regular visits to myself! In those moments, with the sun flooding through the windows, and the background sounds of my husband chatting away to Narayan, I made a vow. No matter what, I'd create time each day to come into stillness and pay attention to my experience. But there was a "back door": How long I sat didn't matter.

Ever since, I have made the time. I usually meditate thirty to forty-five minutes in the morning, but there have been days, especially when Narayan was young, when it didn't happen. Instead, I'd sit on the edge of my bed right before going to sleep, and would intentionally relax my body, opening to the sensations and feelings that were present. Then, after a few minutes, I would say a prayer and climb under the covers. As my body has changed and long sittings have become more difficult, I'll often do a standing meditation. Still, the commitment to daily practice "no matter what" has been one of the great supports of my life.

For some people I know, my approach is a setup for self-punishment. Something happens—a bad cold, falling asleep early, simply forgetting—and the promise has been broken. The bottom line is to enjoy, not stress over, a meditation practice. As Julia Child famously said, "If you drop the lamb, just pick it up. Who's going to know?" If you miss practice for a day, a week, or a month, simply begin again. It's okay.

Unless you feel enriched by meditation, you will not continue. It's hard to feel enriched if you get mechanical, if you practice out of guilt, if you judge yourself for not progressing, or if you lock into the grim sense that "I'm on my own." One of the best ways to avoid these traps is to practice with others. You might look for an existing meditation class with a teacher, or find a few friends who are interested in sharing the experience together. If you are able, attending a weekend or weeklong residential retreat will deepen your practice as well as your faith in your own capacity to become peaceful and mindful. This is a wonderful time to be practicing meditation! Meditators have a growing pool of resources—CDs, books, podcasts, teachers, and fellow meditators—to support and accompany them as they walk this path (see "Resources," on page 291).

OFF THE CUSHION: MEDITATION TRAINING AND DAILY LIFE

Author and Buddhist scholar Robert Thurman jokes that the Buddhists are always talking about practice: "Practice, practice, practice," he says. "What I want to know is, when is the performance?" There is no performance, but there is the possibility of being more awake in the moments of daily life that used to be lost to trance.

For Jeff and Arlene, the married couple from the beginning of the chapter, meditation practice was central to reclaiming their relationship. Their strategy (which is used by many couples I work with) was to take a meditative "time-out" whenever they became caught in one of their reactive dances of anger and defensiveness. Either one of them could call for this intentional pause, and both agreed to honor such a request. They would sit quietly—separately or together (they experimented with both)—and draw on the skills they had been cultivating in formal practice: Recalling their aspiration (to choose presence, to decide on love); stepping out of stories of blame; relaxing and quieting with the breath; and bringing presence to their own hurts and fears. After ten or fifteen minutes of this minimeditation, they'd check in with each other to see if they felt ready to resume talking. Their guideline for being ready was feeling in touch with their own vulnerability rather than focused on blame. If either needed more time, they'd allow for that, and on several occasions they agreed to wait until the next day to talk. But for the most part, after a short period of meditation they were better able to identify their real feelings and communicate them openly. By learning to pause and choose presence, they discovered a level of understanding and care they had not dreamed possible.

Meditation students often ask me what will help them remember presence in the thick of things. My first response: "Just pause." My second response: "Pause again, take a few conscious breaths, and relax." Our lives are constantly tumbling into the future, and the only way back to here and now is to stop. Even a few moments of suspended activity, a minimeditation of just being still, can reconnect you with a sense of aliveness and caring. That connection will deepen if, during those moments, you intentionally establish contact with your body, breathe, and relax.

A game I play with myself is to see if I can spontaneously remember to pause in situations I usually charge right through. Washing the dishes. Walking from my office to the kitchen. Moving through e-mails. Eating popcorn. Pausing is a wonderful and radical way of plucking myself out of virtual reality and discovering myself once again at the hub, awake, open, and here.

A deliberate meditative pause helps us to savor the often-forgotten goodness and beauty that is within and around us. One client, Frances, felt crushed when her two daughters chose to spend a holiday with their father (her ex-husband) rather than going on a trip with her. "You're no fun, Mom, you don't know how to relax," one had said. When she protested, they pointed out that she was "all business" and was even grim about setting up vacation activities. Frances recognized herself in their words. The oldest of five, she had prematurely become the caretaker of her siblings when her own mother had grown ill. "I don't know how to play," she confessed sadly. "I'm much more comfortable staying busy, getting things done."

Shaken by what she felt to be her daughters' rejection, Frances began a daily practice of meditation to learn how to relax. But when she met with me for guidance, her stiff posture and tightly knitted brows let me know that her approach to meditation was as grim as her approach to the rest of life.

I suggested that she find a beautiful place to walk and do some of her meditation practice there. Her assignment was still to wake up from thoughts when she became aware of them; but rather than the breath, her home base was all of her senses. She would become aware of the pressure of her feet on the earth, the images and smells and sounds of the natural world. I asked her to pause anytime something struck her as beautiful or interesting and to offer that experience her full attention.

When we met several months later, Frances gave me a meditation report: "Tara," she said, "my walks are one long linger!" She went on to tell me about the pleasure she was finding in other parts of life—eating a peach slowly and savoring its texture and flavor, taking long hot showers, and increasingly, during sitting meditation, simply relaxing with the movement of her breath. Most important, Frances was experiencing her daughters in a new way, appreciating one's infectious laugh, the other's grace. "I'm enjoying them," she said, smiling, "and they seem not to mind hanging out with me!" Frances was discovering the blessing of choosing presence—becoming intimate with the life that is right here, right now.

TRUSTING YOUR HEART
AND AWARENESS

At a conference in India with the Dalai Lama, a group of Western Buddhist teachers asked him for the most important message they could bring back home to their meditation students. After a few thoughtful moments, the Dalai Lama nodded and smiled broadly. "Tell them that they can trust their hearts and awareness to awaken in the midst of all circumstances."

We long to trust our capacity to handle difficulties, to grow, to love well, and to be all that we can be. Often we start meditation as a way of connecting with our hearts and awareness, and of living with more confidence in ourselves. Yet I've seen how for many people, the single biggest challenge to sustaining a meditation practice is the sense of doubt: "I'm not doing this right. I'm not getting it. This isn't working." Students tell me that they can't control their thinking, that they are not able to maintain any experience of openhearted presence. They wonder why meditating is so hard.

Training our attention *is* hard. We're going against the grain of countless hours lost in thought and unconsciously driven by wants and fears. It's as though we've spent our lives on a bicycle, pedaling hard to get away from the present moment. We pedal to resist what is happening, we pedal to try to make something happen, we pedal to try to get somewhere else. The more we feel like something is missing, or something is wrong, the faster we pedal. Even in the midst of a meditation we might realize we are pedaling—straining to be with the breath, chasing after a fantasy. Meditation is a setup for feeling deficient unless we respectfully acknowledge the strength of our conditioning to race away from presence. These tendencies toward false refuge are strongly grooved neuropathways: *It's not our fault!* Given this conditioning, how can we follow the Dalai Lama's advice and trust our heart and awareness?

The purposeful "doings" in meditation (naming our experience, mindfully scanning through the body, or focusing on the breath) help us to pause and open ourselves to the life of the moment. Yet because we can get so hooked by the need to do something more, we help ourselves most deeply by our intention to *let go.* For Pam, whispering "I consent" opened her to loving presence during her husband's last days; for me, reflecting on entrusting myself to the waves relaxed my tendency to control life and connected me with a spacious awareness. More recently I sometimes remind myself of a line from poet Rainer Maria Rilke: "Let everything happen to you, the beauty, the terror . . ." Feel free to experiment with self-reminders. What word or phrase helps you to stop pedaling, to relax your habitual "doing" and simply be?

Hindu teacher Swami Satchidananda was once asked by a student if he needed to become a Hindu to go deeply into the practice of yoga. Satchidananda's response was, "I am not a Hindu, I am an undo." Just so, when meditation frees us, it does not turn us into something better or different, nor does it get us somewhere. We are not pedaling toward some spiritual achievement. Rather meditation allows for an undoing of our controlling behavior, an undoing of limiting beliefs, an undoing of habitual physical tensing, an undoing of defensive armoring, and ultimately, an undoing of our identification with a small and threatened self. By undoing all the doings, we discover the vast heart and awareness that is beyond any small-self identity; the heart and awareness that gives us refuge in the face of any life situation. This is the gift of meditation practice—we find we can trust who we most deeply are.

Guided Meditation: Coming Back

The practice of mindfulness is a direct gateway to natural presence. "Coming back" guides you in returning to presence when you have become distracted. This will help you maintain a focused attention in the present moment.

⸺ ❧ ⸺

Find yourself a comfortable seated posture. You will be most wakeful and alert if you sit on a chair, cushion, or kneeling bench with your back and posture as upright, tall, and balanced as possible. Around an erect posture, let the rest of your skeleton and muscles hang freely. Let the hands rest comfortably on your knees or lap. Let the eyes close, or if you prefer, leave the eyes open, with the gaze soft and receptive.

Take several full deep breaths, and with each exhale, consciously let go, relaxing the face, shoulders, hands, and abdominal muscles. Then, after resuming a natural rhythm of breathing, choose an anchor for your meditation. Often the most useful anchors are sensory based. You might attend to:

- *The breath as it enters and leaves the nostrils.*
- *Other sensations that arise with breathing, such as the rising and falling of the chest or the expanding and contracting of the abdominal area.*
- *Sounds within or around you.*
- *Other physical sensations that arise as you experience the sitting posture from the "inside out": This might include tingling in the hands, warmth or coolness anywhere in the body, tightening or loosening of particular muscles.*

Take some moments to bring a full, relaxed, and intimate attention to your anchor. You might imagine that your entire awareness is right here, open to the moment-to-moment flow of your breathing (or other sensations or sounds). You don't need to force your attention; rather, see if it is possible to receive the experience and to relax with the changing expression of your chosen anchor. Sense how your anchor connects you with the wakefulness and "hereness" at the hub of the wheel.

Whatever your anchor, you will very soon discover that your mind is distracted, leaving the hub and circling around in thought. These distractions are totally natural—

just as the body secretes enzymes, the mind generates thoughts! There is no need to judge the thoughts or make them the enemy; rather, whenever you notice a thought, honor that moment of recognition as a moment of awakening. This respectful attitude is key to coming home and reconnecting with a full presence.

When you realize you've been lost in thought, you might find it is helpful to ac-knowledge that by saying to yourself, "This is a thought" or "Thinking, thinking." Then just pause—there is no need to rush back to your home base. You will naturally return to presence by taking a few moments to listen to sounds; to again relax your shoulders, hands, and abdomen; and to relax your heart. Notice the difference between any thought and the vividness of hereness! Then gently guide your attention back to your anchor as a way of sustaining presence at the hub of the wheel.

Continue to practice with the intention of recognizing thoughts and, over and over, return to a relaxed focus on your anchor. This simple practice of coming back to the hub of the wheel is a powerful way of establishing the atmosphere for mindful aware-ness. Even as you expand your meditation practice, this training can continue as a key element in your daily routine.

Guided Meditation: Being Here

"Being here" directly cultivates the openness and clarity of mindful awareness—the alert stillness at the hub of the wheel. Together, "coming back" and "being here" introduce some of the key mindfulness skills that comprise vipassana meditation.

⸻⟨⟩⸻

Set yourself in a sitting position that allows you to be alert and relaxed. Allow your attention to scan through your body and if you notice areas of obvious tension, see if it is possible to soften some and let go. Then bring your attention to your chosen anchor and take whatever time is necessary to practice "coming back." While at first the mind might be restless and distracted, after a few minutes you might notice there are larger gaps between the thoughts, and more moments of resting with your anchor at the hub of the wheel.

Continue with a steady but light attention on your chosen anchor, yet also include in awareness whatever you notice in the background of your sensory experience. For instance, you might be using the inflow and outflow of the breath as your home base, while also being aware of the sounds in the room, a feeling of restlessness, an itch, heat. For a time, these experiences may come and go without drawing your attention away from your anchor. But if an experience has a compelling quality—if it calls your attention—then allow it to replace your anchor in occupying the foreground of your attention. Perhaps you will become strongly aware of feeling sleepy. Your job is simply to recognize and allow *whatever you experience about "sleepy." Sense sleepiness as a constellation of sensations in your body. Notice where you are most aware of the feelings, and what they are like. Is there burning behind the eyes? Weight or pressure at the chest? Fuzziness in the mind? Notice how the sensations change: Do they get stronger, stay the same, or fade? Continue to attend to sleepiness—noticing what it is like and "letting be"—until it no longer calls your attention.*

Sometimes you'll find sleepiness has morphed into something else that is compelling, perhaps anxiety about being sleepy. You might be having thoughts about wasting your time in the meditation, or fear about being tired throughout the day. Be aware of the thoughts ("thinking, thinking") and feel the sensations of fear in the body. Is there tightness in the chest? A sore or squeezing feeling? Just as with sleepiness, notice how the sensations move and change in intensity, and let them be just as they are. When they no longer call your attention, return to your anchor. In this way, whatever arises—thoughts, emotions, sensations—is included in the hub of the wheel, received with a nonjudging presence. Your practice is simply to recognize and allow what is here.

As a support in being here, you might make a mental note when strong experiences arise. Naming your sensations ("burning, burning"), emotions ("fear, fear"), and types of thoughts ("worrying, worrying") can help you to more clearly recognize what is happening inside you, without leaving the presence at the hub of the wheel. Let the tone of your mental whisper be gentle and accepting: The purpose of the noting is to help you connect with your actual experience without judgment or resistance. There is no need to work at finding the right label, or to try to name everything that is going on. If the noting feels distracting or clumsy—if it interferes with the flow of presence—then either use it quite sparingly or put it aside altogether.

If your mind is somewhat busy and continues leaving the hub of the wheel, it is natural that your meditation include a fluid movement between "coming back" and deepening presence with "being here." Yet if you find the mind becomes fairly settled, you might explore letting go of your anchor. Without any effort to direct your attention, rest in the still alertness at the hub of the wheel and receive whatever arises in awareness. Thoughts might come and go, the sensations of the breath, a sound outside, a twinge of fear. Let your only intention be to recognize and allow what is happening, moment to moment to moment. By letting go of control and relaxing with the changing flow of experience, you will begin to inhabit the fullness of natural presence. Notice how the hub of the wheel is actually quite boundless; how rather than a particular location of "here," experience is arising and passing in the wakeful openness of awareness itself. Rest in this awareness, allowing all of life to live through you.

FOUR

THREE GATEWAYS TO REFUGE

Sometimes you hear a voice through the door calling you,
As a fish out of water hears the waves . . . Come back. Come back.
This turning toward what you deeply love saves you.

RUMI

The great gift of a spiritual path is coming to trust that you can find a way to true refuge. You realize that you can start right where you are, in the midst of your life, and find peace in any circumstance. Even at those moments when the ground shakes terribly beneath you—when there's a loss that will alter your life forever— you can still trust that you will find your way home. This is possible because you've touched the timeless love and awareness that are intrinsic to who you are.

Looking back through history, and across many religious and spiritual traditions, we can recognize three archetypal gateways that appear again and again on the universal path of awakening. For me, the words that best capture the spirit of these gateways are "truth," "love," and "awareness." Truth is the living reality that is revealed in the present moment; love is the felt sense of connectedness or oneness with all life; and awareness is the silent wakefulness behind all experience, the consciousness that is reading these words, listening to sounds, perceiving sensations and feelings. Each of these gateways is a fundamental part of who we are; each is a refuge because it is always here, embedded in our own being.

If you're familiar with the Buddhist path, you may recognize these gateways as they appear in their traditional order:

Refuge in the Buddha (an "awakened one" or our own pure
    awareness)
Refuge in the dharma (the truth of the present moment; the
    teachings; the way)
Refuge in the sangha (the community of spiritual friends or love)

However, in the chapters that follow, I've sequenced the gateways differently, in the way that I've found makes them most accessible. For
many people, especially those training in meditation, contacting the
truth of the present moment is the first opening to inner refuge. For
others, it is awakening love. Usually it is after becoming familiar with
these gateways of truth and love that we explore turning toward formless
awareness itself. In time, reflection on any of the gateways will naturally
lead to the others. They are truly inseparable.

The same gateways are central to the Hindu path and denoted in
Sanskrit terms: *sat* (ultimate truth or reality); *ananda* (love or bliss); and
chit (consciousness or awareness). And they appear again in some interpretations of the Christian trinity: Father (source or awareness); Son
(awareness in form or the living reality/truth); and Holy Spirit (love, the
love between father and son).

Does all this seem rather abstract, out of reach when we're caught up
in our daily struggles? How can we enter these gateways in our everyday
lives? If you look again, you'll see that each domain of refuge has both
an outer and an inner aspect. The outer expressions of the refuges are
the sources of healing, support, and inspiration that we find in the world
around us. We can learn from wise teachings (truth). We can be nourished by the warmth of good friends and family (love). We can be uplifted by the example of spiritual leaders (awareness). Every religion and
spiritual path offers these outer refuges. If we are willing to engage with
them, they can offer us immediate, concrete help in living our daily lives.
Yet each outer refuge also offers something more: It is a portal to the
inner refuges of pure awareness, the living flow of truth and boundless
love. As we inhabit these expressions of our true nature, the trance of
separation dissolves and we are free.

The Outer and Inner Aspects of Refuge

OUTER REFUGE	INNER REFUGE
TRUTH Meditation; Ethics; Teachings	Realizing the nature of reality; embodying living presence
LOVE Conscious relationships with self and other	Realizing oneness; embodying loving presence
AWARENESS Inspirational spiritual figures	Realizing and embodying empty, luminous awareness

THE GATEWAY OF TRUTH

In Pali, the language of the earliest Buddhist scriptures, the word *dharma* can mean "path," "way," or "nature of things." When I and other Buddhist teachers offer "dharma talks" at our classes and retreats, we address three ways we can begin to take refuge in truth: working with our inner life through meditation practice; dedicating ourselves to wise, ethical behavior; and understanding the teachings or truths that guide us on the spiritual path.

Meditation: Awakening to Truth

You may have been introduced to mindfulness training—without any reference to Buddhism—in a health clinic, in psychotherapy, or in a corporate seminar. Simply realizing that we can purposely direct our attention can be a radical and wonderful discovery. Even when we are just beginning to practice, we can experience the calm centeredness that arises from waking up from thoughts and resting with the breath, and the lucidity of becoming mindful of our moment-to-moment experience.

Many people first come to my Wednesday night meditation class primarily for health reasons or for stress relief. They are sometimes surprised by what they discover.

Terrance was a superior court judge in Washington, D.C. He came up to me after his first class to talk about his work. He often felt overwhelmed by the crowded courtrooms and the sheer magnitude of suffering he observed day after day. What could he do, he asked me, to find more breathing space in the midst of it all? Taking a cue from his words "breathing space," I suggested a daily meditation practice that used the breath as an anchor. Then, even at work he would be able to pause and quickly establish a connection with his breath, and find some inner clarity and ease.

Terrance was disciplined. He joined a course we taught for a group of other court justices and practiced half an hour a day on his own. At the end of the course, he sought me out again. "It works, Tara," he said with a smile, "but not quite the way I expected. I'm calmer for sure. But there is something else. Each person who approaches the bench these days has become a real person, someone who deserves my respect. More than that . . . each is really 'not other' than me, in some most basic way. I've tapped into a love and a consciousness I'd understood intellectually but never experienced directly."

The popular benefits attributed to meditation are concrete, quantifiable, and immensely valuable, but the Buddha had a more fundamental intent: Cultivating a relaxed and attentive mind allows us to see directly into the truth of who we are. Terrance was beginning to experience moments when compassion and connection weren't just ideas, but lived experiences.

Ethics: Living Aligned with Truth

The Tibetans teach that we should allow our minds to be as vast as the sky and our daily conduct to be as fine as a grain of sand. This reflects a basic truth: How we live today—the ways we treat others, the energy behind our words, our habits of relating to the earth—affects our own consciousness and ripples out into the world around us. In each moment, what we choose to say and do plants the seed of our future. Remembering this truth and allowing it to guide our actions is essential in opening the heart and mind to the inner refuge of truth.

Like many other spiritual leaders, the Buddha taught a fundamental reverence for life and a commitment not to cause harm. His precepts guide us to refrain from killing, stealing, lying, abusing intoxicants, or causing harm through sexual activity. They also call us to compassionate living: to cherish and preserve life, to be generous, to speak the truth with kindness, to take care of our bodies and minds and bring consciousness and respect to relationships.

I've seen how these teachings can provide people with a lifeboat in rough waters. One of my meditation students, Manny, was a project leader for an innovative business that had created a number of successful software applications. Much of the creative brilliance behind these developments had sprung from a young man and woman on his team. Yet in his meetings with company executives, he never mentioned their work. One day, as Manny reflected on his actions, he felt a jolt of self-disgust: It was stealing. He had taken for himself the credit that was due to others. It was also lying: He had not acknowledged what was true. From then on, he made a point of honoring the contributions of his team, both to the team members themselves and to his superiors. He noticed that his mind became clearer and he felt more at ease with himself.

A friend jokes that we can't expect to spend the day lying, stealing, and beating people, and then come home for a nice peaceful meditation sitting. Acting in ways that are violent or manipulative directly affects our nervous system and mood. In the same way, living ethically fosters a happy, contented heart. Even if we're not fully in touch with our own wisdom and compassion, when we make a conscious effort to act in ways that are helpful and kind, there is an "outside-in" effect. We become more energetically balanced and aligned, and more at peace with how we are relating to the life within and around us.

Yet having a commitment to nonharming does not mean that we should beat ourselves up when we've said something hurtful or had too many beers. Rather, our commitment can be a powerful incentive to pause and notice what is going on in the midst of activity. As we learn to deepen our attention in this way, we become increasingly connected with our inherent reverence for life.

Teachings on Truth: Accepting What Is Real

About twenty years ago, a close friend and I drove to southern Virginia to attend a retreat led by Vietnamese Zen teacher Thich Nhat Hanh. At the closing ceremony, he asked us to choose a partner—I turned to face my friend—and bow to each other. He then instructed us to hug our partner while taking three conscious and full in-breaths and out-breaths. With the first breath, he said to reflect, "I'm going to die"; with the second, "You're going to die"; and with the third, "And we have just these precious moments." After slowly releasing our embrace, my friend and I looked at each other through our tears. Thich Nhat Hanh had, in a beautiful way, turned us toward the refuge of truth.

Facing and accepting the realities of our existence is not easy. We are deeply conditioned to try to hold on to whatever we hope will give us security and pleasure, and to protect ourselves from pain. Holding on locked my friend Paul into two decades of conflict in his marriage. An extrovert who thrived on being with others, Paul felt shut out by his wife, Karen. "She would rather be alone with our cat and her poetry," he'd complain, "than spend time with me." Hurt and angry, he'd accuse her of abandoning him emotionally, of not caring about him, of not showing up. Her response would be to withdraw even more. Then, during a weekend when Karen was away visiting their adult daughter, he had a stunning realization. "Week after week, year after year, I was assuming she *should* be different, that our relationship should be different . . . And Karen is the way she is." He realized he and Karen would never achieve his dream of intimacy. The more he directly opened to his own hurt and loneliness, the more he began to accept Karen as she was. Their relationship relaxed and became more fundamentally honest, respectful, and caring. "When we came to the decision that we wanted to separate, it was not because we were at war," Paul told me. "It was because we were being honest . . . accepting how it was." Then he added wistfully, "It's sad how we covered over our love through all those years of wanting each other to be different."

When we walk through the gateway of truth, we start by recognizing what's real and intending to accept it. Accepting what is does not mean passive resignation; it is a courageous engagement with the reality of our experience. We might not like what we discover, but we can hold it in compassionate presence. The more we rest in this presence, the more lucid our attention becomes. We see what lies beyond the changing play of thoughts, feelings, and sensations, and discover our inner refuge—the wakeful openness and tenderness that beholds and enfolds all experience.

THE GATEWAY OF LOVE

Participating in conscious community is a beautiful outer refuge, and it offers a powerful way to enter true refuge. In the Buddhist tradition, the word *sangha* originally referred to the congregation of monks and nuns who followed the way of the Buddha. Today in the West, the concept of sangha has expanded. The key element that distinguishes a sangha or conscious community from other social organizations is the commitment to a particular and shared set of values and to shared practices or rituals that serve spiritual awakening. Some of the best-known sanghas in our culture are twelve-step groups, communities whose members help one another stay free from addictive behaviors and transform their lives for the better.

All religions and faith groups have their forms of spiritual community, but you do not need any formal affiliation to experience this kind of belonging. Our meditation community includes people from many traditions, as well as those who are determinedly secular. Within the larger community, participants have started more than twenty-five smaller groups, called *kalyana mitta*, or spiritual friends groups, which explore how to bring the teachings alive in daily life. These groups are open to anyone who is interested. Some members also join affinity groups for particular populations—teens and young adults; people of color; those struggling with addiction; and lesbian, gay, bisexual, transgender, and questioning members.

Of course, we can experience the benefits of sangha even if we are not part of a spiritual group. It's with family and friends that we often experience our most ongoing, challenging, and profound awakenings. Our hearts open wide when we celebrate births and weddings, when we mourn the loss of loved ones, when we gather at a holiday meal, when we confide a difficult truth, and when we help one another through sickness and stress. In the intimacy of these moments, we glimpse who we are beyond the trance of small self.

The refuge of love continues to come alive for me in poignant and simple ways. It happens when I'm silently keeping a friend company in the midst of his or her pain, when my husband, Jonathan, is escorting me and my computer through a technological minefield, when our community's board listens respectfully to one another's conflicting opinions. It happens when I'm working with others for a shared purpose, whether it's writing something, solving a problem, cooking a meal, or helping our world in some small but real way. My sense of "me" becomes looser and more permeable. I'm part of something larger, no longer contracted by the pain and fear of separation.

People often enter our meditation community with the expectation that everyone will be kind, thoughtful, and generous. We're a spiritual group, after all! They can become disillusioned and disappointed when their fellow meditators make insensitive or judgmental remarks, get defensive about being "right," and lock into conflict. They can also become disillusioned when they come face-to-face, once again, with their own feelings of woundedness and with their familiar ways of getting offended, of creating distance with others.

But even when habits of blaming or defensiveness arise, something profound can change if those involved bring a committed presence to what is happening. This is when community becomes a refuge—a place of true awakening.

Charlie, a college senior who came to me for counseling, had been neglected by his mother, abused by his father. When he joined Narcotics Anonymous, he found himself unable to trust that his sponsor cared about him or that the members of his local group really wanted him there. I encouraged Charlie to stay and commit himself not just to abstinence but to engaging fully with others in the program. While it took many months of regular meetings, he came to feel he had finally found a real family.

Some of us, like Charlie, have always been on the outside looking in. Others have needed to be in control and have not felt truly close with others. We might feel that we are often in conflict, either overly aggressive or defensive with others. Whatever our history, the capacity to have intimate and authentic relationships remains within us, and it comes alive with practice. This happens as we learn to be purposefully attentive, in the present moment, with ourselves and one another. We can do this in relationships with any person or group where there is a commitment to "staying," a commitment to kindness, a commitment to awakening together.

Having spiritual friends is not a superficial comfort. It helps free us from a trance of separation so deep that we are often not aware of it. Conscious relationships shine a direct light both on our layered feelings of unworthiness and loneliness, and on the truth of our belonging. We begin to respond more compassionately and actively to the suffering of the world. Our real community, we discover, includes all beings. As we relax and trust this belonging to the web of life, we recognize the one awareness that shines through each being. Our spiritual friends open the way to the inner refuge of unconditional loving presence.

THE GATEWAY OF AWARENESS

Soon after his enlightenment, the Buddha set out to share his teachings with others. People were struck by his extraordinary radiance and peaceful presence. One man asked him who he was. "Are you a celestial being or a god?" "No," responded the Buddha. "Are you a saint or sage?" Again the Buddha responded, "No." "Are you some kind of magician or wizard?" "No," said the Buddha. "Well then, what are you?" The Buddha replied, "I am awake."

I often share this story because it is a reminder that what might seem like an extraordinary occurrence—spiritual awakening—is a built-in human capacity. Siddhartha Gautama (the Buddha's birth name) was a human being, not a deity. When Buddhists take refuge in the historical Buddha, whose name literally means "one who is awake," they are drawing on the inspiration of a fellow human who was able to realize his inner freedom. Like us, Siddhartha experienced bodily pain and disease, and, like us, he encountered inner distress and conflict. For those who follow the Buddha, reflecting on his courageous investigation of reality and his awakening to a timeless and compassionate presence brings confidence that this same potential lies within each of us. In a similar way we might reflect on Jesus or on teachers and healers from other traditions. Any spiritually awakened human being helps us trust that we too can awaken. You may have already touched upon this outer refuge with a caring and wise teacher or mentor. My eighty-six-year-old aunt, a specialist in childhood blood diseases, traces her love of nature and her determination to be a doctor to a science class in junior high school. Very few women entered medical school at that time, but her teacher, a woman of passionate intellect, conveyed a pivotal message: "Trust your intelligence and let your curiosity shine!" An African American friend who leads corporate diversity trainings found refuge and inspiration in his minister, a leader in the civil rights movement and an exemplar of generosity, humor, and wisdom. I found refuge in my first meditation teacher, Stephen: His great love of meditating, and his own unfolding clarity and kindness, helped awaken my devotion to the spiritual path. We respond to our mentors because they speak to qualities of heart and mind, qualities of awareness, that are already within us. Their gift is that they remind us of what is possible and call it forth. Much in the same way, we are drawn to spiritual figures that help connect us with our inner goodness.

About ten years ago I began experimenting with a simple self-guided meditation. I would call on the presence of the divine mother (the sacred feminine) and over the next minute or so, I would begin to sense a radiant openness surrounding me. As I imagined the mind of this awakened being, I could sense vastness and lucidity. Then, as I imagined the heart of the divine mother, that openness filled with warmth and sensitivity. Finally, I'd direct my attention inward, to see how that tender, radiant, all-inclusive awareness was living inside me. I'd feel my body, heart, and mind light up as if the sunlit sky was suffusing every cell of my body and shining through the spaces between the cells.

I've come to see that through this meditation, I was exploring the movement from outer refuge to inner refuge. By regularly contacting these facets of sacred presence within me, I was deepening my faith in my own essential being.

Realizing who we are fulfills our human potential. We intuit that we are more mysterious and vast than the small self we experience through our stories and changing emotions. As we learn to attend directly to our own awareness, we discover the timeless and wakeful space of our true nature. This inner refuge of pure awareness is our ultimate homecoming. It is the fruition of all spiritual practice, and it gives beauty and meaning to our lives.

START WHERE YOU ARE

Whether we are old-timers or new to the path, we need to intuit where best to place our attention at this time in our lives. Depending on your circumstances, temperament, and past experiences, you might find one or another of the outer refuges easier or more natural to enter. Some people feel most enlivened by some form of spiritual support group, others are dedicated to a weekly meditation class, and still others might feel devoted to studying teachings from Buddhism, and other spiritual and humanistic paths. You can trust that wherever you start or whatever refuge you emphasize is the right place to be right now.

The biggest illusion about a path of refuge is that we are on our way somewhere else, on our way to becoming a different kind of person. But ultimately, our refuge is not outside ourselves, not somewhere in the future—it is always and already here. As you will see again and again in the chapters that follow, *truth* can only be discovered in the aliveness of this moment. *Love* can only be experienced in this very heart, here and now. *Awareness* can only be realized as we discover the space and wakefulness of our own mind.

Guided Reflection: Remembering the Most Important Thing

We turn toward the refuges of truth, love, and awareness by listening to the call of our heart. Beyond any meditative technique, it is remembering what most matters to us that awakens and frees our spirit. Again, as Zen master Suzuki Roshi taught, "The most important thing is remembering the most important thing." For most people, realizing and connecting with our deep aspiration takes time and attention. Like peeling back the layers of an onion, we may unfold layers of more immediate wants and fears before we arrive at the source, the light of pure aspiration. As we inhabit this aspiration, it becomes the compass of the heart that guides us home.

———— ✺ ————

Find a comfortable way of sitting, and allow yourself to relax and be at ease. With a receptive presence, become aware of the state of your heart. Is there a sense of openness or tightness? Of peace or anxiety? Of contentment or dissatisfaction? If there is something of particular concern or importance going on in your life, or simply a strong emotion, allow that to express itself. Perhaps at first you will be aware of wishing your partner would treat you differently. You might find that you are wanting to get past a particularly demanding stretch at work. You might long to be free of chronic pain. You may be wanting one of your children to feel more secure and confident.

Whatever arises, allow it to be there, and with interest, ask yourself: "If I got what I wanted, what would that really give me?" Perhaps you imagine if you were treated differently, you'd be less reactive and free to be more loving. Or if you were relieved of chronic pain, you would then be able to relax and enjoy your life more fully.

Continuing your inquiry you might now ask directly, "What does my heart really long for?" It can also be helpful to ask, "What most matters in this life?" Or, "If I was at the end of my life looking back, what would be most important about how I lived today . . . this moment?" As you pose these questions, sense that you are addressing your inquiry directly to your heart.

After asking, simply listen and be aware of any words, images, or feelings that arise. Try to be patient—it can take some time for the mind to open out of its habitual ideas about life and connect with what is most alive and true. You may need to repeat, several times, some version of "What does my heart long for?" and then listen in recep-

tive silence to what arises. As you listen, stay in touch with the feelings in your body, and particularly in your heart.

Your aspiration will probably express itself differently at different times. You might feel a longing to love fully or to feel loved, to know truth, to be peaceful, to be helpful, to be free of fear and suffering. There is no "right" aspiration. Sometimes you will land on an immediate intention that supports your aspiration. For example, you might become aware of the yearning to write poetry or paint. This would be in service of the deep aspiration to live a creative, vital life. What is important is attuning to what is most true for you in this moment.

The signs of arriving at a clear intention or deep aspiration are a felt sense of sincerity, innocence, energy, or flow. Some people describe an inner shift that gives them fresh resolution, openness, and ease. If there is no real sense of connecting with what matters, that's fine. You might sit quietly and open to whatever naturally arises, or choose to continue this exploration at another time.

If you sense you've arrived at what feels like a pure and deep aspiration, allow yourself to inhabit the fullness of your longing. Feel the very essence of your longing in a cellular way as it expresses through your whole body and being. Let your aspiration be the prayer of your awakening heart.

You can practice reflecting on your aspiration at the beginning and end of each day, and at the beginning and/or end of a meditation sitting. In addition, as you move through the day, try to pause periodically and inquire as to what most matters to you. In any moment that you remember what you care about, you have opened your heart to the blessings of true refuge.

PART II

THE GATEWAY
OF TRUTH

FIVE

RAIN: CULTIVATING MINDFULNESS IN DIFFICULT TIMES

Between the stimulus and the response there is a space and in that space lies our power and our freedom.

VIKTOR E. FRANKL

The quickest way to be happy is to choose what you already have.

WERNER ERHARD

Imagine you just found out that your child was suspended from school.

Imagine your boss just told you to start over on a report you'd worked on for a month.

Imagine you just realized you'd been on Facebook for three hours and have finished off a pound of trail mix in the process.

Imagine your partner just confessed to an affair.

It's hard to hang out with the truth of what we're feeling. We may sincerely intend to pause and be mindful whenever a crisis arises, or whenever we feel stuck and confused, but our conditioning to react, escape, or become possessed by emotion is very strong.

Yes, there are times when being present feels out of reach or too much to bear. There are times when false refuges can relieve stress, give us a breather, help lift our mood. But when we're not connected to the clarity and kindness of presence, we're all too likely to fall into more misunderstanding, more conflict, and more distance from others and our own heart.

About twelve years ago, a number of Buddhist teachers began to share a new mindfulness tool that offers in-the-trenches support for working with intense and difficult emotions. Called RAIN (an acronym for the four steps of the process), it can be accessed in almost any place or situation. It directs our attention in a clear, systematic way that cuts through confusion and stress. The steps give us somewhere to turn in a painful moment, and as we call on them more regularly, they strengthen our capacity to come home to our deepest truth. Like the clear sky and clean air after a cooling rain, this mindfulness practice brings a new openness and calm to our daily lives.

I have now taught RAIN to thousands of students, clients, and mental health professionals, adapting and expanding it into the version you'll find in this chapter. I've also made it a core practice in my own life. Here are the four steps of RAIN presented in the way I've found most helpful:

R   *Recognize* what is happening
A   *Allow* life to be just as it is
I   *Investigate inner experience* with kindness
N   *Non-identification*

RAIN directly deconditions the habitual ways in which you resist your moment-to-moment experience. It doesn't matter whether you resist what is by lashing out in anger, by having a cigarette, or by getting immersed in obsessive thinking. Your attempt to control the life within and around you actually cuts you off from your own heart and from this living world. RAIN begins to undo these unconscious patterns as soon as we take the first step.

RECOGNIZE WHAT IS HAPPENING

Recognition is seeing what is true in your inner life. It starts the minute you focus your attention on whatever thoughts, emotions, feelings, or sensations are arising right here and now. As your attention settles and opens, you will discover that some parts of your experience are easier to connect with than others. For example, you might recognize anxiety right away, but if you focus on your worried thoughts, you might not notice the actual sensations of squeezing, pressure, or tightness arising in the body. On the other hand, if your body is gripped by jittery nervousness, you might not recognize that this physical response is being triggered by your underlying belief that you are about to fail. You can awaken recognition simply by asking yourself: "What is happening inside me right now?" Call on your natural curiosity as you focus inward. Try to let go of any preconceived ideas and instead listen in a kind, receptive way to your body and heart.

ALLOW LIFE TO BE JUST AS IT IS

Allowing means "letting be" the thoughts, emotions, feelings, or sensations you discover. You may feel a natural sense of aversion, of wishing that unpleasant feelings would go away, but as you become more willing to be present with "what is," a different quality of attention will emerge. Allowing is intrinsic to healing, and realizing this can give rise to a conscious intention to "let be."

Many students I work with support their resolve to "let be" by mentally whispering an encouraging word or phrase. For instance, you might feel the grip of fear and whisper "yes," or experience the swelling of deep grief and whisper "yes." You might use the words "this too" or "I consent." At first you might feel you're just putting up with unpleasant emotions or sensations. Or you might say yes to shame and hope that it will magically disappear. In reality, we have to consent again and again. Yet even the first gesture of allowing, simply whispering a phrase like "yes" or "I consent," begins to soften the harsh edges of your pain. Your entire being is not so rallied in resistance. Offer the phrase gently and patiently, and in time your defenses will relax, and you may feel a physical sense of yielding or opening to waves of experience.

INVESTIGATE WITH KINDNESS

At times, simply working through the first two steps of RAIN is enough to provide relief and reconnect you with presence. In other cases, however, the simple intention to recognize and allow is not enough. For instance, if you are in the thick of a divorce, about to lose a job, or dealing with a life-threatening illness, you may be easily overwhelmed by intense feelings. Because these feelings are triggered over and over again—you get a phone call from your soon-to-be ex, your bank statement comes, you wake up to pain in the morning—your reactions can become very entrenched. In such situations, you may need to further awaken and strengthen mindful awareness with the *I* of RAIN.

Investigation means calling on your natural interest—the desire to know truth—and directing a more focused attention to your present experience. Simply pausing to ask, "What is happening inside me?" might initiate recognition, but with investigation you engage in a more active and pointed kind of inquiry. You might ask yourself: "What most wants attention?" "How am I experiencing this in my body?" or "What am I believing?" or "What does this feeling want from me?" You might contact sensations of hollowness or shakiness, and then find a sense of unworthiness and shame buried in these feelings. Unless they are brought into consciousness, these beliefs and emotions will control your experience and perpetuate your identification with a limited, deficient self.

When I first shared the RAIN acronym with students, many of them had problems with the investigation step. Some said things like, "When fear arises, my investigation just takes me into thinking about what is causing it and how to feel better." Others reported, "I can't stay in my body long enough to investigate where an emotion lives in me." For many, investigation triggered judgment: "I know I'm supposed to be investigating this shame, but I hate it . . . and I hate myself for having it."

All these responses reflect our natural resistance to feeling uncomfortable and unsafe: Thoughts swarm in our head, we leave our body, we judge what is happening. What my students were telling me was that RAIN was missing a key ingredient. In order for investigation to be healing and freeing, we need to approach our experience with an intimate quality of attention. We need to offer a gentle welcome to whatever surfaces. This is why I use the phrase "Investigate with kindness." Without this heart energy, investigation cannot penetrate; there is not enough safety and openness for real contact.

Imagine that your child comes home in tears after being bullied at school. In order to find out what happened and how your child is feeling, you have to offer a kind, receptive, gentle attention. Bringing that same kindness to your inner life makes inquiry, and ultimately healing, possible.

NON-IDENTIFICATION: REST IN NATURAL AWARENESS

The lucid, open, and kind presence evoked in the *R, A,* and *I* of RAIN leads to the *N*: the freedom of *non-identification,* and the realization of what I call natural awareness or natural presence. Non-identification means that your sense of who you are is not fused with or defined by any limited set of emotions, sensations, or stories. When identification with the small self is loosened, we begin to intuit and live from the openness and love that express our natural awareness. The first three steps of RAIN require some intentional activity. In contrast, the *N* of RAIN expresses the result: a liberating realization of your natural awareness. There's nothing to do for this last part of RAIN—realization arises spontaneously, on its own. We simply rest in natural awareness.

APPLYING RAIN TO BLAME

Some years ago, on the day after Christmas, I found myself surrounded by family and annoyed by every person I'd looked forward to spending time with. No one was really being mean spirited, but I found myself spinning in my own irritable, judgmental orbit. After someone interrupted my father at lunch, he became upset and withdrew into an aggrieved silence that ruined the mood for the rest of us. Then my son, Narayan, skipped out to meet a friend instead of helping wash the dishes as he had promised. My mother complained that Narayan was barely around; one of my sisters was sulking because this meal, like several others, showed insensitivity to her food preferences; and my other sister snapped because she hadn't been consulted about the timing of an outing. Even the dogs were misbehaving—hanging around the table and begging for food. As far as I was concerned, each person (and animal!) was exhibiting his or her well-worn version of being a victim or martyr, of being needy or oblivious. Moreover, my own needs for space and harmony were not being met. Here it was, only two days into our visit, and I was churning with resentment.

During the months before our holiday gathering, it had become increasingly clear to me how my habit of judging created a painful separation from others. Motivated by this suffering, I had committed myself to add a specific focus to my spiritual life: I began to intentionally bring RAIN to my feelings of aversive judgment and blame. For the next several weeks, I tried to notice how my body and heart felt when my mind produced stories that diminished others. Each time my inner critic made demeaning comments, I looked to see what underlying beliefs were speaking. Investigating this experience of judgment and blame opened my eyes to the reality of how many moments I was living with a closed heart. This recognition deepened my commitment: The more I saw the pain of this false refuge, the more I sensed the freedom and openheartedness that lay beyond it.

Despite my new commitment, I wasn't at all in the mood to examine my inner life that afternoon. Grumpy and tired—with all the judgments about my family ricocheting in my mind—I considered burying myself in a good book. But I just couldn't get away from that niggling inner voice reminding me of my promise to bring RAIN to blame.

Grudgingly, I threw on my parka and boots and headed outside into the gray December afternoon to see if I could find my way to more presence and peace.

Walking through the light drizzle, I began to reflect on each family member and to watch my mind poke blame at them. I witnessed my judgments: "You get so indignant and huffy, Dad, when others interrupt. What's the big deal? And you, Narayan, you're so irresponsible, never keeping your word . . ." So I began to practice RAIN by recognizing my reactivity: I clearly saw how I disliked the way my family was acting, how I found each in some way wrong.

As a way of allowing—the second step of RAIN—I took some time to acknowledge the blaming thoughts and then just let them be. Rather than judging my own judging mind, I made an effort to remind myself, "This is just what is happening." As I stayed with my experience, I became aware of a tight sore area in my chest. This became a natural focus for the next step in RAIN—investigation. With some interest, I began attending to my body, and soon the tightness turned into a sharply edged knot compressing my heart. While there were many different complaints running through my mind, I noticed that they were all arising from the same irritated, squeezed place.

Now I asked that knotted place a question: "What does life look like through your eyes . . . from your perspective?" In the past, this type of question had helped me get "inside" an experience. In response to my inquiry came a realization: Buried inside my reaction to each person was the experience of feeling bad about myself. In each case their behavior had triggered my own feelings of falling short—as a family peacemaker, as a responsible parent, as a helpful daughter and supportive sister. My inquiry had started to loosen the knot of blame, and I could now feel what it was masking: a familiar, sinking, sick feeling of personal failure.

Over the past two months, my rounds of RAIN had taught me that when I turn against others, I am also at odds with myself. Yet there is often an initial phase during which I recognize that I've locked onto the "wrongness" of others, but am not yet aware of my self-aversion. Now once again, beneath the blame, I encountered the familiar and painful belief that directly perpetuates the trance of small self: "Something is wrong with me."

In practicing RAIN, the quality of our attention determines how deeply we can contact our inner truth. Knowing this, I consciously slowed my walking pace and with a gentle, receptive attention, let the sense of not-okay self express itself fully. It felt like a wire net compressing my heart, making it small, hard, heavy. In my mind's eye, I was utterly alone; a self cut off from others. Now I could sense how this holiday experience was simply an exaggerated version of what happened regularly in daily life. I would blame members of our organization's board for doing too little to increase diversity in our community, but really feel pained by how little time I had to devote to the critical issue. I would blame my son for forgetting a homework assignment, but under that, I would be suffering over the belief that I was a negligent mother. I would blame my sister for complaining that I was too busy to see her, but beneath that I would feel guilty about how little unrushed time I spent with her and my niece. Whether I was caught in self-blame or blaming others, what stood out was the familiar sense that I was cut off, all alone with my painfully closed heart.

Now I felt an upwelling of sadness. My sense of grievance was shifting to grief, and my attention was becoming more intimate and kind. The ache of grief began rolling through me like a tide, flooding my heart, clearing out all thoughts of blame, all stories of personal failure. Gradually, the raw intensity that had felt so overwhelming began to ease up. As the waves of grief slowed, I found myself resting in a quiet tenderness.

As if acknowledging my inner weather, the skies suddenly let loose. Surrendering to the strong steady rain, I started making my way back home. Once again, I invited my family members to come to mind. One by one, I found that with each, the rain had dissolved my ideas of "wrongness." I no longer experienced them as "problem others . . . out there." Rather, each was a unique being who occupied a special place in my heart.

When I reached my parents' house, I was soaked. No one was around except the dogs, who made a fuss over me. Everyone else was on their computers, napping, or otherwise occupied. That felt fine. I was blessedly unencumbered by stories about how anyone should be different from the way he or she was.

After dinner that evening, my mom went to the piano and started playing Christmas carols. We all joined in, singing off-key, not remembering most of the verses. The program moved on to musicals. We sounded pretty awful and we soon ended up laughing at ourselves. Then we sang some more.

I drifted off to sleep that night with a deep sense of well-being. My family hadn't changed, but in the place of my trance of separation and blame was an openness full of love and ease. This is the blessing of taking refuge in truth.

As poet Dorothy Hunt wrote,

> Peace is this moment without judgment.
> That is all. This moment in the Heart-space
> Where everything that is is welcome.

GUIDELINES FOR PRACTICING
WITH RAIN

You can practice the steps of RAIN during a formal meditation whenever a difficult emotion arises, or, as I did, you can call on it in the midst of daily life. Either way, the key is to be conscious and purposeful as you initiate the practice—knowing that you are offering a committed presence to what is true, here and now.

Here are some more specific suggestions that have emerged as I've taught RAIN to many students and therapists.

Pause

Before you begin RAIN, take the time to pause. The pause might be in the form of a physical time-out that removes you from immediate external triggers. More important, it is an internal time-out from the reactive tumble of thoughts. In a pause, you intentionally create a space in which you set aside distractions and pay attention. This willingness to deliberately interrupt habitual activity and dedicate time to being present will lend increased focus and clarity to your practice.

Give Yourself the Support of a Regular Meditation Practice

A regular meditation practice directly awakens the key ingredients in RAIN—mindfulness, openheartedness, and inquiry. During my evening walk, the skills developed through past meditation training served me in several key ways. My practice in being mindful of thinking helped me to be aware of my thoughts without getting lost in them. Similarly, my practice in bringing presence to unpleasant experiences allowed me to open to the raw feelings and sensations in my body. Maybe most important, my practice with awakening self-compassion, a key element in my own meditative path and in my teachings, enabled me to bring a warm, intimate attention to the onslaught of judgment and blame.

Cultivate Flexibility

You have a unique body and mind, with a particular history and conditioning. No one can offer you a formula for navigating all situations and all states of mind. Only by listening inwardly in a fresh and open way will you discern at any given time what most serves your healing and freedom.

As you practice RAIN, remember that the sequence I've suggested is neither rigid, nor necessarily linear; you may need to adapt the order as you attend to your inner experience. You might find, for instance, that as soon as you feel rising anxiety, you recognize it as a familiar inner weather pattern that happens to you and most everyone you know, and hence does not feel so personal. In moments like these you have already arrived at the N of RAIN; so, rather than any continued "doing," such as investigating with kindness, you might simply rest in natural presence. Similarly, you might end your RAIN practice before formally moving through all the steps or cycle through the process again if you encounter something unexpected.

As you listen inwardly to what is needed, you may also feel drawn to weave other forms of meditation into your practice of RAIN. To ground yourself, you might begin with a body-based reflection (see "A Pause for Presence," on page 15), yoga, or a walking meditation. If strong feelings arise in the midst of RAIN, you might take some time to simply focus on your breath. Or you might find that a few minutes of lovingkindness practice (see page 26) helps you to bring a gentler and more compassionate attention to investigation. This kind of inner listening and adaptability can help you transform what at first might seem to be a mechanical technique into a creative and vibrant means of awakening on your spiritual path.

Practice with the "Small Stuff"

Eighth-century Buddhist master Shantideva suggests that by staying present "with little cares, we train ourselves to work with great adversity." Each time you bring RAIN to a situation that usually causes you to react, you strengthen your capacity to awaken from trance. You might identify in advance what for you is chronic "small stuff"—the annoyance that comes up when someone repeats herself, the restlessness when you are waiting in line, the frustration when you've forgotten to pick up something on your shopping list—and commit to pausing and practicing a "light" version of RAIN, as in the guided meditation at the end of the chapter. By pausing many times throughout the day, and bringing an interest and presence to your habitual ways of reacting, your life will become increasingly spontaneous and free.

Seek Help

Practicing RAIN can intensify your emotional experience. You may find that some forms of Western psychotherapy offer valuable support as you investigate painful or confusing feelings. My work with clients and students has been influenced by Focusing (developing by Eugene Gendlin), a body-based psychotherapy that emphasizes tracking the felt sense of experience with an open and accepting attention. Other mindfulness-based therapies provide similar support in maintaining a healing attention as we explore what is happening inside us.

If you are concerned that you might become possessed or overwhelmed by your feelings, postpone practicing RAIN alone and seek help. Especially if you are working with post-traumatic stress, it can be important, and even necessary, to have the guidance of a therapist or psychologically attuned meditation teacher. The presence of a trusted and experienced person can help you feel safe enough to connect with inner vulnerability and also to find relief if what arises feels like too much. (See chapter 9 for more guidance in dealing with trauma.)

Let Your Senses Be a Gateway to Presence

The practice of RAIN comes alive as you learn to step out of your thoughts and connect with your body's experience. Many people move through daily life possessed by thoughts and, to varying degrees, dissociated from the felt sense in the body. Strong emotional trauma or wounding makes dissociation from bodily awareness particularly likely. Whether you are working through deep fear and shame, or a less acute emotional reaction, your inner freedom will arise from bringing attention to how the experience is expressed in your body. On my evening walk, the pivotal moment came when I could directly feel how layers of judgment, assumed unworthiness, and grief were squeezing my heart.

Be Mindful of Doubt

Doubt acts as a main impediment to RAIN, and more broadly, to any gateway of true refuge. The Buddha considered doubt (along with clinging and aversion) to be a universal hindrance to spiritual freedom. When you are stuck in beliefs like "I'm never going to change," "I'm not cut out for spiritual practice," or "Healing and freedom aren't really possible," you get stopped in your tracks.

Needless to say, some doubt is healthy, as in "I'm no longer certain this job is in line with my values," or "Maybe *I've* been the one who is avoiding intimacy," or "I wonder whether I can trust a spiritual teacher who speaks disrespectfully of other teachers." Like investigation, healthy doubt arises from the urge to know what is true—it challenges assumptions or the status quo in service of healing and freedom. In contrast, unhealthy doubt arises from fear and aversion, and it questions one's own basic potential or worth, or the value of another.

When unhealthy doubt arises, let it be the subject of RAIN. It helps to say to yourself, "This is doubt," consciously acknowledging its presence in your mind. By recognizing and naming doubt when it arises, but not judging it, you immediately enlarge your perspective and loosen the bind of trance. If the doubt is persistent, you can deepen presence by regarding it with kindness. Rather than being controlled, and perhaps paralyzed, by doubt, let it be a call for a clear, mindful presence.

Be Patient

Patience gives you joy in the process of awakening. Without patience, you may find yourself at war with your own forgetfulness or reactivity. Long-term meditators or therapy clients often complain, "I've been dealing with this same issue for decades." They are troubled by their regressions into old feelings of being worthless or rejected, unsafe or ashamed. Such bouts of trance can be accompanied by desperation and the fear that there will be no end to the cycling of unhealthy patterns of feelings and behaviors. While RAIN reduces the grip of trance, it is rarely a one-shot experience. You may need to go through numerous rounds of RAIN, again and again meeting entrenched patterns of suffering with attention and kindness.

The belief and feeling that "something is wrong with me" was a key theme in my first book, *Radical Acceptance,* and it continues to be part of my life. But my many rounds of meeting it with presence have had an effect: The trance is much more transparent, short-lived, and suffering-free. Often it makes a brief appearance, and then there's recognition, "Ah, this again . . ." and a letting go. It's not that "I" am letting go, but rather the old false sense of self just dissolves when it is seen. What remains is an invigorated realization of the heart space that holds this life, and a trust in the tender awareness that lives beyond the trance.

Each time you meet an old emotional pattern with presence, your awakening to truth can deepen. There's less identification with the self in the story and more ability to rest in the awareness that is witnessing what's happening. You become more able to abide in compassion, to remember and trust your true home. Rather than cycling repetitively through old conditioning, you are actually spiraling toward freedom.

Be Sincere

An attitude of sincerity in approaching spiritual practices like RAIN orients your heart and mind toward freedom. Let yourself recall again and again what for you is the most important thing. Perhaps you long to realize the truth of who you are, to love well, to touch peace, or to live more from presence. Whatever you most care about, let this tenderness of heart energize your meditation. The sincerity of your longing will carry you home.

> All you ever longed for is
> Before you in this moment
> If you dare draw in a
> Breath and whisper "Yes."

——DANNA FAULDS

Guided Reflection: Bringing RAIN to Difficulty

Sitting quietly, close your eyes and take a few full breaths. Bring to mind a current situation in which you feel stuck; one that elicits a difficult reaction such as anger or fear, shame or hopelessness. It may be a conflict with a family member, a chronic sickness, a failure at work, the pain of an addiction, a conversation you now regret. Take some moments to enter the experience—visualizing the scene or situation, remembering the words spoken, sensing the most distressing moments. Contacting the charged essence of the story is the starting place for exploring the healing presence of RAIN.

***

R: Recognize What Is Happening
As you reflect on this situation, ask yourself, "What is happening inside me right now?" What sensations are you most aware of? What emotions? Is your mind filled with churning thoughts? Take a moment to become aware of your "felt sense" of the situation as a whole. Can you feel how the experience is living in your heart and body, as well as in your mind?

A: Allow Life to Be Just as It Is
Send a message to your heart to "let be" this entire experience. Find in yourself the willingness to pause and accept that in these moments, "what is . . . is." You can experiment with mentally whispering words like "yes," "I consent," or "let be."

You might find yourself saying yes to a huge inner no, to a body and mind painfully contracted in resistance. You might be saying yes to the part of you that is saying "I hate this!" That's a natural part of the process. At this point in RAIN, you are simply noticing what is true, and intending not to judge, push away, or control anything you find.

I: Investigate with an Intimate Attention
Now begin to explore what you are experiencing more closely, calling on your natural interest and curiosity about your inner life. You might ask yourself, "What about this most wants my attention?" or, "What most wants my acceptance?" Pose your questions gently, with your inner voice kind and inviting.

Notice where you feel the experience most distinctly in your body. Are you aware of heat, tightness, pressure, aches, squeezing? When you have found the most intense part of your physical experience, bring it into your face, letting your expression mirror, and even exaggerate, what you are feeling in your body. What emotions are you aware of as you do this? Fear? Anger? Grief? Shame?

As you continue to investigate, you might find it helpful to ask, "What am I believing?" If this leads to a lot of thinking, drop it. But you might find that a very distinct belief emerges almost as soon as you ask. Do you believe that you are failing in some way? That someone will reject you? That you will not be able to handle whatever is around the corner? That you really are flawed? That you will never be happy? How does this belief live in your body? What are the sensations? Tightness? Soreness? Burning? Hollowness?

As before, send the message of "yes," "I consent," or "let be," allowing yourself to feel the fullness or intensity of the difficult experience. As you contact and allow what is happening, what do you notice? Is there any softening in your body and heart? Can you sense more openness or space? Or does the intention to allow bring up more tension, judgment, and fear? Does it intensify or change what you are feeling?

Now ask the place of most difficulty, "What do you want from me?" or "What do you need from me?" Does this suffering part of you want recognition? Acceptance? Forgiveness? Love? As you sense what is needed, what is your natural response? You might offer yourself a wise message, or an energetic, tender embrace. You might gently place your hand on your heart. Feel free to experiment with ways of befriending your inner life—whether through words or touch, images or energy. Discover how your attention might become more intimate and loving.

N: Non-identification: Rest in Natural Awareness

As you offer this unconditional, kind presence to your inner life, sense the possibility of relaxing back and being that awareness. Like an ocean with waves on the surface, feel yourself as the tender, wakeful openness that includes arising and passing sensations, emotions, thoughts. Can you sense how who you are is not identified by or hitched to any particular wave of fear or anger or hurt? Can you sense how the waves on the surface belong to your experience, but cannot injure or alter the measureless depth and vastness of your being? Take some moments, as long as you'd like, to simply rest in this spacious and kind awareness, allowing whatever arises in your body or mind to freely come and go. Know this natural awareness as the innermost truth of what you are.

Guided Reflection: A Light RAIN: Practicing on the Spot

Pausing for brief periods of RAIN during the day is as important in awakening us from trance as a more full-blown session. A brief and cleansing shower of RAIN might take a minute or so. The steps are essentially the same, just abbreviated.

———— ✇ ————

Recognize *emotional reactivity.*
Pause by taking three full breaths, and allow *your inner experience to be as it is.*
Investigate *with kindness whatever feelings are most predominant.*
Resume activity, and notice if there is more natural presence.

A light RAIN starts by recognizing that you are caught in reactivity—to a perceived slight, unwashed dishes, misplaced eyeglasses, feelings of indigestion, something you regret saying. When you recognize you are stuck, stop everything and take three long, full breaths. These breaths help you disengage from the momentum of your thoughts and activity and make space for your inner experience. Investigate by asking yourself, "What am I feeling?" and bring your attention to your body—primarily your throat, chest, and belly. Notice what sensations (tightness, heat, pressure) and emotions (angry, afraid, guilty) are predominant. Let your intention be to befriend what you notice. Try to stay in touch with your breath as you contact your felt sense of what is happening.

Sometimes it's easy to locate your felt sense, but at other times it might be vague and hard to identify quickly. That's fine. What is important is pausing and deepening your attention. See if it is possible to regard yourself with kindness.

You complete your moments of light RAIN by simply relaxing and reentering activity. As you move into what is next in your day, sense what might have shifted. Are you more aware? Open? Warmhearted? Are you taking things less personally? Is there more access to natural presence, the N of RAIN?

As with practicing the fuller version of RAIN, approach these pauses creatively. You will soon discover what most helps you listen, with a friendly attention, to your inner life.

———— ∞ ————

SIX

AWAKENING TO THE LIFE
OF THE BODY

Trust the energy that
Courses through you. Trust
Then take surrender even deeper. Be the energy.
Don't push anything away. Follow each
Sensation back to its source
In vastness and pure presence.

DANNA FAULDS

Here in this body are the sacred rivers: here are the sun and moon, as well as all the pil-
grimage places. I have not encountered another temple as blissful as my own body.

TANTRIC SONG

"What does numb feel like?" I asked. Jane stared stonily at the floor and, after a few moments, whispered, "Blocking everything, nothing can get in or out. It's like a blanket around my heart."

It was the third day of a weeklong retreat, and Jane had come to let me know that she was stuck. She avoided my eyes as she entered the room. Once seated, she frowned and then nervously ran her fingers through her severely cut short blond hair.

"I've been thinking of coming to a retreat for years," she began, "but I finally signed up because I've felt so hopeless recently . . . it's like I'm either constantly anxious or shut down and depressed." For more than ten years she'd been totally immersed in her work as a sociologist, researching and teaching at a large university. But the competition to publish seemed increasingly meaningless, and she'd become aware of an inner deadness. "I was hoping that meditation would help me feel more alive."

But now Jane feared that it was a mistake to have come. "I'm doing something wrong," she stated flatly. "In the group this morning, people talked about their hearts opening, feeling buried grief, or having deep insights." Jane shook her head. "But for me, nothing's happening. I have no idea what I'm feeling. When I meditate either my mind is churning or I'm getting bored trying to follow my breath. I'm just numb." That's when she described the blanket around her heart.

"Can you say more about this blanket?" I asked. "I hate it!" she blurted out. She shot me a quick look before continuing. "I've done enough therapy to know that not feeling things is screwing up my life. It makes it so that I can't have meaningful relationships. It stops me from knowing what I really want or looking forward to anything." She shook her head. "I know there's stuff buried inside me, but something in me doesn't want to go there. So here I am, finally at a retreat . . . and I'm just not getting it."

"Jane," I said, "it's important for you to know that you're not doing anything wrong." She shifted uncomfortably in her seat. "You're honestly recognizing and naming your experience as it is," I said. "And that's an essential part of meditation."

I had already taught RAIN to the group and I reminded her that by recognizing what was happening inside of her, she was practicing the *R* of RAIN. "Would you like us to explore the next steps in using RAIN?" She nodded her agreement. "Good," I said. "You might begin by pausing and bringing your attention to your body." I waited a few moments and then asked, "What is happening inside you right now?"

After crossing and then uncrossing her legs, Jane sat back in her chair and rearranged her hands. "I'm restless . . . as you can probably tell. It's hard to sit here right now. It's like I feel when I'm at home trying to meditate. I want to get up and go online or grade papers . . . anything but just sit there." "So there is restlessness," I said. "Can you agree to let it be there for now? Allow it to be as it is, so that we can investigate a little?" Jane gave a small smile. "Yeah, sure."

"Good. Now, where in your body are you most aware of that restless feeling?" At first Jane just shook her head, but then she took a deep breath and closed her eyes. A few moments later she started rubbing the center of her chest, right over the breastbone. "Jane," I said, "bring your attention fully to the place where your hand is on your chest . . . and let me know what you are feeling there." She responded quickly: "There's an uncomfortable, shaky feeling here. It's really unpleasant."

I let her know that this was a fine example of the *I* of RAIN, investigation. Then I asked, "Are you willing to try an experiment?" Jane nodded. "Okay, just for a few moments, find out what happens if you allow those shaky, unpleasant feelings in your body to be there, just as they are—as if you are simply pausing in the middle of them." Noticing that she had frozen with her hand on her chest, I added, "Try keeping your hand right where it is, and breathe in and out of where the sensations are strongest. This can help you stay connected with the experience."

Jane sat without moving, fingers touching her chest. After a minute or so she opened her eyes, looked briefly at me and then at the floor. Her frown was back, and when she spoke, her voice was resigned. "First there was an anxious feeling, but then that disappeared and I was numb again." She paused for a moment and then shrugged. "As usual, I couldn't feel much of anything."

OUR CHAIN OF REACTIVITY

When I meet with people at retreats or in counseling sessions, some, like Jane, will tell me they feel numb, lost in thoughts, and disconnected from life. Others might tell me they are overwhelmed by feelings of fear, hurt, or anger. Whenever we are either possessed by our feelings or dissociated from them, we are in trance, cut off from our full presence and aliveness.

Both Buddhist and Western psychology tells us that our trance of emotional reactivity begins with a universally conditioned reflex: Consciously or not, we continually assess whatever is happening as pleasant, unpleasant, or neutral. The smell of fresh-baked cookies—probably pleasant. A thought about a recent argument—probably unpleasant. The sound of cars passing outside—usually neutral. "Pleasant" arouses our conditioning to grasp. We may start craving the cookies and fantasize about eating them. "Unpleasant" sensations trigger our conditioning to contract and avoid them. Thoughts of an argument might lead to physical tensing, feelings of anger, and plans for proving our point. When something is neutral, we tend to ignore it and turn our attention elsewhere.

While these mental and emotional reactions are natural, it's easy for us to become identified with them, retreating to a space-suit self. For instance, as our attention fixates on our craving for cookies—how we want them but maybe shouldn't eat them—we contract and become ensnared in the sense of a wanting self. As our attention fixates on an argument—how insulted we feel and what else we should have said—we contract and become ensnared in the sense of an angry, offended self. Our thoughts and feelings start to loop—the more we think about what is upsetting us, the angrier we get: the more anger we feel, the more we generate angry thoughts. When we are caught in this chain of reactivity, we are in trance. We have pulled away from a larger sense of who we are and what matters in our life.

In Buddhist meditation training, awakening from trance begins with mindfulness of sensations. Sensations are our most immediate way of experiencing and relating to life. All our other reactions—to thoughts, to external situations, to people, to emotions—are actually in response to physical sensations. When we are angry at someone, our body is responding to a perceived threat. When we are attracted to someone, our body is signaling comfort or curiosity or desire. If we don't recognize the ground level of sensation, we will continually be lost in the swirl of thoughts, feelings, and emotions that make up our daily trance.

TOUCHING THE GROUND

One of the best instructions I've heard for meditation practice was given by Thai Buddhist teacher Ajahn Buddhadasa: "Do not do anything that takes you away from your body." The body lives in the present. When you are aware of the body, you are connected with living presence—the one place where you can see reality, see what is actually happening. *Awareness of the body is our gateway into the truth of what is.*

This gateway to refuge was crucial to the Buddha's own awakening. When Siddhartha Gautama took his seat at the base of the bodhi tree—the tree of awakening—he resolved to stay there until he found full freedom. He began his meditation by collecting his attention, quieting his mind, and "coming back" to a full and balanced presence. But then, as the story is told, the demon Mara appeared, accompanied by a massive army, and with many deadly weapons and magical forces at his disposal. Mara is a tempter—his name means "delusion" in Pali—and we can also see him as Gautama's shadow self. Mara's intent was to keep Gautama trapped in trance.

Throughout the night Mara hurled rocks and arrows, boiling mud and blistering sands to provoke Gautama to fight or flee, yet he met these attacks with a compassionate presence, and the missiles were all transformed into celestial flowers. Then Mara sent his daughters, "desire, pining, and lust," surrounded by voluptuous attendants to seduce Gautama, yet Gautama's mind remained undistracted and present. Dawn was fast approaching when Mara issued his final challenge—doubt. What proof, Mara asked, did Gautama have of his compassion? How could he be sure his heart was awakened? Mara was targeting the core reactivity that hooks and sustains the sense of small self—the perception of our own unworthiness.

Gautama did not try to use a meditative technique to prove himself. Rather, he touched the earth and asked it to bear witness to his compassion, to the truth of what he was. In response, the earth responded with a shattering roar, "I bear you witness!" Terrified, Mara and his forces dispersed in all directions.

In that instant of acknowledging his belonging to the earth, Gautama became the Buddha—the awakened one—and was liberated. By claiming this living wholeness, he dissolved the final vestiges of the trance of separation.

For us, the story of the Buddha's liberation offers a radical and wonderful invitation. Like the Buddha, our own healing and awakening unfolds in any moment in which we take refuge in our aliveness—connecting with our flesh and blood, with our breath, with the air itself, with the elements that compose us, and with the earth that is our home. Whenever we bring our presence to the living world of sensation, we too are touching the ground.

ENTERING THE BODY

For Jane, finding her way into the world of sensation seemed crucial. Before we ended our meeting, I encouraged her to take some time during her meditations to feel the life of her body from the inside out. It would be easier to do this, I told her, if she started by learning to become aware of neutral or pleasant sensations. To give her a taste of what I meant, I asked her to close her eyes. "Let your hands relax, resting effortlessly and easily in your lap," I suggested. "Now imagine you could place your awareness inside your hands. See if it's possible to soften your hands a little bit more and sense the life that's there." I paused. "Can you sense the vibrating, the tingling? Can you feel heat or coolness? Can you feel places of pressure where your hands contact your legs, and where your fingers touch each other?"

Jane sat very still, and then with a slight smile she nodded. "Good," I said. "Now try to feel that same aliveness in your feet. Just take a moment and sense the vibrating, the tingling, the shifting sensations in your feet." After a pause, she nodded again. "Jane, the same aliveness that is in your hands and your feet exists throughout your body. Now try widening the lens of your attention and sense the whole field of sensations in your body. These might be pleasant or unpleasant . . . just allow them to come and go, noticing whatever is predominant. And to help you stay connected and relaxed, try sensing how your breath is moving through it all."

When Jane opened her eyes to meet mine, they seemed softer and brighter. She looked around the room as if she was taking in her surroundings—the candles, the clock, the box of tissues—for the first time. "Tara," she began, "I couldn't feel much through the rest of my body, but just feeling my hands and feet, feeling my breath for a few moments was . . . well . . . I felt like I was actually here!"

I let Jane know that when people first begin training in mindfulness of the body, some find it difficult to feel sensations in the stomach, chest, or throat. But with practice and patience, I assured her, our awareness of the body awakens. Over the next few days, her job was to take some time in each meditation to first explore neutral or pleasant sensations by feeling her hands and feet from the inside out; and then to open to as many bodily sensations as possible.

I also suggested a more challenging job: When she encountered a difficult state of mind—restlessness, anxiety, sadness, anger—I urged her to ask herself, as I had, "What is happening inside you right now?" To help her as she opened to the sensations underlying these feelings, I reminded her to keep some of her attention on her breath: "Especially when sensations are unpleasant, your breath can be a safe home base . . . it's good company."

Mindful awareness of sensations is the "ground level" in practicing with RAIN. I hoped Jane could discover how a state of mind expresses itself as a felt sense, even before it coalesces into a thought. "Any experience you have is rooted in your body, and contacting that experience— letting yourself feel the sensations—will help you feel more grounded and aware," I told her.

"Even feeling the blanket of numbness?" she asked with raised eyebrows and a hint of playfulness. "Yes," I said, smiling. "That too."

As Jane was to find, whatever arises in the present moment is exactly the experience that can open the door to healing.

IF IT FEELS LIKE TOO MUCH

Many years ago, when I first started going to vipassana retreats, the instructions we received were fairly uniform. We were given the anchor of the breath, but if something intense or unpleasant emerged, we were told to contact those sensations with a full attention. This included opening to feelings of numbness and terror, despair and rage. While this led to valuable insights for most students, for some I knew—people who were living with untreated trauma—it was harmful. Instead of new insights and greater awareness, they were flooded by emotions and overwhelmed with helplessness. The experience only reinforced their sense of being threatened and powerless. This is one reason why I encouraged Jane to develop her home base; I did not know what her numbness was protecting.

The conditioning to pull away from pain is part of our survival equipment. When we have experienced deep emotional wounding or physical or emotional trauma, dissociation from raw sensations and acute fear is a powerful self-protective reflex. Yet until the trauma is felt and processed, these painful energies continue to be held in our tissue and nervous system. Because they express themselves as recurrent physical or emotional pain, we develop ongoing strategies to avoid what we're feeling—tensing or numbing the body, generating distracting thoughts, engaging in addictive behaviors, acting aggressively. Focusing attention on the body can begin to undo these protective strategies and open us to intense and often disruptive energies. While ultimately this "undoing" is an essential part of healing, we may become overwhelmed and possibly retraumatized if our mindfulness is not stable or strong enough.

Most people live with emotional wounding, and many, with some degree of trauma. As Jane put it, there is "stuff buried inside." How do we know when it is safe to connect with these long-avoided feelings? Some students fear that if they intentionally open to what is inside them, they will fall apart and become emotionally paralyzed or dysfunctional. They wonder what style of meditation is right for them.

These critical questions deserve careful attention. While there is no clear formula, I've found that mindfulness of the body requires a sufficient sense of safety and stability—in other words, some initial sense of refuge. I often recommend seeking the guidance of a qualified teacher or therapist attuned to mindfulness and to healing trauma. If someone is feeling shaky and vulnerable, he or she might feel safe enough practicing with a group of fellow meditators, and/or knowing that a mindfulness teacher, therapist, or trusted friend is available to provide support as needed. As Jane and I started working together, I could tell by her willingness to explore her experience that she felt a reasonable sense of trust in my support. One powerful aspect of the refuge of love is what I call "being accompanied." The presence of another person who cares for our well-being can become a kind of healing "container" for our intense internal energies. (I will explore this refuge more fully in chapter 9.)

Our sense of safety and stability also grows as we cultivate our own inner resources—the meditative skills that settle the mind, calm the body, and steady the attention. Here we are taking refuge in truth, in practices that ready us for a full, embodied presence. For instance, I began working with Jane by asking her to connect with pleasant or neutral feelings in her body. Strengthening this skill would help her relax her mind and give her a sense of her body as a potentially safe place. We also worked on developing the use of her anchor (the breath) as a reliable and comforting home base; she needed to know she could calm herself if something felt like too much. As I suggested, this same anchor could then support her—be "good company"—as she moved toward presence with more difficult emotions.

I recently counseled a young man who had served in Iraq and was suffering from post-traumatic stress. When he first came to me, paying attention to any part of his body other than his feet triggered terror. We worked together to build two resource anchors: the sensations in his feet—which helped to ground him—and a mantra, or set of sacred words, that reminded him of the protection of a loving universal spirit. For many months, his primary practice was to reflect on his mantra, repeating it inwardly over and over again, and to feel his feet on the ground. After about six months, when he was feeling more grounded and protected, he gradually began to include the sensations in the rest of his body in his awareness. He called this his "journey back to being alive and whole."

One woman at a weeklong retreat I led was suffering from what she called a "stranglehold" of anxiety. She learned to work with it by intentionally contacting and then moving away from intense sensations. She would imagine she was stepping into the river of her fears, and she'd let herself open to the clutching and squeezing and soreness that lived inside her. Then she would visualize stepping out of the river and sitting on the bank. There she would take some moments to intentionally awaken her senses—open her eyes, look around—including in her awareness the sounds outside the room, the sense of air and space around her, the feeling of her breath, the support of the chair beneath her. By widening her attention she could remain aware of the grip of anxiety, but without feeling so overwhelmed. In a single sitting she might do several rounds of stepping into the river to contact her fears directly, and then stepping out to rest on the calm and spacious bank. Gradually she discovered that the energies that seemed so fearsome were, as Tibetan teacher Chögyam Trungpa puts it, "workable."

Some of the same questions about working with emotional pain also come up with physical pain. Students want to know if they should stop meditating when their pain is intense and distracting. "Why would I want to feel that migraine?" they ask. "Why would I choose to attend to that queasiness, that stomachache?" "What should I do if my body's pain feels like too much?"

Sometimes the notion of pain itself is a setup for assuming the experience is bad or too much. When I teach about being with pain, I encourage students to investigate the dance of sensations they have labeled as "pain." Under the solid concept of pain is a changing constellation of experience—burning, pinpricks, twisting, pressing, soreness, stabbing. Simply bringing interest to how these sensations move and unfold, how they become more or less intense, can make the experience less personal, and will enlarge your sense of presence.

I often recommend widening the attention before contacting unpleasant sensations. Pain can narrow our focus so much that we lose contact with what else is present. At these times it's helpful to scan the body for neutral and pleasant sensations, and to rest in those areas for a while. Then experiment with moving back and forth between the neutral/pleasant sensations and the unpleasant ones. Alternately, as I advised Jane, you might stay in contact with a neutral/pleasant anchor like the breath as you investigate the difficult spots.

You can also widen the attention by attuning to the space around unpleasant sensations, or simply to the space around your body, and then move back and forth from there. Rather than a small self who is tensed against pain, you will gradually open to a more spacious awareness that can be present with the difficult sensations without reacting or recoiling.

Yet there are times when attempting contact with any pain has diminishing or negative returns. If you are reacting with agitation or distress, it is usually best to take a break. Switch to a concentrative practice with a pleasant or neutral anchor—such as resting in the breath, listening to the sounds around you, or reciting a mantra. When you feel more equanimity, then you might bring a soft attention back to the stronger sensations. Alternatively, you might end your sitting for now, and instead, with mindfulness, seek whatever remedy—medication, stretching, a hot shower, a cup of tea—provides relief.

Being present with difficulty is not an endurance test. It is not yet another domain where you need to prove that you can succeed. Sometimes you simply need to prepare the ground and find ways to feel more safe and stable. Sometimes in the face of great pain, you might stay present for just thirty seconds, a minute, five minutes. All that matters is how you are *relating* to pain. Refuge is always waiting for you; it is here in the moments that you regard what is happening with a kind and gentle presence.

RECOGNIZING UNLIVED LIFE

Two days after Jane and I first met, she sent me a note to say that she was getting the knack of feeling both pleasant and unpleasant sensations in her body. Then, late the following afternoon, she and I met again privately. Eyes red from crying, Jane told me what had happened earlier that day. "I was thinking about my mother, who died a couple of years ago. We'd always had a distant, uneasy relationship—she was a single mom, also a college professor, who was immersed in her work and glad to have me out of the house—so I didn't really grieve her death. While I was meditating I could feel that numb heaviness of the blanket. It was like the blanket was between me and her, me and everything. As you'd said, I just let that numbness and heaviness be there, trying to feel how it was in my body. My throat got very tight and I started swallowing repeatedly. Then a memory took over . . . something painful I had totally forgotten.

"I must have been about seven. I had golden hair that flowed down to my waist. I loved my hair. After school I'd wrap myself in fancy scarves and dance around and feel like I was a beautiful princess. Then one afternoon my mom told me we were going to the hairdresser, that my hair was a nuisance. I knew that word, 'nuisance.' It meant pestering her for a puppy at a pet store, or getting a new dress dirty because I'd played in it, or trying to get her attention while she was grading papers. Being a nuisance often led to closed doors and being alone. This time I pleaded, I promised to keep my hair in a ponytail, I cried and cried, but she just dragged me to the car and told me it was time to grow up.

"The hairdresser could see how upset I was, but she just laughed at me. 'You'll be cooler in the summer,' she said, and then went ahead and chopped off my long locks." Jane's hand instinctively rose toward her head, as if feeling for the phantom hair that was no longer there. "Sitting there at the beauty parlor, something in me knew that I didn't matter. What I was feeling didn't matter. I was invisible, no one cared." Jane stopped abruptly, her mouth pressed tight, both hands now in her lap and clenched in fists. Then, in a defeated voice she said, "That's probably when a part of me stopped living."

Jane's voice was barely audible when she started talking again. "You know, Tara, I've become just like her. Joyless. A hardworking, uptight, dried-out woman. She shut down after Dad left, ignored her hurts and needs . . . and mine." Jane was quiet for a moment, as if letting herself take in what she had just said out loud. Then she continued: "Well, I've shut down too. Now I know what I'm most afraid of. It's of dying like her, without having lived."

Carl Jung wrote, "Nothing has a stronger influence psychologically on their environment, and especially on their children, than the unlived life of the parents." The outer domain of our unlived life includes all the places where we've held back from pursuing and manifesting our potential—in education and career, in relationships and creativity. But it is the inner domain of our unlived life that sets this suffering in motion. Here we find the raw sensations, the longings and hurts, the passions and fears that we have not allowed ourselves to feel. When we pull away from the energetic basis of our experience, we turn away from the truth of what is. We make a terrible bargain. When we separate from the felt sense of our pain, we also separate from the visceral experience of love that allows for true intimacy with others. We cut ourselves off from the sensory aliveness that connects us with the natural world.

When there is unlived life, we can't take good care of ourselves, our children, or our world.

The feelings you are trying to ignore are like a screaming child who has been sent to her room. You can put in earplugs and barricade yourself in at the farthest end of the house, but the body and the unconscious mind don't forget. Maybe you feel tension or guilt. Maybe, like Jane, you are baffled by intimacy or haunted by a sense of meaninglessness. Maybe you fixate on all the things you need to get done. You can't live in a spontaneous way because your body and mind are still reacting to the presence of your distressed child. Everything you do to ignore her, including becoming numb, only strengthens your link with her. Your very sense of who you are—your identity—is fused with the experience of pushing away a central part of your life or running from it.

In shutting down the passion, hurt, and pain she had experienced as a young girl whose precious hair was butchered, Jane had locked herself into a numb and anxious fragment of who she was. Yet something in her was calling her to live more fully. By beginning to contact her body's experience, by touching the ground, she was opening the door to what she had been running from.

COMING ALIVE THROUGH THE BODY

After Jane named her fear of dying without having lived, she dropped into silence. I asked her if she would like to bring the presence of RAIN to what was going on inside her, and she nodded in agreement. "Okay," I said gently, "start by letting yourself sense that fear and where it is living in your body." She gestured to the middle of her chest, and then, as before, she placed her hand there. "You might investigate by noticing what it feels like, from the inside," I suggested.

Jane sat still for a few moments. Then, after deepening her breath, she responded: "It's like a claw that's pulling and tearing at my heart." I reminded her to let those sensations be there, and to allow them to express themselves however they wanted. She was breathing deeply, letting the breath help her stay with the experience of her body. "The tearing is pulling me open, there's lots of heat . . . Now it's this huge screaming blowing apart everything . . . It's my voice, screaming at my mother."

"Jane, if there are words, and you want to, it's fine to say them out loud."

Eyes squeezed tight, at first she seemed to be fighting back the words. Then they burst out: "I *hate* you for cutting my hair. How could you do that to me? How could you?" Jane's voice broke, and then she put her face in her hands, weeping. "You just wanted me out of the way so I wouldn't bother you. You didn't love me . . . you couldn't love me."

Jane cried deeply for several minutes, hugging herself and rocking. I encouraged her to take all the time she needed to feel what was in her heart and, if she wanted, to name what was happening. "There's a hurt that's stabbing," she whispered as she continued to hold herself. Then, a minute or two later, she spoke in a softer, more tender voice, emphasizing each word: "Now deep . . . aching . . . sadness." When the sobs subsided, we sat together in silence. After drinking some water, she looked up at me. For the first time, her eyes held mine in intimate contact.

"Tara, while I was quiet just then, the sadness turned into a kind of sweet, peaceful energy and it was like my whole body was tingling with it. I felt totally alive . . . for the first time. Then I heard a different voice, like the gentlest whisper, blessing me. It was giving me permission to live my life from this place of aliveness. I had a glimmer that this whisper was coming from the real me, the living spirit that has been invisible all these years, but never actually went away." Jane's eyes glistened with tears. "More than anything, I want to trust this spirit, to stay connected with who I am."

Jane was on the path of true refuge. By investigating her body's experience with a committed, intimate presence she had tapped into her unlived life. Now a wise and hopeful voice was emerging from her depth, one that expressed an awakening from years of troubled sleep.

PLANTING OURSELVES IN
THE UNIVERSE

In the early part of the last century, D. H. Lawrence found himself in a society devastated by war, a landscape despoiled by industrialism, and a culture suffering from a radical disconnect between mind and body. Published in 1931, Lawrence's words from "A Propos of *Lady Chatterley's Lover*" have lost none of their urgency:

> It is a question, practically of relationship. We must get back into relation, vivid and nourishing relation to the cosmos and the universe. . . . For the truth is, we are perishing for lack of fulfillment of our greater needs, we are cut off from the great sources of our inward nourishment and renewal, sources which flow eternally in the universe. Vitally, the human race is dying. It is like a great uprooted tree, with its roots in the air. We must plant ourselves again in the universe.

When we disconnect from the body, we are pulling away from the energetic expression of our being that connects us with all of life. By imagining a great tree uprooted from the earth, we can sense the unnaturalness, violence, and suffering of this severed belonging. The experience of being uprooted is a kind of dying. Jane felt it as an "inner deadness," and described herself as mechanically trying to keep herself going day after day. Some people tell me about the despair of not really living, of skimming the surface. Others have the perpetual sense of a threat lurking around the corner. And many speak of being weighed down by a deep tiredness. It takes energy to continually run away from pain and tension, to pull away from the life of the present moment. Roots in the air, we lose access to the aliveness and love and beauty that nourish our deepest being. No false refuge can compensate for that loss.

Several years after that retreat, Jane came to D.C. for a conference and made an appointment with me. I didn't immediately recognize the woman with long, flowing blond hair who walked into my office. Relaxed and smiling, she looked me directly in the eye and joked about boycotting beauty salons. She told me she had continued to practice mindfulness of the body, using the steps of RAIN whenever she encountered her old patterns of anxiety or depression. While she still sometimes became anxious and uptight, her life had changed in many unexpected ways. The most important had to do with her heart: "When I bring my attention to the young girl who got her hair cut and feel her hurt in my body, I sometimes find myself crying for my mom who never really knew how to relax and live life. I feel her suffering in my body too, the loneliness and loss that she maybe never allowed herself to feel. There's room in my heart to include her life, and a feeling of love I never touched upon when she was living."

Jane and I sat quietly together for a few moments, sharing each other's company. Then she went on: "When I'm present and awake in my body, I'm larger than any old idea or feeling I had about myself. That living spirit I reconnected with at retreat is really what I am." We sat for another moment savoring her realization, and then we said our good-byes.

Like the Buddha touching the ground, we reclaim our life and spirit by planting ourselves again in the universe. This begins when we connect with the truth of what is happening in our body. The mysterious field of aliveness we call the universe can only be experienced if we are in contact with the felt sense of that aliveness in our own being. For Jane, the simple practice of feeling the life of her hands expanded to include the wounds of her unlived life, and then opened her to the pure aliveness of her heart and body. By connecting with her inner life, by bringing presence to the truth of her immediate experience, she had begun to re-plant herself in the universe.

Guided Reflection: Bringing RAIN to Pain

We release the suffering that can accompany pain by relaxing our resistance to unpleasant sensations and meeting them with an open, allowing presence. This meditation is especially useful when you are currently experiencing physical pain. If at any point the pain feels like too much, turn the attention with mindfulness and compassion to whatever will ease and soothe you. Then you can return to this direct practice of mindful and open presence when ready.

Find a comfortable position, sitting or lying down. Take a few moments to become still, relaxing with the natural rhythm of the breath. Gently move your attention through your body, relaxing your brow and jaw, dropping your shoulders, and softening through your hands. Try not to create any unnecessary tension in your body.

Begin the R of RAIN (recognize) by scanning through your body and recognizing if there are areas of strong discomfort or pain. If so, bring a gentle, receptive attention directly to the unpleasant sensations. Continue the R of RAIN by discovering what happens as you begin to be present with the pain. Is there an attempt, however subtle, to push it away? To cut it off, block it off, pull away? Is there fear?

Because of the tendency to resist unpleasant sensations, it is essential to awaken an allowing, open presence, the A of RAIN (allow). To establish this openness, you might imagine a great blue sky and let the mind mingle with that vastness. Open your senses to include sounds, listening with a full, receptive attention. As you listen to the sounds, sense the space in which they are happening. Then begin including in your awareness areas in your body that have neutral or even pleasant sensations. This might be your hands, feet, cheeks, the area around your eyes. You might also sense these areas, or your whole body, as an open field of sensations that is suffused with space.

Investigation (the I of RAIN) is a deepening of attention. It begins as you remain aware of this background of openness and simultaneously contact the unpleasant sensations. Let your attention move toward the place or places where the sensations are the most intense or unpleasant. If it feels difficult, take some more moments resting the attention in the space around the area of unpleasantness, establishing a sense of openness. Gently move back and forth, touching the pain and then sensing the space around it, until you feel more able to enter fully into the center of the unpleasantness without resistance.

As you directly contact the pain, allow the sensations to express in whatever way is most natural and real. Where are the unpleasant sensations? What is the shape of the pain? What is its intensity (on a scale of one to ten, ten being strongest)? As you sense the location, shape, and intensity, see how fully you can say "Yes" or "I consent," surrendering any resistance and genuinely letting this life be just as it is. Continue to feel both the pain, and the background field of sensations and space. What happens to the unpleasant sensations when there is no resistance?

It is natural to move through several rounds of this stage of the meditation. Once you can experience your awareness as the soft open space that surrounds the pain, move again toward the center of the unpleasant sensations. Let your awareness soak into the pain like the gentlest falling rain. Is it possible to merge your attention into the center or heart of the pain? Can you sense the openness diffusing the painful sensations? Or can you sense the painful sensations dissolving into openness? Continue to notice what is happening as you surrender over and over into the experience of the painful sensations.

Let the body become like open space, with plenty of room for unpleasant sensations to arise and dissolve, fade and intensify, move and change. No holding, no tension. Explore what it means to have a surrendering presence, releasing resistance over and over. When there is no resistance whatsoever, is there any sense of a self who owns the pain? A self who is a victim of the pain? Discover how you can inhabit the sea of awareness, including the changing waves of sensations, but not be identified with them. This is the N of RAIN: Not identified, you touch the freedom of natural presence.

Guided Reflection: The Buddha's Smile

In many statues and pictures, the Buddha is depicted with a slight smile. Research now shows that even a small smile relaxes our reactivity and inclines us toward feelings of ease and well-being. This short reflection can be done during a formal meditation or at any time during the day.

———∞∞∞———

Close your eyes, take a few full breaths, and with each exhale sense a letting go of tension, a softening and relaxing of the body. Imagine a smile spreading through your eyes, gently uplifting the corners and softening the flesh around them. Feel a real yet slight smile at the mouth and also sense the inside of the mouth smiling. Relaxing the jaw, notice the sensations that arise through the mouth and cheek area.

Imagine smiling into the heart. Sense the smile spreading through the heart and chest, creating space for whatever you might be feeling. Allow the sensations and feelings in the heart area to float in this tender space.

Imagine smiling into the navel area, letting the curve of a smile spread through the belly, softening any tension there. Notice awareness awakening deep inside the torso.

Now imagine the atmosphere of a smile enlarging to include your whole body. Take a few more full breaths, sensing the aliveness that fills your entire body held in the openness of a smile. Rest for as long as you like in that felt sense of aliveness and openness.

———∞∞∞———

SEVEN

POSSESSED BY THE MIND: THE PRISON OF COMPULSIVE THINKING

You think too much, that is your trouble.
Clever people and grocers, they weigh everything.

NIKOS KAZANTZAKIS

Be empty of worrying.
Think of who created thought!
Why do you stay in prison
When the door is so wide open?

RUMI

Near the beginning of his career, the great magician Harry Houdini traveled throughout Europe visiting small towns where he would challenge local jailers to bind him in a straitjacket and lock him in a cell. Again and again he delighted the crowds with his quick escapes from seemingly impossible restraints. But in one small Irish village he ran into trouble. In front of an avid group of townspeople and news reporters, Houdini easily broke free of his straitjacket, yet despite his repeated efforts to solve the puzzle of the lock, he failed to open his cell door.

After everyone had left, Houdini asked the jailer, "What kind of new lock do you have on your cell?" "Oh," said the jailer, "it's a very ordinary lock. I figured that you'd have no difficulty opening it . . . so I never bothered locking it at all." Houdini falsely assumed that he was trapped, and his very efforts to free himself had locked him in!

When I first heard this story, I thought about how many of us, like Houdini, perpetually assume that life is a problem we have to solve. Our challenge is that we are hooked on thinking—it is our way of trying to control life itself. It's only when our incessant inner dialogue quiets that we realize the cell door is already open.

"LOST IN THOUGHT"

When a student asked renowned Thai teacher Ajahn Buddhadasa to describe the consciousness of today's world, he answered simply: "Lost in thought." When we live inside an incessant stream of thoughts, we become identified with our mental creations. We react to the people or events in our minds as if they were real, and we believe that the self portrayed in our mental stories is actually who we are. Severed from the direct experience of the present moment—from the truth that is here and now—*we are lost in a virtual reality.*

We're usually aware of painful obsessions like nagging thoughts about a dreaded job interview, or persistent fantasies about having a drink when we've sworn to be abstinent. But compulsive thinking also takes the shape of everyday obsessing, the familiar stream of worries and plans that are an ever-present part of our lives. This kind of obsessing is free floating; it will affix itself to whatever object is available. We might anxiously obsess about an unfinished project at work, complete it, and then immediately transfer our obsessing to what needs to be done next. Or we might have a strong craving for acknowledgment, or a burning desire to buy something new and, after satisfying it, find we are grasping after the next fix. Even a vague sense of anxiety or stress can lead to dozens of hours lost to worrying or planning, judging or figuring things out.

While the intensity of compulsive thinking varies, the common denominator is that whenever we're lost in thought, we are disconnected from our body and our senses. We are cut off from the perceptiveness and receptivity that underlie our natural intelligence and kindness.

In all this, I certainly don't mean to devalue thinking. Thinking is a crucial part of our evolutionary equipment, our primary means for surviving and thriving. Everything we humans bring forth into the world—

buildings, computers, pianos, and poems—begins as an idea in the mind. And yet this same thinking brain is responsible for unspeakable violence toward our own species and other animals, it drives the over-consuming that threatens to destroy our living planet, and it generates much of our emotional misery. Just as Houdini locked himself in his cell, our thoughts can imprison us in a painful and sometimes night-marish trance.

COMPULSIVE THINKING IS A
FALSE REFUGE

Compulsive thinking is the primary strategy of the space-suit self. For many of us, it is the easiest and quickest way to temporarily control stress or escape from the raw tension of wants or fears in the body. Our thoughts keep us from feeling powerless—we're not just sitting around helpless, we're doing something . . . we're thinking! As Descartes said, "I think therefore I am." Thinking continually reconstructs the self-sense, and it reassures us that this self exists.

Yet the notion that compulsive thinking helps us is an illusion. On the most fundamental level, compulsive thoughts arise from fear-based beliefs. When we are in their thrall, we take on the identity of a self who is in trouble, a self who is isolated and endangered. We become ruled by the underlying message that "something is wrong with me," or "Some-thing is wrong with you." Compulsive thinking keeps us from seeing clearly the root of suffering—our own and others'—and it keeps us from responding to that suffering with the kindness and clarity that can bring true healing.

My students sometimes object that obsessing can be beneficial. "What about creative obsessions—like the poet who spends days trying to find just the right word, or the scientist obsessed with a problem? Don't we need those?" But this kind of focus, this intense, mindful en-gagement, is different from the churning of obsession. When the inten-tion behind thinking is to deepen our understanding, to communicate clearly, to awaken spiritually, or to nurture the life around us, then our thinking is not primarily focused on protecting the small self. Our thoughts are not circling around what will hurt or help us (or those who are close to us). Rather than possessing us, our thoughts become our tools, and can be guided by our natural compassion, intuition, and creativity.

I'm also asked about situations when we really are endangered. Isn't there a value to compulsive thinking then? Fear-based thinking does serve a critical function when we need to protect ourselves. Just as the body prepares itself for danger by directing blood flow to the extremities and tensing the muscles, so the mind mobilizes to orchestrate a strategic response to threats. But when that orchestration never ends, when we become completely identified with our stream of fearful thoughts, we lose touch with the actual feelings and circumstances that require our attention. Our repetitive thoughts have no exit or outcome. They simply loop. Worse, they lock us into fear.

STRANGLED BY OBSESSION

I first came face-to-face with the pain of mental obsessing during my sophomore year in college. I had gone into therapy, and I remember the March day when I brought up my current prime-time fixation: how to stop binge eating. No matter how committed I felt to my newest diet plan, I kept blowing it each day. I mercilessly judged myself for being out of control; when I wasn't obsessing on how I might concoct a stricter, more dramatic weight-loss program, I was getting caught up in food cravings.

My therapist listened quietly for a while, and then she asked a question that has stayed with me ever since: "When you are obsessing about eating, what are you feeling in your body?" As my attention shifted, I immediately noticed the painful, squeezing feeling in my chest. While my mind was saying "something is wrong with me," my body was squeezing my heart and throat in the hard grip of fear.

In an instant I realized that when I was obsessing about food—craving it, wanting to avoid it—I was trying to escape from these feelings. Obsessing was my way of being in control. But then I realized something else. "It's not just food," I told her. "I'm obsessing about everything." Saying it out loud unlocked something inside of me. I talked about how I obsessed about what was wrong with my boyfriend, about exams, about what to do for spring break, about when to fit in a run. I obsessed about what I'd tell her at our next therapy session. And most of all, my tireless inner critic obsessed about my own failings: I'd never change; I'd never like myself; others wouldn't want to be close to me.

After pouring all this out, my mind started scratching around again—this time for a new strategy for changing my obsessive self. When I started down that track, my therapist simply smiled and said kindly: "If you can notice when you're obsessing and then feel what's going on in your body, you'll eventually find peace of mind."

During the weeks that followed, I kept track of my obsessing. When I caught myself planning and judging and managing, I would note that I was obsessing, try to stop, and then ask how I was feeling in my body. Whatever the particular focus of my thoughts, I'd find a restless, anxious feeling—the same squeezing grip I had felt in my therapist's office. While I didn't like my obsessing, I *really* didn't like this feeling. Without being conscious of pulling away, I'd start distancing myself from the pain almost as soon as I'd contacted it, and the relentless voice in my head would take over again. Then, after a month or so of this, I had an experience that really caught my attention.

One Saturday night, after my friends and I had spent hours dancing to the music of a favorite band, I stepped outside to get some fresh air. Inspired by the full moon and the scent of spring blossoms, I sat down on a bench for a few moments alone. Suddenly the world was deliciously quiet. Sweaty and tired, my body was vibrating from all that dancing. But my mind was still. It was big and open, like the night sky. And filling it was a sense of peace—I didn't want anything or fear anything. Everything was okay.

By Sunday morning, the mood had vanished. Worried about a paper due midweek, I sat down to work at noon, armed with Diet Coke, cheese, and crackers. I was going to overeat, I just knew it. My mind started ricocheting between wanting to eat and not wanting to gain weight. My agitation grew. For a moment I flashed on the evening before; that quiet, happy space was like a distant dream. A great wave of helplessness and sorrow filled my heart. I began whispering a prayer: "Please . . . may I stop obsessing . . . Please, please." I wanted to be free from the prison of my fear-thinking.

The taste of a quiet, peaceful mind I'd experienced the night before had felt like home, and it motivated me not long after to begin spiritual practice. In the years since, I've become increasingly free from the grip of obsessive thinking, but awakening from this mental trance has been slower than I initially imagined. Obsessive thinking is a tenacious addiction. Yet like all facets of trance, it responds to awareness—to an interested, good-humored, forgiving presence. We can listen to the energies behind our obsessive thinking, respond to what needs attention, and spend less and less time removed from the presence that nurtures our lives.

IN THE GRIP OF EMOTION

I recently read in the book *My Stroke of Insight* by brain scientist Jill Bolte Taylor that the natural life span of an emotion—the average time it takes for it to move through the nervous system and body—is only a minute and a half. After that we need thoughts to keep the emotion rolling. So if we wonder why we lock into painful emotional states such as anxiety, depression, or rage, we need look no further than our own endless stream of inner dialogue.

Modern neuroscience has discovered a fundamental truth: *Neurons that fire together, wire together.* When we rehearse a looping set of thoughts and emotions, we create deeply grooved patterns of emotional reactivity. This means that the more you think and rethink about certain experiences, the stronger the memory and the more easily activated the related feelings become. For example, if a young girl asks her father for help and he either ignores her or reacts with irritation, the emotional pain of rejection may become linked with any number of thoughts or beliefs: "I'm not loved," "I'm not worth helping," "I'm weak for wanting help," "It's dangerous to ask for help," "He's bad. I hate him." The more the child gets this response from either parent—or even *imagines* getting this response—the more the impulse to ask for help becomes paired with the belief that she will be refused and the accompanying feelings (fear or hurt, anger or shame). Years later, she may hesitate to ask for help at all. Or, if she does ask, and the other person so much as pauses or looks distracted, the old feelings instantly take over: She downplays her needs, apologizes, or becomes enraged. Unless we learn to recognize and interrupt our compulsive thinking, these ingrained emotional and behavioral patterns continue to strengthen over time.

Fortunately, it is possible to break out of this patterning. Researcher Benjamin Libet discovered that the part of the brain responsible for movement activates a quarter-second before we become aware of our intention to move. There is then another quarter-second before the movement begins. What does this mean? First, it casts an interesting light on what we call "free will"—before we make a conscious decision, our brain has already set the gears in motion! But second, it offers an opportunity. Say you've been obsessing about having a cigarette. During the space between impulse ("I have to have a cigarette") and action (reaching for the pack), there is room for a choice. Author Tara Bennett-Goleman named this space "the magic quarter-second," and mindfulness enables us to take advantage of it.

By catching our thoughts in the magic quarter-second, we are able to act from a wiser place, interrupting the circling of compulsive thinking that fuels anxiety and other painful emotions. If our child asks us to play a game and we automatically think "I'm too busy," we might pause and choose to spend some time with her. If we've been caught up in composing an angry e-mail, we might pause and decide not to press the send button.

The basic mindfulness tools for working with compulsive thinking are "coming back" and "being here." If you recall the wheel of awareness from chapter 3, you can visualize how easily our mind fixates on the thoughts circling around the rim. But when we notice that our attention has left home, and come back to our anchor (such as the breath), we reconnect with the presence at the hub. This builds a critical muscle—our capacity to wake up, to "come back," when we are lost in thought.

Then, when we practice "being here"—noticing the changing sensations in our body, the sounds around us, how feelings come and go—we become increasingly aware of the difference between the virtual reality of thoughts and the truth of what is happening in the moment. If we practice this way of waking up from thoughts during less stressful times, we will be more alert and better equipped to respond mindfully when dealing with strong obsessions. The more familiar we get with the sense that "this is just a thought," the less power thoughts have.

Some thoughts are harder to wake up from than others. If we become mindful of a wispy thought cloud, it usually dissolves, and it is easy to come back to the hub of the wheel. In contrast, when we are overtaken by storm clouds—the compulsive thinking that is driven by intense fear or craving—the trance is more compelling. We are in an emotional tornado—a "wired together" constellation of thoughts and feelings. As soon as we recognize our storm cloud of thoughts, we are no longer inside it. But unless we also acknowledge that cloud's strong emotional charge, its energy will catapult us back into obsession. We will quickly become reidentified with our thoughts, and they will again drive our emotions and behavior. It was this looping dynamic that my therapist was inviting me to notice: "When you are thinking about your struggle with eating, what are you feeling in your body?"

When we wake up from charged thoughts, remembering an anchor such as the breath can initially help us to come back. But to fully be here, we need to mindfully include the sensations that live beneath the thoughts.

Any thought or mental perception is expressed in a corresponding physical feeling; conversely, our feelings also give rise to thoughts. This means that unless we bring both elements of this self-reinforcing loop into conscious awareness, we will continue to be hooked into the identity of an endangered or wanting self. If we are unaware of our thought process, we will buy into the content of our thoughts, which will in turn keep generating feelings of craving or fear. In the same way, if we are unaware of the anxiety in our bodies, we will identify with the felt sense of endangerment or craving, which will generate a new cycle of obsessive thinking. Then an emotion that lasts for a minute and a half can become a weather system that settles in for the long haul.

The Buddha taught that to be free—not identified with or possessed by thoughts or feelings—we need to investigate every part of our experience with an intimate, mindful attention. This kindly investigation, developed in the *I* of RAIN, is an essential tool for working with obsession. When I started therapy in college, my attention was anything but accepting: I was strongly critical of my obsessing and at the same time resistant to contacting the unpleasant feelings underneath. In the years since, I've seen this same reaction in many students and clients. It's a natural part of our conditioning, and it's workable. The key is being honest with ourselves about what's happening and choosing presence as much as possible.

BRINGING RAIN TO
OBSESSIVE THINKING

Jim was a law student who had been attending my Wednesday night meditation class for a year and a half. He made an appointment to see me privately, telling me that he had a compelling obsession that he wanted to address. When he arrived at my office he walked quickly to one of the chairs, seated himself, and jumped in. "I don't know if you work with this kind of thing," he said, "but I'm having sexual problems and I really need some help." He stopped abruptly, and blinked nervously.

I could feel his courage in pushing himself to be so direct, and I wanted to set him at ease. "How about telling me more," I said, nodding a bit to encourage him. "If I'm not the best person to help, we can figure out a good next step."

Jim gave me a grim smile. "Okay, then," he said, "here's what's going on. I'm in a new relationship, one that has some real potential. She . . . Beth . . . has so much that I'm looking for. She's smart, fun, kind. And very attractive." Jim paused, as if acknowledging to himself the realness of her appeal. When he continued, his voice was a defeated monotone: "The problem is, I'm afraid I'm going to blow it with her." Jim's fear was of performing poorly during sex. He said the problem had ruined several prior relationships: He'd obsess longingly about having sex, and he'd obsess anxiously about premature ejaculation. Then, when he started to make love, he'd either climax quickly, or he'd shut down and lose his erection. Ashamed, over a period of weeks or months he'd become increasingly distant from his partner until she reacted with hurt or anger. Then he'd call it quits.

"I don't want to do this to Beth, or to me," he stated bitterly. "I *hate* how I obsess about sex—wanting it, fearing what will happen—*it's my mind that's ruining my sex life* . . . and it's also screwing with my ability to study." Sitting back, he shook his head in disgust. "We've slept together a couple of times, and the same old thing is happening . . . What to do?" he asked, not really expecting an answer.

I suggested that while we could talk some more, we could also use RAIN to explore what was going on. Jim had heard about RAIN in class but had not yet tried it on his own. "Let's go for it," Jim said. "I've talked this to death in my own head already."

When we practiced RAIN together, Jim noted the fear and shame underlying his thoughts, but he quickly shifted from connecting with the feelings to analyzing what was happening. "I'm fixated on the past," he said scathingly, "and can't get it that now is now!" Drawing his attention to his harsh attitude toward both the feelings and the obsessing, I suggested that as he continued this investigation on his own, he might intentionally offer some message of acceptance or care to whatever felt painful or unwanted.

This turned out to be a real sticking point for Jim. At our next meeting several weeks later, he confessed that whenever he'd tried to work with RAIN on his own, he could acknowledge his feelings, but he definitely couldn't allow or accept them. Instead, within moments of recognizing his shame and fear, he'd flip right back again into the stories of past embarrassment and the anticipation of future humiliation. Then he'd judge himself. "No matter what was going on, I was doing something wrong," he told me.

Finally, after more than a week of this, Jim realized he had lost confidence that RAIN could help him. The crisis came late one evening. Craving relief, he cast about for anything that might distract him and subdue his mental fixation. He focused on his breath, he tried substituting other thoughts, he put on his favorite music, and then he finally picked up a novel. When he realized he wasn't taking in the words on the page, Jim threw the book aside in desperation. "I knew I was running away," he told me, "and that it was making things worse."

Then he finally surrendered to what was happening inside him. "There was a mix of bad porn and dumb soaps dominating my mental screen . . . with nobody controlling the remote," he recalled. "It was obvious that 'I' couldn't do anything. So something in me stopped fighting and softened." As the charged thoughts kept playing through his mind, Jim mindfully noted them as "obsessing." Soon he recognized the familiar undercurrents of fear and shame. But this time, he spoke to them with a gentle inner whisper: "It's okay, it's okay." To his surprise, the fear and shame gave way to a deep loneliness. Again he offered the message "It's okay," and he felt his eyes well up with tears. When his mind lurched back into sexual fantasy, and then into judgment, he noted that, and remembered to whisper "It's okay." He was accepting both the fantasy and his aversion to it. Gradually, as he continued to make room for what was arising, Jim realized he was utterly sad. But it was okay. He felt real and, as he put it, "fully present in my skin."

Jim had found his way to the accepting presence that is key to RAIN. I encouraged him to continue to pause whenever he realized he was feeling stuck and reactive, to give himself time to come back and be here, and then inquire with interest into whatever was going on inside him. "Try to be patient," I told him. "It can take a while to decondition our emotional looping . . . but you can trust it's happening!"

In the weeks that followed, Jim discovered that whenever he could stop the war and offer an unconditional presence to his experience, the circling of obsessive thoughts and unpleasant feelings began to dissipate. The more he mindfully named and accepted his scenarios of future failure, the more he could see them as thoughts, not reality. He didn't have to believe their story line. And by opening without resistance to the fear in his body, he reconnected with a mindful presence that included the fear, but was not possessed by it. Jim was more at home with himself, but when I asked him about his relationship with Beth, he shifted uncomfortably in his seat and looked down at the floor. "We've got a ways to go," he said, "but I'm working on it."

Our next session was a month later. Jim told me that the week before, he and Beth had been on the verge of breaking up. On several occasions during the past weeks the sex had been what he called passable. "It worked," he said flatly. But there were other times when he had avoided being intimate because he felt the old insecurities lurking in the background. Beth too had pulled away a few times after they had begun hugging or kissing. One night after dinner she tried to break the tense silence, asking him if they could talk about what was going on between them. Jim felt himself shut down completely. He gave her a tired look and attributed everything to the pressures of law school. When he left early, saying he needed to study, she didn't even walk him to the door.

When he was back at home, Jim did some honest soul-searching. He asked himself what really wanted his attention, and the response in his body was immediate. An ache of sadness filled his chest and strangled his throat. "It was a lifelong loneliness . . . and it felt unbearable," he said. "When I asked that place of loneliness and sadness what it wanted from me, the response was 'acceptance,' but that was not all." Jim waited, listening inwardly as he relived his experience. "It wanted me to be as real with Beth as I was being with myself." He looked at me with a self-effacing smile and shook his head. "I was scared shitless!" His mind raced forward to the moment when he would confess his shame about falling short sexually. He could see her being polite and kind, but having to mask the pity and disgust she was feeling. "Impossible. Forget it," he told himself. "I might as well break it off now." But when he imagined losing Beth, something cracked open. "Tara," he said, looking at me with tears in his eyes, "I had to take the chance."

He called her on the spot and asked if he could come back over that night. "She agreed . . . it was almost like she was expecting the call." Initially Beth sat on the other end of the couch, frosty and quiet. But as soon as Jim started talking, she realized that he wasn't there to break up with her. "Beth shocked me, because she just started crying. That's when I realized how much our relationship mattered to her." From that point on, he said, their conversation was nothing like what he had imagined. The more he told her about his embarrassment and fear, the more he realized that his feelings were in the safest, most caring hands possible. "Beth was hurt that I hadn't trusted her enough to tell her," Jim told me. "She had thought I was losing interest . . . we were both afraid of rejection." Jim was quiet for a few moments as if weighing what he wanted to say next. "That night was the first time I could really say I made love with someone."

The adage "what we resist, persists" is a deep truth. If we try to fight obsession and the raw emotions that underlie it, we end up reinforcing them. For some people this might lead to acting out in rage or taking drugs. In Jim's case, it meant being unable to maintain a sexually intimate relationship. Even without acting out, resisting our obsessive thoughts or feelings traps us in the suffering of a small, deficient, separate self.

As Jim was discovering, the best medicine for obsession is taking refuge in the truth of the present moment. We learn to recognize what's going on, and accept the fact that it's happening. When we become mindful of a thought as a thought, our sense of identity is not unconsciously fused with its content and felt sense. Thoughts and feelings can come and go without disconnecting us from our natural openness, intelligence, and warmth. For Jim, this homecoming freed him to be intimate with another person. He could contact and accept his own inner life without believing limiting stories about himself. And he could see past the veil of stories about Beth that had been keeping him separate from her. She became an authentic, vulnerable human, and that allowed true loving to flower.

REAL BUT NOT TRUE

Tibetan Buddhist teacher Pema Chödrön writes,

> Being preoccupied with our self-image is like being deaf and blind. It's like standing in the middle of a vast field of wildflowers with a black hood over our heads. It's like coming upon a tree of singing birds while wearing earplugs.

The next time you awaken from a long train of thoughts, take a moment to ground yourself in presence—in your immediate experience of sensations, feelings, sounds—and then compare being here to where you've been. Waking up from thought is much like waking up from a dream. While we're in it, the dream experience is real; we react to its story line with real emotions, pleasure, and pain. But the dream is not true. Its pictures and sound bites represent only fragments of the living world. Similarly, thoughts are real (they are happening, they create a felt experience) but they are not true. When we are caught in the virtual reality of thinking, we inhabit a sliver of experience that is dissociated from the vividness and vastness and aliveness of the here and now.

I first heard the phrase "real but not true" from Tibetan Buddhist teacher Tsoknyi Rinpoche, and I've found it to be a great tool for breaking through the trance. In the midst of obsessing about our own failings, about what will go wrong, how others perceive us, what's wrong with others—some inner wisdom reminds us: "real but not true." Mindfulness can then reconnect us with the vibrating sensations in our hands, this inflowing breath, the pressure or ache in our heart, and we open to the larger awareness that holds all our thoughts and feelings. As we will explore in the next chapter, distinguishing between our story and living truth is critical when our relationships and happiness have been undermined by painfully limiting beliefs. If we can realize that our fear thoughts are real but not true, they lose their power to possess us and shrink our world. We are free to inhabit our wholeness and vitality, and to appreciate the wildflowers and singing birds.

> Move outside the tangle of fear-thinking.
> Live in silence.
> Flow down and down in always
> Widening rings of being.

> —RUMI

Guided Reflection: My Top-Ten Hits

Cultivating an alert and friendly relationship with your "Top-Ten Hits"—the issues and themes that regularly take over your mind—is the beginning of awakening from their grip. Both this exercise and the RAIN meditation that follows build on the basic skill of recognizing thoughts in the "Coming Back" meditation in chapter 3.

———— ✺ ————

For several days keep a journal where you identify and record your primary areas of obsessive thinking. This might include obsessing about

> *How someone (or people) are treating you*
> *Mistakes you are making; ways you are falling short*
> *What you need to get done*
> *What others are doing wrong*
> *Your worries about another person*
> *How you look*
> *Symptoms of being sick; what your symptoms mean*
> *What you can do about a relationship problem*
> *How you want someone (people) to change*
> *What is going to go wrong*
> *What has already gone wrong*
> *How you need to change*
> *Something you are craving*
> *Something you really want to happen*
> *Something you really wish was different*

Once you have your list, select two or three obsessions that you know regularly take over your mind and trap you in anxiety, shame, anger, or discontent. Find a name that describes each of these obsessions—several words that are simple, easy to remember, and not derogatory. It could be something like "worrying about my daughter," "wanting a drink," "judging myself for doing a bad job." For example, one of my obsessions is strategizing how I'm going to get everything done. I call this "checking-things-off list." Another arises when I enter a cycle of joint pain and physical weakness, and my mind spins with thoughts about what is causing it, what will help, how much worse it will get over time, and how much exercise I can get away with. These are "sickness thoughts." Yet another obsession is anticipating upcoming stressful events. This is "leaning ahead."

For the next week or two as you move through the day, try to notice when you are caught in one of these preidentified obsessions. When you become aware that you are circling in the obsession, mentally whisper its name and pause.

In the moment of identifying an obsessive thought, the most important thing to do is offer a nonjudging, friendly quality of attention to your experience. *In fact, the more friendly the better! Gently remind yourself that the thought is "real but not true." Honor that this is a moment of awakening, of stepping out of virtual reality into the actuality of what is here. In that spirit, take a real interest in what is happening inside you. You might feel the inflow and outflow of your breath as you check into your body and ask what it is feeling. Is there tension in your chest? Knots in your stomach? Numbness? Pressure? Are you aware of fear? Anger? Anxiety? Craving? Breathe with whatever sensations or emotions are there, sensing the energy that underlies obsessive thinking.*

Do not try to change the feelings you encounter in any way. Rather, just offer them a respectful, allowing presence. Depending on your situation, this step of attending to your feelings might take thirty seconds to a minute. Then, take a few full breaths, relaxing with each out-breath, and resume your daily activity. Notice the difference between being inside the virtual reality of an obsession and being awake, here and now.

Practice with your first two or three obsessions for as many days, weeks, or months as seems fruitful, and then when you feel inclined, either add or substitute a different set. Use a journal if that helps. You might also find it helpful to team up with an "obsession buddy" for company and support. Let each other know the name of the obsessions you are working with, and find a time each week to check in and share what you are discovering.

Reflect on the following: What helps you to recognize when you are lost in obsession? What do you notice when you first pause? How are you relating to the obsession (kindly? with curiosity? feeling victimized by it? discouraged?)? Have you noticed any changes in the strength and duration of the obsessive thinking? More generally, how has the obsessive thinking affected your life, and how might that be changing?

Guided Reflection: Bringing RAIN to Obsession

Here is a practice for when obsessive thinking arises in the midst of a meditation, or when you are obsessing during daily activity and have the time to stop for a fuller investigation.

—⁘—

Sitting in a posture that allows you to be alert and relaxed, let your attention focus on whatever obsessive theme is appearing in your mind. If you have not already named it, find a few words as a mental label. It might be that you note "anxious about . . ." or "wanting so and so to . . ." or "judging . . ."

After naming the obsession, pause and let the whole experience of obsessing—the images and words, the reality that you've been obsessing, the mood surrounding obsessing—be as it is. You are not trying to fight obsessive thought; rather, you are recognizing what is and allowing it.

With curiosity and gentleness, begin to investigate what is going on inside you. As you attend to the theme of obsession—what you are worried about, what you are wanting—also bring your attention into where that fear or wanting lives in your body. Pay particular attention to your throat, chest, and belly—to the midline of your body. Where is your experience most distinct? What sensations do you notice (heat? pressure? tightness?)? What emotions are you aware of (fear? shame? anger?)?

Continue to investigate by speaking directly to whatever experience feels most compelling. Ask that part of you, "What do you want from me? What do you most need?" Perhaps you are feeling fear, and the fear wants forgiveness for being there or wants to trust that you will pay attention to it. There might be a part of you that is craving food and wants to be soothed, to feel held in love. Listen with an intimate attention to what the emotional energies in your body are asking for under the obsessive thinking.

As you listen to your wants and fears, watch for any words, images, or feelings that arise in response. Perhaps you will feel your heart soften with acceptance or care. Perhaps you will have an image of that vulnerable part of you filled with light or warmth, or feel that place being bathed in loving attention. No need to invent or force anything; simply sense any natural response you may have.

You might find that instead of a tender response, there is another wave of reactivity. Perhaps you'll notice judgmental thoughts ("I don't deserve love") or fear ("Something really is wrong, this won't help"). Whatever arises, recognize it and say yes, including it in your attention. As before, you can investigate by discovering how it expresses in your body and what it needs. Again, sense the possibility of offering it the tenderness, acceptance, or love it might want.

By continuing to investigate and offer a caring presence to the layers that make up obsessive thought, you are enlarging the awareness that heals and frees you. When you rest here, obsession will have less power to obscure who you really are.

EIGHT

INVESTIGATING CORE BELIEFS

Reality is always kinder than the stories we tell about it.

BYRON KATIE

Your beliefs become your thoughts
Your thoughts become your words
Your words become your actions
Your actions become your habits
Your habits become your character
Your character becomes your destiny.

MOHANDAS GANDHI

Can you imagine understanding, even loving, someone who belongs to a group of people responsible for killing your father or brother or best friend? Can you imagine growing close to someone whose people have driven you from your home, humiliated your family, and turned you into a refugee in your own country? Twenty-two teenage girls from Israel and Palestine were flown in to a camp in rural New Jersey, where they would live together in the face of these questions. As part of a program called Building Bridges for Peace, these young people were called upon to examine beliefs that seemed central to their identity, beliefs that had fueled estrangement, anger, hatred, and war.

Even though they had volunteered for the program, the girls were initially mistrustful of one another, and sometimes overtly hostile. One Palestinian teen drew a line in the sand right from the start: "When we're here, who knows, maybe we're friends. When we return, you are my enemy again. My heart is filled with hatred for the Jews." In another exchange, an Israeli girl told a Palestinian: "You expect to be treated as a human being, but you don't act like one. You don't *deserve* human rights!"

Yet from this harsh beginning, some of the girls left camp having formed deep bonds, and for most, it became impossible to see each other as the enemy. What allowed for this change of heart? The girls contacted the truth of one another's pain and the truth of one another's goodness. Reality, when we let it in, dismantles the iron grip of our beliefs. As one Israeli girl put it, "If I don't know you, it's easy to hate you. If I look in your eyes, I can't."

SUFFERING: THE CALL TO INVESTIGATE BELIEFS

The Buddha taught that ignorance—ignoring or misunderstanding reality—is the root of all suffering. What does this mean? He surely did not mean to deny the inevitable pains and losses in our lives, but he wanted his followers to grasp how their beliefs about what is happening— their thoughts about themselves, others, and the world—represented a contracted and fragmented view of reality. This distorted view, described by the Buddha as a dream, fueled the cravings and fears that confined their lives.

As with all thoughts, our beliefs are real but not true. The Buddha illustrated this with an ancient teaching story that we still repeat to our children. A king instructs a group of blind men to describe an elephant. Each man feels one part of the elephant's body—the tusk, the leg, the trunk, the tail. Each gives a detailed—and very different—report about the nature of the elephant. Then they come to blows about who is right. Each man is honestly describing his immediate and real experience, yet each misses the big picture, the whole truth.

Every belief we hold is a limited snapshot, a mental representation, not the full truth of reality itself. But some beliefs are more fear-based and injurious than others. Like the teens in Building Bridges, we may believe that certain people are evil. We may believe that we can't trust anyone. We may believe that we are fundamentally flawed and can't trust ourselves. These beliefs all arise from the primary fear-based belief that the Buddha identified: that we are separate from the rest of the world, vulnerable and alone. Whether our beliefs arouse self-loathing, trap us in self-destructive addictions, ensnare us in conflict with a partner, or send us to war with an enemy, we are suffering because we are mistaken about reality. Our beliefs narrow our attention and separate us from the living truth of how things are. They cut us off from the full aliveness, love, and awareness that is our source.

The sage Sri Nisargadatta teaches that "illusion exists . . . because it is not investigated." If we are attached to untrue beliefs, it is because we have not examined our thoughts. We have not met them with the mindful investigation of RAIN; we have not asked whether they truly represent our current, living experience of reality. *Suffering is our call to attention, our call to investigate the truth of our beliefs.* For the teenage girls in Building Bridges, the call to investigate was the hatred tearing at the fabric of their lives and society. For a parent, the call might be the stranglehold of worry about a child's welfare. For a social activist, it might be exhaustion and despair in the face of seemingly endless war and injustice. For a musician, it might be the disabling terror that accompanies performance. Wherever we feel most endangered, most separate, most deficient—that is where we need to shine the light of investigation.

THE PORTAL OF ADDICTION

Jason's call to attention was the addiction that was threatening to destroy his marriage and career. As a lobbyist for an important industrial group, he was constantly scanning his environment for people who might thwart him, and obsessing about the situations that might undermine his reputation as a powerful and connected person. The man who came to see me was fit, attractive, and seemingly confident. Yet, as I learned, he'd been priming himself with alcohol and cocaine in order to get through the many meetings and social gatherings that were essential to his work.

Jason had come to the United States from Argentina in his early teens. He'd thrived academically on scholarships, and over the years had climbed the corporate ladder. He and his wife, Marcella, seemed to be living the American dream, but it was in danger of falling apart.

For about a year, Jason had been an intermittent member of Narcotics Anonymous. But he had recently found a sponsor he really liked and the sponsor invited Jason to join him at my weekly meditation class. After several sessions Jason e-mailed me for an appointment.

At our first meeting, Jason jumped right in. "I'm abstinent right now," he told me, "but part of me still thinks I can do this my way." He admitted that cocaine and alcohol had been causing real trouble, but he believed that he could get away with occasional use. Cocaine in particular made him feel competent and in control, an experience that, in Jason's words, "is difficult to swear off."

But Jason knew he was in a bind. The president of his trade association had insisted that he go into a twelve-step program, and his wife had made it clear that their relationship was at risk unless he abstained totally. After telling me that he was committed to keeping his job and preserving his marriage, Jason shook his head and frowned. "I know this should be a no-brainer, Tara. But it's hard."

I've worked with many clients and students who've been stuck in similar ways. They are trying to make a life change that seems healthy and wise—giving up smoking, losing weight, abstaining from affairs, refraining from lashing out at loved ones—yet some inner resistance or impulsiveness either makes them unwilling or sets them up to try and fail repeatedly. This is a signal that strongly held beliefs are in control; it is a call for investigation.

When I asked Jason how he felt about his situation he spoke without hesitation. "Right now I'm angry. I can deal with my own problems, so it pisses me off when Marcella and my boss nose into my business."

"Can you agree to let the anger be here?" I asked. "Just to allow it and feel it?" After a few moments Jason nodded, then added, "I get mad a lot. Mostly when people are getting in my way, trying to control things."

"Jason, take a moment to remember a recent time when someone was doing that . . . trying to control things." He nodded and with a grim smile said, "It happened a few hours ago."

"Okay," I said. "Now rerun the situation and stop when you are most aware of reacting." It took him only a few seconds. "Got it."

"Bring your attention to the place in your body where your feelings are the strongest . . . it might be your throat, your chest, your belly . . . just check in and sense what's happening, what you're feeling."

Jason clenched his hands into fists. I asked him what he was feeling, and at first he hesitated. "It's . . . it's . . . well, my stomach's in knots. It's . . . fear."

WHY CORE BELIEFS ARE SO POWERFUL

Our core beliefs are often based on our earliest and most potent fears—we construct our strongest assumptions and conclusions about life from them. This conditioning is in service of survival. Our brains are designed to anticipate the future based on the past; if something bad happened once, it can happen again. Our brains are also biased to encode most strongly memories of experiences that are accompanied by feelings of endangerment. This is why even a few failures can instill feelings of helplessness and deficiency, which many later successes may not be able to undo. As the saying goes, "Our memories are Velcro for painful experiences and Teflon for pleasant ones!" We are very inclined toward building our core beliefs out of experiences of hurt and fear, and holding on to them (and the underlying fears) for dear life.

Imagine that you are a child trying to get your mother's attention: You want her to look at your drawing, to get you a drink, to play a game with you. While she sometimes responds to your needs, at other times she explodes in anger at being disturbed. She yells at you to leave her alone and threatens to spank you. Years later, you may not remember most of these incidents, but your brain registered her anger and rejection, and your hurt and fear. Over time, these encoded memories may constellate into negative beliefs about yourself and what you can expect from others: "I am too needy . . . people won't love me"; "If I bother someone, I'll get punished"; or "Nobody really wants to spend time with me."

The greater the degree of early life stress or trauma, the greater the conditioning, and the greater the likelihood of deeply entrenched fear-based beliefs. If you grew up in a war zone, your survival instincts would ensure that you automatically distinguish between "us" and "them," and you would easily classify "them" as bad and dangerous. If you were sexually abused as a child, any intimacy might seem dangerous, a setup for abuse. Alternately, you might be drawn to aggressive and domineering people, because the connection feels so familiar or even "safe." If you are an African American male, you might believe that you will be seen as inferior, held back no matter how hard you try, or unfairly targeted as a criminal. If you were poor and went hungry, you might believe that there will never be enough, that you will never be secure, no matter how rich you become.

Although they're rooted in the past, our core beliefs feel current and true. The thoughts and feelings associated with them filter our experience of what is happening right now, and they prime us to respond in a certain way. If your partner seems preoccupied when you ask her a question, it can set off a very old feeling of not mattering, and that feeling may trigger a reflex to become apologetic, withdrawn, or aggressive. If your boss asks you to redo part of a project, it can set off old feelings of failure and a reflex to give up or to become angry and resentful. Your core belief narrows your current experience to a single interpretation: You are threatened and alone.

This picture is complicated, of course, because current experience may reinforce old beliefs. If, like the Building Bridges teens, you believe that your enemies want to kill you, every suicide bomber, every home destroyed by the army, deepens your conviction. For these girls, danger is a daily reality. But the interpretation of that reality—that the hatred is personally directed at a self, that only by striking back will the self be safe—is not necessarily true. As we will see, if we can attend to the whole truth of our current experience, a space opens up, and we can begin to glimpse other possibilities.

IN THE GRIP OF FEAR-BELIEFS

For Jason, the first step was to investigate the fear he'd discovered underneath his anger. I asked him to try an experiment. "As you feel the fear in your stomach, just allow your face to express it." Jason's eyes widened and hardened and his gaze fixed on the floor. His jaw was clenched, his mouth pressed tight. "Now," I said, "see what happens when you look at the situation through the perspective of your fear. What is your fear trying to tell you? What does it believe is going to happen? What does it believe about you, about your life?

"You don't have to *think* about an answer," I went on. "Actually feel that you are inside the fear and sense how it is experiencing the world." This is an important reminder, because investigation can easily become a mental activity quite removed from the experience of the moment. Jason seemed to understand that he should stay in direct contact with his feelings: He tilted his head slightly as if he were listening to the frightened place inside him.

When he spoke, it was in a soft, low voice: "My fear tells me that if I don't take control, someone will control me, disrespect me, hurt me." Again he paused and seemed to look inward. Finally he said, "It believes that I'm a failure, just a bag of hot air . . . and that everyone will find out how weak I am. Then they won't respect me . . . or like me."

By giving his fear a voice, Jason had revealed the core beliefs that were driving his life. During our next two sessions he told me about growing up outside of Buenos Aires. He had been bullied and shamed by an alcoholic father, and then by his older brother. "When I was a kid," he said, "they were the real men. That's how men were. Tough, always putting down the weaker ones . . ." He was quiet a moment. "I wasn't like my brother, big and loud. I liked books, even as a kid. And I didn't like to fight. So in front of the whole neighborhood my father would call me *una niña*—a girl. It was the worst when he was drinking . . . Right after he lost his job he beat me up badly."

Jason remembered the day he decided to start working out at the gym. His family had moved the year before to live with relatives in the Bronx, and he was a freshman in high school. "My brother and his friends would hang out by a gas station, and I'd have to pass them walking home from school. That day it was raining, and I was walking fast, toting a pile of books. They started hooting at me, making fun of me." Then one of the boys shoved Jason and he went sprawling over the curb. A car ran over a couple of textbooks, and the others thought this was hilarious. "That was it, Tara," he said. "I wasn't going to let anyone mess with me again." Within a year, that skinny kid had changed. "I was ripped," Jason told me, "and cruising the streets with the older guys. For a while, I was as mean as the worst of them."

Jason had to hide the fact that he studied hard and got good grades. "I just acted bad, and stayed up late at nights, finishing assignments." Recognizing his potential, two of his teachers steered him toward a scholarship at a prestigious state university. "I was playing everyone," he confided. "The teachers thought I was 'clean,' but I was drugging and partying up a storm . . . and my friends thought I was one of them, but I knew I was leaving the hood." After a thoughtful pause Jason gave me a level look. "I'm still playing everyone, aren't I?"

OUR BELIEFS BECOME OUR DESTINY—
UNLESS WE SEE THEM

Jason had found strategies that gave him a sense of control and temporary security, whether it was building his muscles, getting good grades, drugging, or presenting a "take charge" persona. But now these same strategies, like all false refuges, were backfiring. Constantly manipulating others reinforced his sense of being a flawed person who had to struggle to stay on top. Alcohol and drug use had become addictions that threatened both his job and his marriage. His very efforts to stay in control were preventing him from actually facing and healing his deep insecurity. Jason was caught in a vicious cycle that would continue as long as he bought into his core beliefs.

If we pay close attention, we can see how our beliefs about ourselves and the world give rise to the very behaviors and events that confirm them. If you believe that nobody will like you, you'll behave in ways that broadcast your insecurities. When people pull away, your sense of rejection will confirm your belief. If you believe that others are waiting to attack or criticize you, you'll probably act defensive or aggressive. Then when people push back, your fears will be justified.

The Buddha taught that if your mind is captured by the fear and misunderstanding of limiting beliefs, "trouble will follow you as the wheel follows the ox that draws the cart." Traditional translations of Buddhist texts speak of the mind as "impure," but this can be understood as "distorted," "colored," or "tainted." Today, many twelve-step programs draw attention to "stinking thinking," the deluded self-justifications that are the precursor to relapse. Similarly, a cognitive therapist might help a client recognize the assumptions behind his interpretation of events, and show how they shape his responses. If we are primed to believe that others don't care or understand, how will that affect our search for intimacy? If we believe it is dangerous to stand out, how does that affect our creativity and self-expression? As the Buddha put it, "With our thoughts we make the world."

There is only one way to free ourselves from the grip of limiting beliefs, and that is by bringing a full presence to the raw feelings that drive them. Yet contacting these feelings—the fear, the shame, the grief—can be painfully difficult, even intolerable. That is why we can spend years or decades reacting to the world out of our beliefs, rather than investigating their emotional roots. For some people it's wise, or even essential, to have the support of a trusted healer, teacher, or therapist as they face those underlying feelings. Yet whether we are working with core beliefs on our own or with support, healing arises out of our willingness to bring the entire interdependent tangle of beliefs and emotions into awareness.

INTO THE BLACK HOLE

When Jason came back to see me, he was in crisis. During our first three meetings, he'd uncovered the beliefs that had shaped his life. But he quickly began to numb out this awareness. He plunged into a major project with a new client, and then one Friday night he became very anxious and he broke his abstinence by going to a bar after work and drinking several martinis. When he got home, Marcella angrily confronted him. "I hadn't called my sponsor, I hadn't been going to meetings or even meditating. Marcella told me I had destroyed her last shred of hope." She insisted that he sleep in his study and told him she was consulting a divorce attorney on Monday.

"Marcella and I haven't talked since the weekend. I know what I want to say to her, but I just can't."

I waited, and he nodded, gathering himself to say the words. "I want to beg her . . ." His voice cracked, and he took a few breaths. "I want to beg her to give me another chance . . . but that is so . . . weak. So pathetic." Now there was a flare of irritation in his eyes, and stiffening in his shoulders. "If she sees me like that, how could she ever want me?"

"So," I inquired, "wanting her to give you another chance is weak?"

"Well . . . it's just that . . . letting her know that my world would collapse without her, without our life together . . . that . . . that I need her." Jason began tearing up, but then wiped his eyes briskly. His hands clenched again, and he gave me an embarrassed shrug.

"Jason, for a very long time something in you has believed that you are weak and unworthy . . . I want to ask you, is this the truth? Are you unworthy of respect? Unworthy of Marcella's love?"

"I . . . I don't know." He was shaking his head, confused. "Intellectually I understand that I'm worthy, but I just somehow feel too pathetic for her, anyone, to respect or love me . . ."

As Jason's voice faltered, his body slumped back in the chair. His face seemed to drain of color. I asked him to pay attention to his body, to sense his heart, and to let me know how it felt to believe what he did: that he was unworthy of Marcella's love. He spoke in a low voice. "I feel ashamed. And totally alone." Again the tears began welling up: "These feelings—shame, loneliness—feel very old . . ."

"Where are you feeling the shame and loneliness?" I asked. Jason silently brought one hand to his belly and began making small circles. Again I invited him to tell me what it was like. "It's a deep hollowness. Aching. Like I've been building my abs for years to cover this hole."

As he spoke, I noticed that the circles he was drawing with his hand were getting larger. I pointed this out and he nodded. "It's huge—like a black hole that has pulled in my heart and everything else."

I encouraged Jason to simply breathe and let the hole, the ache, the hollowness be as large as it wanted to be. He agreed, his body motionless, his head shaking slightly from side to side.

"It's important to notice," I said, "that when you believe that you're weak or unworthy, *that's* how the belief is living in your body. It's that feeling of a gaping black hole. And you've been living with *that*, the loneliness, the shame, under the surface, for a long time." He bowed his head, nodding sadly.

We were silent for some moments, and then I went on. "Take a moment, Jason, and let yourself be aware of how believing you are unworthy has affected your relationships—with Marcella, with your colleagues and friends." Again he nodded and after a long pause he spoke, his voice so soft that I had to lean forward to hear him. "It's kept me apart from everyone." Then gesturing toward his chest, "My heart has been lost in a black hole, my life . . ." He stopped talking and closed his eyes, as if the loss was too much to try to name with words.

I invited him to take his time and just allow the feelings to unfold. He was very still for a few minutes, then said, "It feels like deep pain—a kind of squeezing and ache—from when I was young, and now it's spreading into different parts of my body." I suggested that he stay with his experience, and if it was helpful, to breathe with it. When he opened his eyes a few minutes later, there was more brightness and life in them. "After the pain spread, it started dissolving . . . and now it's gone."

I smiled, honoring his unfolding process, and for a few moments rested quietly with him in presence. Then I asked him a question that invited a shift in attention: "Jason, what would it be like to live without the belief that you are weak and unworthy?" As Jason was considering this, I added, "Who would you be if you no longer believed you were weak and unworthy?"

Looking at me directly, Jason responded. "I don't know who I would be." He paused thoughtfully, and then continued, "But somehow that not knowing feels good . . . like all of a sudden there's space and I'm more alive." Jason took a few full breaths, as if he were allowing himself to open to and savor that space. "What is clear," he said, "what I do know is, if I didn't believe I was unworthy, I could relax *here* . . ." Jason gestured toward his heart. "I could trust that Marcella really does care, I could trust enough to tell her the truth . . . That I love her."

Jason began weeping, and this time he did not try to wipe away his tears. His hands unclenched as if to allow the enormity and intensity of all these feelings to move through him. As he consciously recognized the raw pain of his beliefs and allowed that pain to express itself, Jason's heart was opening. He was discovering the freedom of "real but not true."

When the intensity of feeling had passed, Jason took a long deep breath and sat quietly. We both knew that there was not much more to say. He whispered a sincere "Thank you," and then added, "My work's cut out for me." He left with a soft yet determined look in his eyes: Not so bound by his unseen beliefs, Jason now had the capacity to reconnect with his own heart and with his wife.

THE POWER OF INQUIRY

Fear-based beliefs are creatures of the dark. They are sustained outside the light of awareness and they dissipate upon mindful inspection. As author Byron Katie teaches in her groundbreaking work, "You're either attaching to your thoughts or inquiring. There's no other choice." Inquiry into what is true is central to Byron Katie's work and to meditative practices like RAIN. By inquiry (or in RAIN, investigation) I mean asking questions like those I asked Jason, questions that invite a deepening of attention. The ultimate purpose of inquiry is that it allows us to pause, rather than ride along on the habitual track of our assumptions about reality. In the space of a pause, truth can shine through.

"What am I believing?"

Emotional suffering is a flag that you are in the grip of unexamined, fear-based beliefs. If you are caught in anger or depression, hurt or fear, the simple question "What am I believing?" can reveal what is driving your mood. As I suggested to Jason, this inquiry needs to be directed to the feelings themselves. You are asking, "Sadness, what are you believing?" or "Fear, what are you believing?"

"Is this really true?"

When we assume a belief is truth, there is no room for other possibilities, for new information, for a larger perspective. Pausing and questioning our belief can begin to open the windows of our mind to the fresh air of reality.

One client began to ask himself this question during a painful stand-off with his teenage son. He had assumed that if he didn't express his anger and judgment, his son would never become a responsible and pro-ductive adult. Asking the question "Is this really true?" stopped him in his tracks. He realized that he really didn't know whether angrily con-fronting his son was helping. As he continued to ask that question, pause, and listen to what came up, he became increasingly open to other possibilities. "Maybe it's more important that he gets that I trust him . . . that he's basically a good kid," he said, "than always hearing from me about what is wrong."

"What is it like to live with this belief?"

Beliefs are always accompanied by a felt sense in the body. If we pay at-tention, we can discover how our body feels when we are in the sway of a limiting belief. Is there tightness in certain areas? Heaviness? Hollow-ness? Cramping? Trembling? Are these sensations associated with par-ticular emotional states? Are we feeling embarrassment? Fear? Anger? Self-hatred? We can also investigate more broadly, asking, "How has this belief influenced my way of relating to myself, to other people, to life?" Our answers to these questions may point to any part of our lives—to a persistent shortness of breath, to our surges of irritation, to an ongoing conflict with our spouse. Body, emotions, thoughts, and behaviors—all express our beliefs.

When I investigate how believing "something is wrong with me" af-fects my life, I can sense how it blocks me from feeling loving and loved. It creates a tension that keeps me restless, edgy and distracted, and un-able to enjoy what I'm doing. It prevents me from being attuned and sensitive to others. Sometimes I become aware of how long I've been judging myself harshly, and of how many moments of my life have been lost to this familiar trance. This often brings up what I call "soul sad-ness," a tenderness that is full of compassion. In these moments I am living in a presence that is not confined by my belief.

"What stops me from letting go of this belief?"

Even when you've seen the pain of a belief, it's easy to get rehooked and to buy into its message again. Your newfound freedom may vanish the moment someone acts insensitively toward you or you make a mistake. Sometimes the old belief reasserts itself with a vengeance: "I must have been a fool; no one will ever really understand or care about me," or "That proves it: If I let down my guard, people do take advantage of me" or "What was I thinking? I'm a fundamental loser. I'll screw up any good thing that comes my way."

The truth is that people don't always understand, and people do hurt us. The truth is that we will continue to make mistakes. However, it is not true that no one will ever love or understand us, or that "you're bad" or "I'm bad." Yet our fear-based conditioning holds on tight. The mind gathers evidence to support our limiting beliefs, and it is biased toward fixating on that evidence. When you ask, "What stops me from letting go of this belief?" you shine a light on this basic strategy of self-protection. It is based on another core belief: "If I know what is wrong, at least I can control things. Keeping my attention on this will help me avoid greater pain in the future." On some level, we believe that our beliefs are serving us.

You can challenge these underlying assumptions by again asking, "Is this really true?" If you hold on to the belief that "no one will ever really care," will you avoid more suffering? If you hold on to the belief that "I'm a fundamental loser," will you start to improve in some way? If you hold on to the belief that "if I let down my guard, people will take advantage of me," will you feel safer and more at peace?

"What would my life be like without this belief?"

Take a minute right now to reflect on a fear-based belief that you have already identified. Maybe you believe that you will never be really intimate with anyone, or that you are a disappointment to others, or that you don't deserve love. Maybe you believe that you have to work constantly to win approval. Maybe you believe that you are too old for anyone to really be interested in you. Whatever the belief, take a moment to sense how it has affected your life. Can you connect with the pain of living with this belief? Now ask yourself, "What would my life be like without this belief? How would my relationship with myself change? How would my relationship with others change?"

When Jason asked himself these questions, he immediately sensed that without the belief in his unworthiness, he'd have more space, more aliveness. He also realized that without the belief, he'd truly be able to trust the love he shared with his wife. Some people who ask themselves this question can feel their bodies spontaneously unwind from a deep, habitual tightness that they didn't know they were carrying. Others imagine how they might walk through their days with a sense of true openness, creativity, and wonder. Still others glimpse the possibility of loving without holding back. Even these small tastes of freedom actually awaken our intrinsic awareness and wisdom, further releasing our attachment to the belief.

"Who (or what) would I be if I no longer lived with this belief?"

When your sense of self has been organized around a belief like "I don't deserve love," and you come to see that the belief is not true, you may feel disoriented and confused. Like Jason, you might even say, "I don't know who I would be." You don't know who you are anymore! For Jason, not knowing created a space that allowed him to unclench, breathe, and begin to relax. Others experience a sense of groundlessness that can be enlivening, fascinating, or even frightening.

There is great spiritual power in asking, "Who would I be if I no longer lived with this belief?" The question dissolves the questioner, the sense of separate self. Losing yourself opens the way to the *N* of RAIN: non-identification. When you lose yourself, the space suit of small self cracks open, and you discover that you can move and breathe without the constricting layers, without the helmet and air tube. Losing yourself makes it possible to realize the true mystery and wholeness of who you are.

LIVING BEYOND BELIEFS

The next time Jason and I met, he told me about the evening he'd spent with Marcella after our previous session. At first he had talked, and

Marcella had listened. "I told her things I've never said out loud. Mostly I let her know about the ashamed, scared kid inside of me . . . the one who is always trying to control things to protect himself . . . and also about the man who loves her." He paused, his eyes becoming moist in remembering. "I told her how even if she left me, at least now she would know the truth."

Marcella had been equally honest, and Jason was able to listen without becoming defensive. She let him know the extent of her rage and despair and loneliness at not finding intimacy in their marriage. While this was not the first time she had expressed her pain and dissatisfaction, it was the first time Jason had actually stayed still and attentive, that he heard her out. "I guess I'm getting better at being present," he said with a bit of pride. "I really wanted to know what was true for her . . . to understand her experience, even if it didn't feel good to hear it."

"She ended," Jason said, "by telling me I had been living in my head and was unreachable, and that now, maybe I was moving from my head to my heart." When they were done with words, they had just held each other. In the silence he could feel the tenderness of giving love, the deep pleasure of receiving it—and something more. "My mind wasn't telling me a story about what could go wrong and what I needed to do next to manage things. So I just disappeared. All I knew was the loving that was there, just loving awareness."

Jason left my office that day with a sense of gratitude and openness to whatever might unfold next, and I didn't see him again for almost a month. At that next session he greeted me with a smile and started in eagerly: "No surprise, the insecure one who assumes he's got to take charge has made his appearance again." He paused, then said, "But I've found some ways to deal with him." When the urge to have a drink resurfaced, Jason was able to respond with a new sense of confidence. "I heard a prayer at our twelve-step meeting that another man uses . . . It's perfect for my life: 'Not my will, but my heart's will.' When I start thinking about drinking or drugs, or when I realize I'm trying to control a situation, I'm back to believing I'm unworthy. When I'm anxious or angry, I'm back to believing I'm unworthy. But now, as soon as I catch the belief, I tell myself to listen to my heart's will . . . You know what, Tara, it works. I'm not hiding anything. I'm not playing anyone. My life is cleaner, and things at home are only getting better."

Our fear-based beliefs trap us in the trance-identity of an insecure self that is hypervigilant in managing life. We rationalize, we justify ourselves, we defend, we blame. Our will, our capacity for conscious, purposeful action, is commandeered by a frightened ego. For Jason, this had landed him in addiction and almost destroyed his marriage. But this same purposeful energy can be guided by a deeper intelligence. When he called on his "heart's will," Jason recognized fear-thinking, and rather than subscribing to his limiting beliefs, he allowed his life choices to emerge from the depths of his own inner wisdom.

REFUGE IN TRUTH

The Building Bridges program reminds us that beliefs can be dismantled, even in the most difficult circumstances. At an early Building Bridges camp, a Palestinian girl told the rest of the campers about how Israeli soldiers had barged into her family's house, beaten up everybody, and then left without apology after finding out they were at the wrong place. The group facilitator, using a technique called "compassionate listening," asked an Israeli teen to repeat the story in first person, including the feelings—the rage and terror—that she might have felt. After listening to the Israeli retell her story, the Palestinian girl began to weep. "My enemy heard me!" she said. The two girls cried together and, through their time together, became close friends.

But what happens to the bonds between these girls after they return to their war-torn homelands? Since its beginnings in 1993, hundreds of teenagers have attended Building Bridges camps, and follow-up studies have shown that even a short exposure to a larger reality—the realness and heart of the "enemy"—creates real change and opens the door for continued bridge building. This has been an internal process for some, and more public for others. A few of the young women have become peace activists. One Palestinian woman is a leading environmentalist who works with both sides to save their shared fragile desert ecosystem, and another is a schoolteacher who introduces a larger, more compassionate reality to her students. A number of the attendees have maintained their friendships with one another. After her school was bombed, one Palestinian girl was touched to get a call from an Israeli teen even before she heard from any of her Palestinian friends. This same young woman broke down in tears when an Israeli bus was bombed, even while her cousins cheered around her.

The trance of separation, of "us" against "them," is powerful. Yet, as the Buddha taught: "Greater still is the truth of our connectedness." Beliefs lose their force whenever we take refuge in actual experience. If we really pay attention to another person, if we really listen and try to enter his or her experience, we may begin to discover who he or she is beyond any preconceived notions.

Henry Wadsworth Longfellow wrote, "If we could read the secret history of our enemies, we should find in each man's life sorrow and suffering enough to disarm all hostility." This is not a naive claim. It does not mean that other people—even people we've befriended—won't harm us. Nor does it mean that we should set aside the wise discrimination that guides us to protect ourselves. What it does mean is that our hearts need not be armored by beliefs that obscure the "secret history" of another's suffering or that shut off the possibility of mutual understanding and care.

In just the same way, when we bring full presence to our own experience, we see beyond the confining stories we tell ourselves about our own unworthiness, badness, unlovableness. Rather than living from these stories, we become increasingly free to trust and live from our natural intelligence, openness, and love. Then, like the poet Rumi, we might realize:

> I've gotten free of that ignorant fist that was pinching and
>   twisting my secret self.
> The universe and the light of the stars come through me.

Guided Reflection: Beliefs Inventory

The more you are mindful of your beliefs, the less force they will exert on your psyche. A skillful way of strengthening this mindfulness is to create an inventory of your strongly held beliefs. Take some time to reflect on your limiting, fear-based beliefs and write them down. Perhaps some of the following examples will feel familiar:

"I need to work hard for approval or love."
"I am not worthy of being loved; I don't deserve to be happy."
"Anyone I get close to will hurt me."
"I will hurt anyone I love."
"I need to protect myself or I will get hurt."
*"I need to be different (more attractive, intelligent, confident, successful) if I
      am to be loved or loving, happy, or at peace."*
"Other people don't understand or appreciate me."
"I am invisible to others."
"I am special, smarter, better than others."
"It is dangerous to appear weak or needy."
"I can't trust anyone not to take advantage of me."
"If I don't 'get even' others will continue to hurt me."
"I am fundamentally flawed."
"I am a failure; I will fail at anything I do."
"God (life, other people) has betrayed me."

Guided Reflection: Catching Beliefs on the Fly

You can develop your mindfulness muscles for "catching beliefs" by experimenting with situations that bring up moderate, rather than full-blown, emotional reactivity.

---

1. *When you feel calm, identify and write down several situations that regularly produce anxiety, irritation, or discouragement. Some examples: "communicating with my boss," "getting my son ready for school," "being caught in rush-hour traffic," "approaching a deadline for a project," "feeling fatigued at work," "being criticized by my partner."*

2. *With your belief inventory on hand, take some time to reflect on each situation. Ask yourself, "What am I believing?" You might need to ask several times, "What am I really believing?" or "What is the most disturbing thing that I'm believing?" in order to uncover the most basic form of the belief. Write it down, trying to capture the belief in a few easy-to-remember words: "Believing I'm falling short," "Believing I'll be punished (rejected) if I fail," "Believing I have to try harder to be okay."*

3. *Set your intention to be mindful when the situations you identified arise. See if it is possible to pause in the midst of them and recognize what you are believing. Notice if this shifts how you feel or gives you fresh choices as to how you respond.*

At your own pace, you might tag new situations for "catching beliefs." As you become more confident in your capacity to meet your beliefs and feelings with mindfulness, you will be able to practice with increasingly charged situations.

PART III

THE GATEWAY OF LOVE

NINE

HEART MEDICINE FOR TRAUMATIC FEAR

How
Did the rose
Ever open its heart
And give to this world
All its
Beauty?
It felt the encouragement of light
Against its
Being.
Otherwise,
We all remain
Too
Frightened

HAFIZ

When Ram Dass suffered a massive cerebral hemorrhage in 1997, he had more than four decades of spiritual training to help guide him. One of the American pioneers in bringing Eastern spirituality to the West, he had explored meditation practices from Hindu, Buddhist, Advaita, and other traditions and introduced several generations to meditation and the path of devoted service. Nonetheless, in the hours after his devastating stroke, he lay on a gurney staring at the pipes on the hospital ceiling, feeling utterly helpless and alone. No uplifting thoughts came to rescue him, and he was unable to regard what was happening with mindfulness or self-compassion. In that crucial moment, as he put it bluntly, "I flunked the test."

I sometimes tell Ram Dass's story to students who worry that they too have "flunked the test." They have practiced meeting difficulties with RAIN, but then they encounter a situation where the fear or distress or pain is so great that they just cannot arouse mindful presence. They are often left with feelings of deep discouragement and self-doubt, as if the door of refuge had been closed to them.

I start by trying to help them judge themselves less harshly. When we're in an emotional or physical crisis, we are often in trance, gripped by fear and confusion. At such times, our first step toward true refuge— often the only one available to us—is to discover some sense of caring connection with the life around and within us. We need to enter refuge through the gateway of love.

Ram Dass passed through this gateway by calling on Maharajji (Neem Karoli Baba), the Indian guru who had given him his Hindu name, and who had died twenty-four years earlier. In the midst of his physical anguish, powerlessness, and despair, Ram Dass began to pray to Maharajji, who to him had always been a pure emanation of love. As he later wrote, "I talked to my guru's picture and he spoke to me, he was all around me." That Maharajji should be immediately "there," as fully available as ever, was to Ram Dass pure grace. At home again in loving presence, he was able to be at peace with the intensity of the moment-to-moment challenge he was facing.

The gateway of love is a felt sense of care and relatedness—with a loved one, with the earth, with a spiritual figure, and ultimately, with awareness itself. Just as a rose needs the encouragement of light, we need love. Otherwise, as poet Hafiz says, "We all remain too frightened."

THE LEGACY OF TRAUMA

Dana had been coming to our weekly meditation group for four months when she approached me one evening after class. She told me that she needed more help in dealing with her fear. "Trust doesn't come easy for me," she said, "but listening to you calms me down . . . I get the sense that you'd understand, that I'd feel safe working with you."

Dana did not appear insecure or easily intimidated. A tall, robust African American woman in her late twenties, she had a tough job as a parole officer for a state prison facility. She also had an easy smile and lively eyes, but her words told a different story. "I can be just fine, Tara," she told me, "and then if I get tripped off . . . I'm a totally dysfunctional person." Especially when a strong male got angry with her, she said, she'd get "tongue-tied." "It's like I'm a scared little girl, a basket case."

I asked Dana to tell me about some recent times when she'd been tongue-tied with fear. She sat back in her chair, crossed her legs, and began nervously tapping the floor with one foot. When she spoke, it was in a rush of words. "One place it happens is with my boyfriend. He drinks—too much—and sometimes he'll start yelling, accusing me of things that aren't true . . . like that I'm flirting with other men or talking about him behind his back." She stopped for a moment and then continued. "When he gets on my case, you know, threatening me," she said, "my insides just huddle up into a tight little ball, and it's like the real me disappears." At these times she was unable to think or talk. All she was aware of was the pounding of her heart and a choking feeling in her throat.

Her boyfriend was not the first man to violate her. It soon emerged that Dana had disappeared into that tight ball over and over again, ever since she was eleven years old and her uncle began to molest her. For four years, until he moved out of state, Dana had lived in fear that he would drop by when her mother was at work. After each assault, he would swear her to secrecy and threaten to punish her if she told. He often accused her of "asking for it"—if she had dressed or acted differently, he said, it never would have happened. Even then, a part of her knew this wasn't true, but something else in her believed him. "It still does," she said. "It's like there's some badness in me that is always waiting to come out."

Dana was clear about the source of her fears, but that clarity didn't protect her from feeling anxious, guilty, and powerless. The next time I saw her, Dana told me that after our first session, the old terrors of her uncle's threats had resurfaced. Had she betrayed her boyfriend? Would she be punished for "telling"? Now, just sitting down in my office plunged her into an old and familiar spiral of fear. She stopped talking, her face froze, and her eyes became fixed on the floor. I could see that she was trembling and her breathing had become shallow. "Are you disappearing inside?" I asked. She nodded without looking up.

I was fairly sure that Dana was having a post-traumatic stress reaction. She seemed to have tumbled back into the past, as defenseless and endangered as when her uncle was standing over her. In that moment, I knew it was unlikely that Dana could access a sense of mindful presence. The fear contraction was too strong.

I've found that what a person usually needs when fear is intense is to "be accompanied"—an experience of another person's caring, accepting presence. If a child is hurt or frightened, showing that we understand and care about her feelings is more important than looking for a Band-Aid or explaining why everything will be all right. The core of vulnerability is feeling alone in one's pain; connection with another person eases fear and increases the sense of safety. However, when a person has been traumatized, it is also important that he or she control the degree of contact. Otherwise, contact itself could be associated with the traumatizing situation.

"Dana," I said gently, "would you like me to sit next to you?" She nodded, and patted the cushion right next to her on the couch. When I moved to her side, I asked her if it was okay for me to sit so close, and she whispered, "Sure . . . thanks." I suggested that she make herself as comfortable as possible. Then she could focus on feeling how her body was being supported by the sofa, and how her feet were contacting the floor. When she nodded again, I encouraged her to notice the felt sense of what it was like for us to be sitting together.

Over the next few minutes, I checked in several times, letting her know I was there with her and asking her if she was okay. She nodded and remained silent, but gradually she stopped trembling and her breathing became deeper and more regular. When I asked again how she was doing, she turned her head enough to catch my eye and gave me a small smile. "I'm settling down, Tara. It's better now." I could tell by the way she was engaging—with her eyes and smile—that she no longer felt so trapped inside her fear.

I returned to my chair facing her so we could talk about what had happened. "I don't know what's wrong with me," she began. "I should be able to get it together on my own, but when I get stuck like that, it's embarrassing. I just feel so broken." Dana realized that she had been traumatized, and yet she still considered her "episodes," as she called them, to be a sign of weakness and cowardice. Worse, they were evidence that she was spiritually bereft. As she put it, "I have no spiritual center, it's just darkness there . . . no soul."

One of the most painful and lasting legacies of trauma is self-blame. Students and clients often tell me that they feel broken, flawed, like "damaged goods." They may understand the impact of trauma rationally, but they still feel self-revulsion and shame when they feel or act out of control. Their underlying belief seems to be that no matter how awful our experience, we should be able to subdue its terror, quiet our catastrophic thinking, and avoid false refuges like addictive behavior or withdrawing from intimacy. In other words, the self, no matter how distressed, should always be in control.

Inevitably, the small self "flunks the test." When we're inside the trance of a separate, traumatized self, we are trapped in a loop of suffering: Our brains and bodies continuously regenerate the physiology of fear, reinforcing our sense of danger and powerlessness. The healing of trauma, and of the shame that surrounds trauma, requires waking from the trance of separation. Dana needed to discover that she could take refuge in belonging even while the raw feelings of trauma were arising. Our close, personal contact during those disturbing moments in my office was an important first step.

UNDERSTANDING TRAUMA

Trauma is the experience of extreme stress—physical or psychological—that overwhelms our normal capacities to process and cope. When we're in a traumatized state, we are gripped by primitive survival strategies, and cut off from our own inner wisdom and from the potential resources of the world around us. Our entire reality is confined to the self-sense of being isolated, helpless, and afraid. This profound state of disconnection is the core characteristic of trauma, and to some degree, of all difficult emotions.

I've worked with many people whose lives have been painfully imprinted by trauma, yet who have not recognized trauma as the cause of their struggles. They are so familiar with their own personal history that they discount the impact of the violence they have endured. Others, like Dana, have recognized the trauma, yet feel ashamed and undeserving of compassion. It can help to know just how pervasive trauma is: For example, somewhere between seventy-five million and one hundred million Americans have experienced sexual or physical abuse during childhood. The conservative American Medical Association estimates that more than 30 percent of all married women, as well as 30 percent of pregnant women, have been beaten by their spouses, often repeatedly. Less recognized sources of trauma include difficulties in our own process of being born, undergoing surgery, or the sudden loss of a loved one. Millions more endure trauma during wars or natural disasters. When the clients and students I work with can acknowledge that they too have suffered from trauma, they begin to regard their own lives with a deeper and more sympathetic attention.

Not all trauma unfolds into the chronic condition called post-traumatic stress disorder (PTSD). According to clinician and writer Peter Levine, trauma generates the suffering of PTSD if the strong biological energies it provokes cannot be successfully processed or resolved. When we are threatened, fear mobilizes us toward some action—fight or flight—that will protect us from danger. In traumatic situations, some people are able to escape from the danger, strike back, help others to safety, or find a strong ally to protect them in the future. The sense of being endangered is mitigated, the survival energies are discharged. But if there is no way to mobilize a response, as was the case for Dana when she was repeatedly raped by her uncle, the backup reaction is to freeze. In this state, the thwarted fear-based energies of fight/flight remain trapped in the body, and the mind cuts off or dissociates from the felt sense of their raw intensity. This dissociation, which may be experienced as numbness or a feeling of being "unreal," is a core feature of PTSD.

These frozen traumatic memories may be evoked at any time. When a similar situation arises, the unprocessed, temporarily dissociated energies of terror, rage, or helplessness are rearoused. We experience the distress of wanting to flee or fight all over again, as if it were happening in the present. For Dana, "telling on" her boyfriend in a therapy session with me set off the stored terror of her uncle's threats to punish her if she "told."

My clients and students are sometimes stunned to realize how many of their thoughts, feelings, and behaviors have become organized around managing the intensity of their past trauma. Together, we explore how often they feel endangered, how often their energies are mobilized for flight or fight, and how these energies express or discharge themselves in a wide range of symptoms: In addition to dissociation and flashbacks, symptoms can include panic attacks, insomnia, nightmares, depression, mental obsession, rage and/or addictive behaviors, and incapacity for sexual intimacy. Dana suffered debilitating fear ("disappearing into a tight ball"), but she would also at times lash out in anger, overeat, and smoke cigarettes. Like other false refuges, the symptomatic behaviors of trauma can temporarily dilute the raw pain of fear, but they prevent us from moving toward the safety and love that bring authentic healing. They also reconfirm our sense of being weak, out of control, and flawed.

People with post-traumatic stress often swing between being fully possessed by an emotion to being dissociated from the felt sense in the body. Caught in a constricting trance, they are ungrounded, cut off from key dimensions of their being. They may lose access to critical cognitive capacities, become unable to recall times when they have coped success-fully, and seem blind to potential resources in the larger world. There is disconnection from their loving bonds with others. And finally, there is the loss of the sense of presence, and with that, a distancing from the very source of spirit. This was what Dana was referring to when she told me she had no spiritual center, no soul.

For Dana, as for others who have experienced the anguish of trauma, the crucial question is, "What will make it safe enough to come home—to this body, to life, to presence?"

TAKING REFUGE IN LOVE

At our next session, Dana told me that the worst part of the sexual abuse was wanting someone to help her, but being too scared to ask. "I would rehearse telling my mother," she said, "and then have nightmares about my uncle finding out and kidnapping and strangling me."

While our last meeting had "tripped off" that old terror, Dana realized that she had recovered more quickly than usual. "When you sat next to me on the couch, it started to fade. There was something about you caring about me and just being there . . . I knew I was safe in that moment, I was okay." She paused for a few moments and then asked a key question: "But what can I do when I'm on my own?"

In the process of healing, there is often a natural movement or progression. First we take comfort in the physical presence of others, and then we discover within ourselves a pathway to safety and love. This is an important and delicate sequence. The traumatized self is fragile and needs an external resource. Yet because the original traumatic wounding often occurs in a relationship, relationships may have become associated with danger. For this reason, a caring and secure relationship is an essential part of the healing work.

In many shamanistic cultures, it is believed that when a person is traumatized, the soul leaves the body as a way of protecting itself from intolerable pain. In a ceremony called "soul retrieval," the traumatized person is held in the love and safety of community as the soul is invited to return. We can translate this to many other healing relationships, where the care of a therapist, friend, support group, or teacher initially provides the safety to reconnect with some degree of presence and well-being.

But as Dana's question implies, the deepest healing allows us to feel loved and safe in any situation, including when we're on our own. Through meditation, our outer refuge—the presence of a caring other—can become a bridge to discovering a trustworthy inner refuge, the love and care sourced in our own being.

More than twenty-five hundred years ago, the Buddha taught his followers a lovingkindness meditation to ward off fear. Each year, before the rainy season in India, hundreds of monks would gather around the Buddha for spiritual teachings and instructions. They would then go off to find a suitable location for a three-month "rain retreat," a period of intensive practice. One year, as the story goes, the monks found an idyllic forest grove with majestic trees and a clean spring of cool water—the perfect place to meditate day and night. They didn't realize, however, that the forest was inhabited by tree deities who felt dispossessed when the monks moved in. The infuriated spirits created terrifying illusions of monsters, ghosts, and demons, filled the groves with dreadful shrieks and moans, and produced a sickening stench. The monks soon became pale and shaky, unable to maintain any concentration or inner balance. Encouraged, the tree deities became even more aggressive, until the monks fled back to the Buddha's encampment.

Much to their dismay, however, the Buddha insisted that they return to the haunted grove. But before they left, he taught them verses of universal love to recite and reflect on, and promised that this would carry them beyond fear to spiritual liberation. As the monks neared the forest, they immersed themselves in this meditation, sending currents of unconditional lovingkindness first to themselves and then outward, to all beings everywhere. The hearts of the tree spirits became so infused with goodwill that they materialized in human form, offered the monks food and water, and invited them to stay. For the remainder of the monks' retreat, the tree spirits basked in the aura of their loving presence and in return, kept the grove free of noise and distractions. And as the story also tells us, each one of the monks attained the pinnacle of spiritual realization.

Like the monks, we suffer whenever we dispossess the energies of shame or hurt, anger or fear. When any part of our inner life is unseen, unfelt, pushed away, or rejected, we feel alone and afraid. And like the tree spirits, these dispossessed energies will haunt us and keep us fearbound until we meet them with a caring presence. As the Buddha taught, there are two expressions of love that naturally heal and free us. The Pali word for lovingkindness, *metta*, means unconditional friendliness, warmth, love, or care, and the Pali word for compassion, *karuna*, means to "feel with," to bear suffering with an active sympathy. In his wisdom the Buddha realized that by purposefully awakening lovingkindness and compassion, we invite the alienated hurts and fears into consciousness, and free ourselves into a wholeness of being.

Today, researchers are discovering what happens in the brains of meditators when their attention is focused on these two expressions of love. Sophisticated brain scans show that the left frontal cortex, a part of the brain that is deactivated during trauma, lights up during loving-kindness and compassion meditations. This brain activity correlates strongly with subjective feelings of happiness, openness, and peace.

When I teach meditations for the heart, I often ask my students to visualize being held by a loved one and/or to offer gentle self-touch as part of the practice. Research shows that a twenty-second hug stimulates production of oxytocin, the hormone associated with feelings of love, connectedness, and safety. Yet we don't need to receive a physical hug to enjoy this benefit: Either imagining a hug or feeling our own touch—on our cheek, on our chest—also releases oxytocin. Whether through visualization, words, or touch, meditations on love can shift brain activity in a way that arouses positive emotions and reduces traumatic reactivity.

This is why my next goal in working with Dana was to help her access feelings of love and safety on her own. She had already learned a traditional version of the lovingkindness meditation in my class, but now we would personalize it, identifying the particular images and words that would allow her to feel held in love.

"Who," I asked, "helps you find a warm feeling of being safe inside?" Dana's eyes lit up. "That's easy. Marin, my friend, or my little sister Serena. I trust both of them, they've totally got my back. And I feel safe . . . with you." She said this a little shyly and I smiled, letting her know that I felt honored to be counted in.

I suggested she picture what I called "her allies" right here in the room, imagining that she was surrounded by the three of us. Closing her eyes, Dana concentrated for a few moments and then said softly, "Okay, I see each of you. You and Marin are on either side . . . each of you is holding one of my arms . . . and my sister's right behind me."

"What's that feel like, Dana?" Without much hesitation she responded. "It's like being in a warm bath!"

"Good," I said. "Now let yourself just soak that warmth in, feel how deep it can go . . . how it can relax the places inside that most need it." I paused and then asked, "As you let in the warmth of your allies' presence, what words might be most comforting to hear and remember?"

Dana was very still and then she nodded. "It's that I'm safe, that I'm loved . . . that's my prayer: May I feel safe, may I feel loved."

I waited a few moments and then said, "Dana, if you contract inside and get huddled up in fear, just imagine each of us here, around you again. Feel the warmth surrounding you and let those words, your prayer, comfort you . . . let the meaning, the feeling of being safe and loved, sink into you. *Let your body have the felt sense of being loved.* You can practice that now if you'd like."

Dana settled back in her chair and her breathing became easier and deeper. She rolled her head in circles a few times to loosen her neck and then was quite still. When she looked up at me again, she smiled and her eyes were clear. "This reminds me that it's *possible* to relax. It's like there's a net around me and I can't fall too far. I feel better than I've felt in a long time."

Before Dana left, I encouraged her to practice calling on her allies at some point each day, during a time of low stress. "Experiment with what helps you feel our presence, our company," I suggested. "You might whisper our names, visualize our faces, feel our touch supporting you . . . whatever connects you with this sense of ease. Then remember your prayer for safety and love . . . and let it fill you."

THE NEED FOR NEW RESOURCES

Discovering a way to contact positive emotions and in particular a sense of care and relative safety is a key element in healing trauma. Recent research has shown that it is the common denominator of all effective trauma therapies. In order to achieve freedom from intense emotions like terror or shame, *the felt sense of that pain needs to be reexperienced within an enlarged, enriched context.* By this I mean that some additional resource like love, safety, or strength needs to be present for the repeating pattern of emotional pain to transform.

This approach also draws on a basic insight of modern learning theory. For new learning to occur, the new information needs to be combined with a known experience. For Dana, this meant experiencing her old fears of punishment while someone—in this case, me—was there who might help her feel safe in the present moment.

Therapies or meditative strategies that do not provide this added resource of care can easily be retraumatizing, because reexperiencing the fear and helplessness of the traumatic event without new resources confirms one's felt identity as an endangered, powerless self. In contrast, developing an inner refuge where we feel loved and safe enables us to reduce the intensity of traumatic fear when it arises. When we are able to contact an inner refuge through our internally generated words, images, or self-touch, our biochemistry shifts. Our fight-flight-freeze reactivity no longer overwhelms potentially adaptive responses, and the mind becomes more spacious and receptive. New associations, new inner resources, new ways of coping and understanding begin to emerge spontaneously. The most basic outcome is a growing sense of self-trust—we know that we have within us whatever is needed to be present with our life.

CULTIVATING AN INNER REFUGE

You can begin to develop a reliable inner refuge on your own by drawing on whatever in your past experience has helped you to feel a sense of connectedness and an increased sense of safety. *This reflection is best done when you are not in the grip of fear.* Once you have tuned in to these existing pathways to refuge, you can deliberately use the power of attention to make these states of mind more readily available.

When I work with students and clients to develop an inner refuge of safety and love, I often start with the following questions.

- With whom do you feel connection or belonging? Feel cared for or loved? Feel at home, safe, secure?

Like Dana, some people immediately identify an individual—a family member or friend, healer or teacher—whose presence creates the feeling of "at home." For others, home is a spiritual community, a twelve-step

group, or a circle of intimate friends. Sometimes the feeling of belonging is strongest with a person who has died, as for Ram Dass with Maharajji, or with a person you revere but may never have met, such as the
Dalai Lama, Gandhi, or Mother Teresa. Many people feel drawn to an
archetypal figure like the Buddha or Jesus, Kwan-yin (the bodhisattva of
compassion), the Virgin Mary, or some other expression of the divine
mother. I've also known a good number of people who feel comfort and
belonging when they call to mind their dog or cat. I assure students that
no one figure is more spiritual or elevated or pure than another as a
focus. All that matters is choosing a source of safe and loving feelings.

• When and where do you feel most at home—safe, secure, relaxed, or strong?

Some people find a sense of sanctuary in the natural world, while
others feel more oriented and secure when they're surrounded by the
noise and vibrancy of a big city. Your safe space may be a church or
temple, your office, or a crowded sports stadium. Some people feel most
at home curled up with a book in bed—others when they're working on
a laptop at a busy coffee shop. Certain activities may offer a sense of ease
or flow, from playing Ping-Pong to cleaning out a closet to listening
to music. Even if you almost never feel truly relaxed and secure, you
can build on any setting or situation where you are closest to feeling at
home.

One client I worked with thrived on solitary walks in the woods, so
I asked him to visualize a spot that was special for him, where a sun-
dappled stream swirled around rocks, and then to tell me what he could
see, smell, hear, and feel. We revisited the stream together several times,
and gradually, as he deepened his attention, he discovered a smooth
flowing sensation in his chest that was linked with this place. Then
whenever he felt overwhelmed by depression or anxiety, he would sum-
mon his sacred space, put his hand on his chest, and breathe in a sense
of aliveness, flow, and ease.

• What events or experiences or relationships have best revealed
  to you your strength, your courage, your potential?

Sometimes what arises is a memory of a particularly meaningful experience—an artistic or professional endeavor, a service offered, an athletic feat—that was a source of personal gratification or accomplishment. Whatever the experience, it's important to explore how it deepens our trust of ourselves.

One man I worked with recalled how he'd joined a picket line to protest the discriminatory hiring policies of his corporation. When he got in touch with the sense of integrity and courage that he remembered from that time, he felt a steady, bright vibrancy radiating from his heart, filling his entire chest, and overflowing into the world around him. "Something very real in me had come forward," he told me.

• What about yourself helps you to trust your goodness?

When we're in the grip of trauma or very strong emotion, it may not be possible to reflect on goodness, our own or others'. But when the body and mind are less agitated, this inquiry can be a powerful entry to inner refuge. I often ask clients and students to consider the qualities they like about themselves—humor, kindness, patience, creativity, curiosity, loyalty, honesty, wonder. I suggest that they recall their deepest life aspirations—loving well, realizing truth, happiness, peace, serving others—and sense the goodness of their hearts' longings. And I invite them to sense the goodness of their very essence, their experience of aliveness, awareness, and heart.

• When you are caught in fear, what do you most want to feel?

When I ask this question, people often say that they just want the fear to go away. But when they pause to reflect, they often name more positive states of mind. Like Dana, they want to feel safe or loved. They want to feel valued or worthwhile. They long to feel peaceful, at home, or trusting. Or they want to feel physically held, embraced. The words that name our longings, and the images that arise with them, can become a valuable entry to inner refuge. Often the starting place is to offer ourselves wishes or prayers such as, "May I feel safe and at home." Like offering the phrases in the classic lovingkindness meditation or placing a hand on the heart, expressions of self-care open us to an experience of belonging and ease.

Sometimes, however, people feel so isolated, so disconnected from love and security, that they can't initially find any inner resources to build on. Bonnie came to a weekend meditation retreat after a biopsy of a suspicious growth in her breast. Her cancer had been in remission for a number of years and at first the fear that it had returned gripped her so strongly she could barely breathe. Then, in a small group meeting, two other people talked about the life-threatening illnesses they lived with. When it was Bonnie's turn to speak, she was trembling, but present. "Listening to your stories let me take the first full breaths I've had in a few days. I realized I wasn't alone." We agreed that for the rest of the weekend Bonnie's practice would be simple: to acknowledge the fear by saying to herself, "This is suffering," and then remind herself, "I'm not alone. Others experience this too." Before leaving she told me, "I've been saying those words over and over. Now just naming it like that and *feeling* that I have company gives me a little space . . . I can let the fear be there for a minute or so at a time. I don't like it, but I can stay present with it." When Bonnie arrived home to find that the growth was benign, she e-mailed me. "I know more about finding true refuge," she wrote. "My cancer may still come back. Everything is uncertain, but now I know what I have to remember. I'm not alone."

Again the phrase "Neurons that fire together, wire together" says it well: When we repeatedly direct our minds toward thoughts and memories that evoke feelings of love (or safety or strength), the very structure of our brains is altered. On a physical and energetic level, we create new neural connections that serve as vital channels for healing. Where attention goes, energy flows.

At the time of his stroke, Ram Dass had studied with, revered, and prayed to his guru, Maharajji, over a period of thirty years. The gateway to a vast loving presence was already open, and in his moment of great need, he could walk through it to healing. But I've seen time and again that the gateway of the heart is still available even for people like Dana who have had little experience with inner training. All that is needed is the longing to heal and the willingness to practice. As poet Hafiz writes, "Ask the friend for love, ask him again . . . For I have found that every heart will get what it prays for most."

"I'M TRUSTING MY SOUL"

For three months, Dana practiced faithfully, calling on her allies daily during moments of relative calm, and feeling embraced by their warmth and her own prayers for safety and love. She and I met regularly during that period, exploring together how her new ability to soothe herself also helped her practice RAIN when she felt anxious, irritated, or upset. But it was on her own, and in the face of extreme reactive fear, that Dana discovered her capacity to awaken from the trance of trauma.

"I'm learning what it means to trust myself," she began. Then she told me what had happened the prior Saturday night. After downing a six-pack, Dana's boyfriend had aimed some taunting remarks at her, and then egged her on to react. "You don't like my talk? Go ahead, bitch . . . try shutting me up . . . see what happens." Dana felt her gut instantly seize up with fear and she knew that if she stayed, she would only become more frightened and frozen. Before she walked out the door, Dana told her boyfriend that this time it was over between them.

And then the fear slammed into her. Afraid to be home alone, she went to her friend Marin's apartment and asked to stay the night. Marin hugged her warmly and they spent over an hour talking about what had happened. But long after Marin was asleep, Dana lay awake on the couch. "I couldn't stop thinking about how he might try to punish me, you know . . . stalk me or something." Feeling a rising tide of terror again, Dana found herself curled up in a ball and shaking. "That was when I remembered that time in your office when I freaked out and we sat on the couch together . . . I knew I had to call on my allies."

Dana sat up and wrapped her blankets around her; she focused on the support of the sofa under her, as I had suggested she do when she felt her fear arise, and she planted her feet squarely on the ground, feeling its solidity. "Then I called out for help," Dana said in a soft voice. "I whispered Marin's name, my sister's name, and yours, Tara. I was gathering my women allies, having them surround me. But even then my heart still felt like it was exploding with fear."

Dana described the fear "like hot, broken glass" tearing up her chest, but she kept whispering our names and bringing her attention to her feet on the ground. "Feeling you all with me, I could hang in there while all hell broke loose!" she told me. Dana sat on the couch hugging herself and imagining that we were all there hugging her, while her body trembled uncontrollably, and fear continued to tear through her. Yet, as she put it, "I kept feeling you all there caring—like I was surrounded by a presence that was caring about me—while my insides were being broken apart. Even though I was freaked out, I didn't feel alone. I could hear the words 'May I feel safe, may I feel loved' going through my mind."

Gradually Dana noticed that something was shifting. "The fear was still there, but it was no longer taking over . . . there was some space. *It was that space of loving that was larger than this scared self.* And as I settled down a little, and the minutes went by, that space became more and more filled with light. Warm, luminous light. It was like I was part of that light . . . and then I realized . . . my *soul* was back. That lit-up space was inside me. I started crying, feeling how all these years I'd been lost, living without this light, living in a broken self."

Dana fell silent. Her hands pressed together as if in prayer, she bowed her head and allowed the tears to flow. When she looked up and spoke again, her voice was soft, yet full. "Tara," she said, "I'm sad, and that's okay. There's something new growing in me. When I told you I am learning to trust myself . . . what I meant is . . . I'm trusting that caring place that lets in love, that is loving—my soul. That's where the safety is. Even though I'll probably have that broken feeling again, even though I'll feel lost, I'll find my way back. This light, this love, is part of what I am."

As Dana and I sat quietly together, I remembered some lines from a poem by Rashani Réa called "The Unbroken":

> There is a brokenness out of which comes the unbroken . . .
> And a fragility out of whose depths emerges strength.
> There is a hollow space too vast for words
> through which we pass with each loss,
> out of whose darkness we are sanctioned into being.

There is a cry deeper than all sound
whose serrated edges cut the heart
as we break open to the place inside
which is unbreakable and whole . . .

FIERCE GRACE: BECOMING WHO WE ARE

In the aftermath of his stroke, Ram Dass described his path of healing as "fierce grace." The stroke had stripped him of tightly held aspects of his identity—he was no longer self-sufficient, he couldn't drive a car, play golf, or speak with his former fluency. Yet in opening to his vulnerability and loss, he found himself more aware of the divine within and around him.

Any deep wound or loss can be transformed into fierce grace when we meet the pain with a caring presence. We can find grace in the immediacy of a frightening experience or in working with long-held trauma. Although the pain of trauma may lead us to believe that our spirit has been tainted or destroyed, that isn't so. No amount of violence can corrupt the timeless and pure presence that is the very ground of our being. Waves of fear or shame may possess us temporarily, but as we continue to entrust ourselves to loving presence, as we let ourselves *feel* loved, our lives become more and more an expression of who or what we are. This is the essence of grace—homecoming to who we are.

Dana had anticipated that the feeling of being broken would resurface, and that she would be able to find her way back home when it did. Luckily, her boyfriend seemed to accept that the relationship was over and did not pursue her. Then, several months after her night on Marin's couch, Dana phoned a recently paroled client who had missed an obligatory relapse-prevention meeting. When she confronted him, the man went on a rant, cursing and yelling, and ended with, "Fuck you . . . you're like all the rest, you don't give a shit about what my life is like." After he hung up on her, Dana's heart raced and her whole body shook. Her mind churned with the notion that she had done something very wrong.

Dana knew she needed to practice with RAIN, but before beginning, she settled herself in her office chair, planted her feet firmly on the rug, and called on her allies. Within a few minutes, she was letting in the message of trust and feeling herself held in a familiar space of care. Settled enough to bring mindfulness to what was happening inside her, Dana deepened her attention. With a kind presence, she was able to investigate the clench of fear in her chest and recognize the familiar belief that somehow she was at risk and might be punished. She gently sent the now familiar words of care inward: "May I feel safe. May I feel loved." The more she relaxed, allowing the sensations and thoughts to come and go, the more she felt reconnected with her true self. "That inner space of warmth and light was back again—my soul. The big me was holding myself with kindness."

Then something happened that really surprised Dana. Just as she had investigated her own inner experience, she began to ask herself about the man who had been so aggressive and threatening. What had he been feeling? Suddenly she could feel the humiliation and fear underneath his anger. Her entire viewpoint shifted. "When I asked myself what *he* most needed," she told me, "it was very clear: someone to help him feel safe, to help him feel like he matters."

Dana was nervous before her client's appointment the following week, but she also felt confident and open. At first the man was sullen and wouldn't look her in the eye. But in response to her questions and obvious concern, he soon became animated, telling her how wild his old friends were, how hard it was trying to stay clean. Before leaving he said, "You know, maybe I got you wrong . . . and I'm sorry about that. Thank you for being on my team."

As she gained confidence in her capacity to handle situations, Dana found that she was becoming more kind. This was a dramatic shift as, in her own estimation, she didn't cut people much slack. "Now I really see how they're hurting," she told me, referring to the people she was working with. "When they go back to the bottle and weed like this man probably did, when they go back to the street, well . . . it's no different from me going for a smoke or getting stuck on the wrong man. So in each case I find that I'm asking myself, 'How can I sit by his side and keep him company? What will help her recover her soul?'"

As Joseph Campbell wrote, "The privilege of a lifetime is being who you are." When we are less identified with fear, the truth of who we are is able to shine through. We might discover a natural empathy, like Dana's, and the capacity to sense the soul, the light and goodness within others. Our truth might express itself as creativity or humor, as curiosity or generosity, as devotion or love. However it is expressed, the path of healing leads us from a narrowed, self-centered existence shaped by fear, to a life sourced in awareness and heart.

Guided Meditation: Lovingkindness: Receiving Love

The trainings of the heart are so central to realizing true refuge that they are found throughout this book. Offering lovingkindness (metta) to ourselves is introduced on page 26, and receiving lovingkindness from others is introduced in the first meditation below. Awakening compassion (karuna) when we are caught in fear is the second meditation below. Compassion is also introduced in the form of forgiveness to ourselves on page 179, and forgiveness to others on page 200. Both lovingkindness and compassion practices are fully extended to include others on pages 223 and 220 respectively.

Fear arises from a sense of separateness and it loses its grip as we perceive our connectedness to others and to life. This version of the lovingkindness meditation can help you develop your capacity to receive love and trust belonging.

Sit comfortably and quietly, and take a few full breaths. With a gentle attention, scan your body and mind, noticing whatever fear or vulnerability you might be feeling. Connect with your longing to feel safe, protected, and loved. Then remember a place—in the world or in your imagination—where you are deeply at home. It might be a spot in nature or in your bedroom, a coffee shop, or a cathedral. Take some moments to evoke it with all your senses, imagining the forms and colors, the smells and sounds of your healing place. Can you feel yourself there, being held by the peaceful, comforting, or beautiful energy around you?

Now bring to mind the face of anyone who helps you to feel loved and safe. It might be your grandmother or a beloved teacher, your dog or your dearest friend. It might be a spiritual figure like the Buddha, Kwan-yin (the bodhisattva of compassion), or Jesus. Whoever appears, sense that they perceive your vulnerability and your longing for safe refuge. Look into their eyes and see them sending you a message of love—"I am here with you . . . I care about you." Feel their physical presence and let their energy surround you and hold you in an embrace of safety. Give yourself some moments to take in the love and ease that is offered. What is it like to feel this care surrounding and holding you?

Now, softly place your hand over your heart or on your cheek and receive the touch as a message of their care and protection.

If you are facing a particularly painful situation in your life, try to contact the underlying fear and feel how that fear is living in your body. Touch your throat, your chest, your belly. As you do, imagine that the love of the being you have called on is flowing through your hand into your most vulnerable and fearful places. You might hear the sound of this being's voice speaking words of kindness and reassurance. Take as long as you'd like, letting in love and opening directly to the sensations and feelings that arise. How does it affect you to receive love? Notice any changes in your breathing, in your shoulders and belly, in your heart and mind. Is there some sign that the message of love and belonging has been received deep within your body and spirit? If you are patient and gentle with yourself, you will learn to connect with a sense of inner refuge when you most need it.

Because we have been wounded in relationships, it can be challenging to trust and let in love. Take your time and explore this practice with as much self-compassion as possible:

- *If you can't find someone who evokes a deep sense of feeling loved or safe, choose a person (pet, spiritual figure) who you believe is intrinsically caring, accepting, and wise. You might also imagine a more formless presence that you experience simply as warmth and light. With practice the sense of living love will awaken.*
- *If you contact pain about feeling unlovable, imagine that being or presence offering kindness directly to your doubt, hurt, or fear. Listen for a message or reminder from this being that might help you relax and trust the presence of love.*
- *Connect with your intention to awaken and free your heart. This will give you the courage to experiment and discover your own pathway to a safe and loving refuge.*

Guided Meditation: Tonglen: A Healing Presence with Fear

The following meditation is a version of the traditional Tibetan compassion practice known as *tonglen*. You will benefit from practicing tonglen in those moments when you become aware of the grip of fear. However, if you are feeling traumatized or overwhelmed, it is safer to start with the lovingkindness meditation or to explore this reflection with the support of a therapist or healer.

———

Find a comfortable place to sit, one where you feel as physically safe and protected as possible. Closing your eyes, gently scan your body, relaxing your brow and jaw, dropping your shoulders, and softening your hands.

Bring your attention to the natural rhythm and sensations of breathing. As the breath flows in, allow your cells to receive this life energy. With each in-breath, relax open in total receptivity, like a balloon gently expanding with air. Be aware of the experience of no resistance, of softening all tension and directly contacting the sensations of the breath.

With the out-breath, experience the actuality of letting go, of releasing what is within the space that surrounds you. Imagine that your entire body and mind could flow outward with the breath and mingle with the vastness of space.

Continue meditating on the rhythm of receiving—being touched with the in-breath—and letting go—sensing openness with the out-breath.

When you feel ready, bring to mind a situation that evokes fear. Ask yourself: "What is the worst part of this situation? What am I really afraid of?" Your inquiry will probably trigger a story at first. But if you stay alert to what's happening in your body, the story can become a gateway to accessing your feelings more fully. Paying particular attention to your throat, chest, and stomach area, discover how fear expresses itself in you. You might kindly invite the fear: "Be as much as you really are."

What does the fear actually feel like? Where in your body do you feel it most strongly? Do the sensations change or move from place to place? Do they have a shape? A color? How do you experience fear in your mind? Does it feel contracted? Is it racing or confused?

Now, as you breathe in, let the breath directly touch the place where you most feel pain and vulnerability. Bring your full attention to the sensations of fear. Then, as you breathe out, sense the openness of space that holds your experience. Also sense the space that exists inside the sensations of fear and release your fear into this continuous inner and outer space. Imagine it floating and untwisting itself in this openness.

You can deepen your healing presence with fear by gently placing a hand over your heart. Let the touch be tender, a gesture of keeping company with the fear. With each in-breath, affirm your willingness to connect with the waves of fear, however unpleasant and disturbing they are. Breathing out, surrender your fear into open awareness and offer yourself a loving prayer: "May I be free of this suffering," "May I feel safe and at ease," "May I feel held in lovingkindness," "I'm sorry and I love you," or any prayer that brings you relief and ease. Sense that the warmth of your touch is helping to communicate the kindness of prayer.

After several minutes, bring to mind other beings who experience fear—people you know and the vast numbers you don't know. Remind yourself that while stories may differ, our human experience of fear is the same. Begin to breathe in on behalf of all those who share this suffering, allowing yourself to receive the intensity and fullness of their pain in your heart. As you breathe out, release this enormity of suffering into boundless space, offering all who suffer openness, peace, care, or whatever you long for most. As your heart opens to the truth of our shared suffering, you become that open healing space. As you offer your care and prayer, your awareness becomes suffused with compassion. Continuing to breathe in suffering and breathe out care, sense that your vast, tender heart can hold the fears of this world.

Adjusting your meditation to your state of mind: *If you feel closed off or numb, focus on the in-breath, and on contacting the physical sensations of fear. On the other hand, if the fear feels like "too much," emphasize breathing out—letting go into openness and safety, focusing on the phrases of lovingkindness and/or on the sensations of your hand over your heart. It can also help to open your eyes or to listen to the sounds around you. With time, you will discover a balance between getting in touch with fear and remembering openness and love.*

The role of the breath: *While the breath can be a powerful support in this practice, the key is receiving or being touched by experience, and then letting go into the larger field of love and awareness. If focusing on the breath distracts or impedes you, feel free to simply focus on these qualities of presence.*

The role of touch: *Self-touch can help you to contact your experience and awaken care. Experiment by varying the placement of your hand and the pressure and duration of the touch to find what best serves your meditation.*

Throughout the day: *Fear often catches us in situations where we are unable* to take a time-out for meditation, but we can do a brief version of this practice that will help contact and heal our feelings as they arise. This way, the energy does not get buried and begin to fester.

Using your breath (should you so choose), breathe in and allow yourself to touch the sensations of fear; breathe out and let go into the space around you, sending the fear openness and lovingkindness. If you sense it helps, place your hand gently on your heart. Notice what happens when you widen your attention to remember and breathe for others who are also struggling with fear.

If the fear is really strong: As soon as you become aware of thoughts and feelings of fear, pause for a moment and take a few full breaths. With each out-breath, see if it is possible to relax areas of obvious tension, softening through your face, letting your shoulders drop back and down, and releasing tension in your arms and hands.

Now silently offer these words to yourself:

> This is the suffering of fear.
> Fear is part of being alive.
> Other people experience this too . . . I am not alone.
> May I be kind to myself . . . may I give myself the compassion I need.

These reminders in working with fear are very similar to phrases author and teacher Kristin Neff recommends in working with all forms of suffering. After you've repeated them several times, reenter your activity with the intention to regard yourself with care. This simple practice can guide you home to a clear, heartful presence and help you face your day with more confidence.

TEN

⊶⊷

SELF-COMPASSION: RELEASING
THE SECOND ARROW

The moment you see how important it is to love yourself,
you will stop making others suffer.

BUDDHA, SAMYUTTA NIKAYA

I never blame myself when I'm not hitting. I just blame the bat and if it keeps up,
I just change bats . . . After all, if I know it isn't my fault that I'm not hitting,
how can I get mad at myself?

YOGI BERRA

The Buddha once asked a student, "If a person is struck by an arrow, is it painful?" The student replied, "It is." The Buddha then asked, "If the person is struck by a second arrow, is that even more painful?" The student replied again, "It is." The Buddha then explained, "In life, we cannot always control the first arrow. However, the second arrow is our reaction to the first. And with this second arrow comes the possibility of choice."

The first arrow is our human conditioning to cling to comfort and pleasure and to react with anger or fear to unpleasant experience. It's humbling to discover that willpower is often no match for these primal energies. We believe we should be able to control our "negative" emotions, then they just storm in and possess our psyches. We think we should be able to stop our obsessive thoughts or compulsive behaviors, but the anxious rehearsing, the cravings for food or attention, hound us throughout the day.

The second, more painful arrow is our reaction to these "failures." Sometimes our self-aversion is subtle; we're not aware of how it undermines us. Yet often it is not—we hate ourselves for the way we get insecure and flustered, for being fatigued and unproductive, for our addiction to alcohol or other substances. Rather than attending to the difficult (and sometimes trauma-based) emotions underlying the first arrow, we shoot ourselves with the second arrow of self-blame.

Awakening self-compassion is often the greatest challenge people face on the spiritual path. Students come to me with complex problems— addictions, family estrangements, crippling performance anxiety, a child in trouble. Yet when we begin to investigate, they discover that the deepest pain is in how they are feeling about themselves—how they are condemning themselves for their cravings, their anger, their inadequacy at work or in relationships.

When we're addicted to the message of the second arrow—"I'm basically not okay"—we become harsh and unforgiving toward ourselves. We're attempting to vanquish our weaknesses and change ourselves for the better, yet the effect is to reconfirm our conviction that we are intrinsically flawed. That core sense of badness then primes the next round of aggression, defensiveness, or paralysis that sustains our suffering. Attacking ourselves is a painful false refuge.

The good news is that we do have some choice about the second arrow. We can stop attacking ourselves for how we are feeling, thinking, and acting. We can learn to recognize when we are at war with ourselves, and decide to pause and deepen our attention. We can allow ourselves to enter the gateway of love.

ADDICTED TO SELF-BLAME

Sam hated himself for his anger. At the office he headed, he was known for being a demanding, impatient, perfectionist boss. He had zero tolerance for excuses and wanted his directives executed quickly and efficiently. When this didn't happen he would hurl accusations of incompetence or apathy. It wasn't much different at home. When his daughter came home late from a concert, he went into a tantrum, yelling and cursing until she ran off to her room and locked the door. When his wife, Jennie, made a mistake in the catering order for their annual holiday party, he blew up at her in front of the delivery crew.

Sometimes, especially with his wife and his daughter, he'd later feel ashamed and disgusted with himself for losing control. He'd try to apologize and find a way to make it up to them. But feeling bad about himself just seemed to set Sam up for the next outburst. When provoked, he'd reflexively snap into feeling "wronged" and then into a self-righteous rage. Somebody was getting in the way of what needed to happen; somebody was screwing things up. He was intentionally being undermined, disrespected.

Sam knew he needed a way to calm down. When he heard from a colleague that a mindfulness-based stress reduction (MBSR) program had reduced his anxiety and insomnia, Sam arranged for a similar program at his company. Mindfulness meditation introduced Sam to a new part of himself. He was struck by the contrast between moments when he was sitting mindfully, aware of his breath, of sounds and sensations, and the times (most of his life) when he was racing around, caught up in busyness and reactive anger. As he later told me, "It was like I was two entirely different people!"

Sam started coming regularly to my weekly class, hopeful that the talks and guided meditations would help him stay more relaxed. After he learned about the practice of taking a mindful pause, Sam tried to stop at certain junctures of the workday—when he first sat down at his desk in the morning, each time he hung up the phone, just before entering a meeting—to reconnect with his breath and his senses. One night he told me that when he could remember to pause, it was "like magic . . . a chance to get centered." But when his temper flared, he said, "I'm a madman, and anything to do with meditation belongs to another galaxy."

Still Sam persisted, and after six months of classes, he signed up for a weeklong retreat. When we met midweek for a private interview, he walked briskly into the room, sat down, and got right to the point: "Mindfulness gets me in touch with hating myself, Tara. With disgust. Here I am, a guy who has so much—stimulating work, financial ease, a fantastic family—and I go around acting like a goddamn jerk." He crossed his arms and sat back hard against the chair. "I'm hurting people with my anger . . . people I love." After a silence he continued. "There is only one thing that matters. I have to get rid of this violent beast inside me . . . I hate the person I've become."

Sam could not have stated our human dilemma more plainly. Beyond all the many targets of our self-judgment lies the same core feeling: aversion toward a defective self.

Many of us cling to our condemning thoughts as a way of controlling and hopefully improving ourselves. Whenever I teach about acceptance and forgiveness, the same questions come up: "What if I am destroying my life with my binge eating . . . isn't that wrong?" "What if I'm really hurting someone . . . isn't that bad?" "Why should I let myself off the hook?" In other words, is self-forgiveness just a way of condoning our shadow, of turning our eyes away from the parts of our being that most need to be uprooted and eliminated? Is it resignation? If we forgive ourselves, do we lose our only chance at change?

I responded to Sam with a different question: "Does hating the beast make it less angry?" Shaking his head, he conceded the point with a smile. As we continued to talk, I assured Sam that when I talk about self-forgiveness, I don't mean we should excuse our hurtful behavior or give ourselves permission to act out. Instead, the aim is to release the self-hatred that closes our heart and contracts our mind.

The first step to freeing ourselves is to pause when we are stuck in self-blame and deepen our attention. Sam's task over the next few days would be to investigate the moments when he turned on himself.

"IT'S NOT YOUR FAULT . . . REALLY."

Two days later Sam shared what he had discovered. "All the second arrows seemed like pinpricks until I thought of Jennie." He took a few full breaths, preparing himself to tell me more. "Two weeks ago she had a mammogram that came out suspicious. The biopsy was on a Tuesday, results were supposed to be in on Friday. But Friday evening when I got home from work, the first thing I saw was a package I'd wanted her to mail still sitting in the hall. I felt a surge of anger and started yelling . . .

totally forgetting about the test results." He stopped, tears welling up. "The look on her face . . . I'll never forget. She crumpled." Sam began sobbing. "Tara," he said, his voice choking, "they caught it early, I think she'll be okay. But her heart? How could I have done that!"

Sam told me that when he thought about Jennie during one of the sittings, he'd had to leave the meditation hall immediately. "I went back to my room and let loose. I was crying and saying, 'I can't help it,' over and over, as if I was trying to get her to understand and forgive me. And then suddenly I was hearing my father's voice, pleading with my mother to forgive him after he'd lost his temper. He'd shattered five wine glasses—slammed them one after the other into the kitchen cabinets. I was standing in the doorway—about eleven years old—he didn't even know I was there. So many times, he lost it . . . with me, with my younger brother, with my mother, yelling on the phone at whoever was on the other end. You never knew what was coming." Sam took a breath and shook his head. "I got it, Tara. I hated him when I was growing up. I remember being in college, freshman year, writing him a letter con-demning him for not getting it together. But he really couldn't control himself. It was like he was on some drug, totally at the mercy of his fury. And he despised himself too." Sam stopped speaking and looked down at the floor. Then he said softly, "When I realized that, I knew that I really can't help it either . . . I think I *should* be different but it just hap-pens. I can't help it."

I was quiet for some moments, honoring his realization. "Sam . . . what you saw—about your dad, and yourself—is true. The out-of-control anger is not your fault." Then I paused and repeated myself. *"It's not your fault . . . really."* Tears welled up in Sam's eyes and I continued. "Please know . . . You can learn to be responsible—able to respond differently—but that's possible only if you realize that you are not to blame."

I've said this to a lot of people, including myself, and it helps. That is because some wisdom deep inside us knows it's true. We'd be better if we could. We don't want to be caught in painful emotions and we don't want to cause suffering in others.

The Buddha taught that the first arrow—the things about ourselves that bring up shame and self-loathing—is often beyond our control.

Our deficits are shaped and sustained by innumerable forces. Many of us are born with genetic tendencies toward anxiety, aggression, or depression; we are brought up in cultures that are plagued by addiction and violence, by deception and greed. Our environment is full of pollutants that effect our nervous system in innumerable and unknowable ways. Our families of origin are often beset by financial difficulties, by conflict and misunderstanding, by trauma carried through past generations. And, crucially, how we treat ourselves and others is molded by how our own caretakers attended to us. Some interplay of these forces generates the first arrow of painful emotions and compulsive behaviors.

If we become mindful of how our experience arises from a complex array of causes, we are at the threshold of an important insight: *The compelling emotions that shape our self-sense are actually impersonal.* Just as recurring blizzards or droughts don't target a particular farm, our inner emotional weather is not owned by or controlled by this particular body and mind. Rather, it arises from causes beyond our individual existence.

I sometimes introduce this idea of impersonality by pointing toward a bronze statue of the Buddha in the meditation hall where I teach. Years ago, a coteacher and I decided to find the perfect Buddha for our community. After looking at many statues, we selected this one for its grace and simplicity. The Buddha was placed on an altar at the front of the hall, and I remember how glad I was when students came up after class to take a closer look. But then I noticed that a small knot of them were gesturing and leaning their heads to the left. I joined them, and one of them pointed out that our new Buddha was leaning. Sure enough, this was an imperfectly cast, off-balance Buddha! Fortunately our community has embraced the leaning Buddha as its own, and the statue has become a reminder that we all are shaped by forces beyond our control. We are imperfect and we can't help it.

Even a taste of this truth, a whisper of "It's not my fault," loosens the identification with self-blame, and it allows us to have more compassion for our actual experience. If we can stop condemning our imperfection, we can reconnect with the healing warmth of our Buddha-hearts. And this opens the door to change.

RELEASING THE SECOND ARROW

Sam got it that he needed to stop blaming and hating himself, but he didn't know where to start, or even if it was possible. "The feeling of being bad is sometimes so strong . . . I just don't know if I can forgive myself for what I put my wife through, my daughter . . ."

"We usually can't forgive ourselves right away," I replied. "It's a process with its own timing. What's important right now is your *intention* to relate to yourself with compassion, with kindness."

Sam and I agreed to end our meeting with a simple guided meditation. "Go back to that situation with your wife, when you first walked in the door," I suggested, "and try to remind yourself of what provoked the anger." He nodded. "Now just let the anger be here . . . mindfully recognizing it, and allowing it. Feel where it is in your body, and invite it to be as full as it is." I waited a few moments, and when I saw Sam's breath get shallow and his face flush, I asked, "From the anger's perspective, what is so upsetting?"

Sam shot back, "It's upset that Jennie didn't do what I asked her to do."

"And what's the worst part of that?" I asked. Now he answered more slowly. "Well . . . behind the anger there's the feeling that I'm not important to her and . . . respected." He paused, then said, "That I'm not cared about. Something like . . . She demeaned me. If she respected me and cared about me, she'd want to help me out." He paused again, and then said, "There's also a feeling of embarrassment or shame, like something must be wrong with me if she doesn't want to do things for me."

I mirrored back what he had said. "So . . . behind the anger is a feeling of not being respected or cared about . . . and some *shame* about that . . . that it means something really must be wrong with you." Sam nodded slowly, taking in the realness of his own insecurity.

"Okay, now take a moment to view yourself as if you could see all this through the eyes of a friend, someone who really cares about you and understands that you are feeling demeaned and ashamed." I paused to give Sam some time to bring this to mind.

"Now," I said, "with that kind of view, begin to send yourself some words of forgiveness and compassion. It might be 'I forgive you,' or 'forgiven, forgiven,' or maybe, 'I care about this suffering.' Offer whatever words communicate understanding and care." Sam practiced silently for several minutes, and when he opened his eyes, they were calm and bright. "Something unclenched, and space opened up," he told me. "It was as if my heart was holding the place in me that gets angry, the place that is insecure . . . and holding my dad as well."

We sat quietly together for a few moments, appreciating this space of kindness and presence. Before leaving Sam said, "For the first time, I'm feeling terribly imperfect, but not *bad*. The anger is part of the mix, but I'm more . . ." He gave me a thoughtful look and then tapped his heart. "I guess I'm opening to the possibility that there's a decent human being in here." Sam and I would work together for many months to come, but in that moment's opening to inner goodness, he had begun to experience the freedom of a forgiving heart.

SEEING BEYOND OUR FAULTS

Contacting the truth of our own suffering is what cracks the heart open to self-compassion and forgiveness. For Sam, this recognition came when he uncovered the feelings that fueled his anger. For Vanessa, a prisoner in a maximum-security prison, it was first awakened through a poem.

Vanessa attended a Buddhist meditation course taught by one of my friends. Standing over six feet tall, Vanessa was a powerful, sinewy woman with hair dyed bright red and tattoos all over her body. Known in her ward as a bully, she protected some women and relentlessly insulted and intimidated others. During the meditation classes, while other participants joined for discussions, she just sat there silent and scowling. But she never missed a session during the eight-week course. At the final class, my friend asked for feedback. After others spoke, she turned to Vanessa. "Well," she began uncertainly, "I couldn't follow some of those Buddhist words." Then she looked around, almost shyly. "What was that one . . . buddhisat . . . ?" The instructor said, "Oh, do

you mean 'bodhisattva'—an awakening being, one with compassion?"
"Yeah," said Vanessa. "That one. I liked that . . . and that poem about
the pirate."

The pirate appeared in a poem by Thich Nhat Hanh that my friend
had read at the prior class:

> I am the twelve-year-old girl,
> refugee on a small boat,
> who throws herself into the ocean
> after being raped by a sea pirate.
> And I am the pirate,
> my heart not yet capable
> of seeing and loving.

"Well, that got me thinking . . . made me know something," Vanessa
said. Then she spoke so softly that everyone had to strain to hear her. "I
always thought I was bad, the problem one, the one that made others
suffer. Now I know *I am suffering too*." Vanessa had tears in her eyes, but
most everyone was looking at the floor, just respecting her words.

After that group "graduated," my friend continued to teach at the
prison, and she heard by word of mouth that Vanessa had changed in a
deep way. She was no longer a bully. She was a sadder and much quieter
person, slowly coming to terms with the reality of her own suffering.

When I heard Vanessa's story I remembered a line from an African
American spiritual that has always moved me: "God looks beyond our
fault and sees our need."

What if we could recognize our faults and look to see what is beyond them? What if we could see, with great tenderness, the painful
unmet needs that have shaped our behaviors? For many of us, this process is the work of a lifetime, one that requires the active support of
loved ones, therapists, spiritual teachers, or healers. Yet it begins the
moment that we are willing to look at ourselves through the eyes of
compassion.

A PARENT'S HEART

Marge, a woman in our meditation community, was in a painful stand-off with her teenage son. At fifteen, Micky was in a downward spiral of skipping classes and using drugs, and he had just been suspended for smoking marijuana on school grounds. While Marge blamed herself—she was the parent, after all—she was also furious at her son. The piercings that she had not approved, the lies, the stale smell of cigarettes, the earphones that kept him in his own removed world—every interaction with Micky left her feeling powerless, angry, and afraid. And the more she tried to take control with her criticism, with "groundings" and other ways of setting limits, the more withdrawn and defiant Micky became.

When she came in for a counseling session, Marge told me, "It's been months since my son and I have had a civil conversation. Basically, he won't talk to me." But she mostly wanted me to know why the entire situation was really her fault. An attorney with a large firm, Marge felt she had let her career get in the way of attentive parenting. She had divorced Micky's father when the boy was entering kindergarten, and her new partner, Jan, had moved in several years later. More often than not, it was Jan, not Marge, who went to PTA meetings and soccer games, Jan who was there when Micky got home from school. Recently, the stress had peaked when a new account increased Marge's hours and demands at work.

"I wish I had been there for him more," Marge said. "I mean, I love him, I've tried, but now it is impossible to reach him. Tara, I'm so afraid he is going to create a train wreck out of his life." I heard the despair in her voice, and when she fell silent, I invited her to sit quietly for a few moments. "You might notice whatever feelings you are aware of . . . and when you are ready, name them out loud." When she spoke again, Marge's tone was flat. "Anger—at him, at me, who knows. Fear—he's ruining his life. Guilt, shame—so much shame, for screwing up as a mother." As she named shame her voice became low, almost inaudible.

"Marge," I said softly, "let's take some time and investigate the shame . . . Is that okay?" She nodded. "You might start by agreeing to let it be there, and sensing where you feel it most in your body." Again she nodded and, a few moments later, put one hand on her heart and another on her belly. "Good," I said. "Keep letting yourself feel the shame, and sense if there is something it wants to say. What is it believing about you, about your life?"

It was a while before Marge spoke. "The shame says that I let everyone down. I'm so caught up in myself, what's important to me. It's not just Micky . . . it's Jan . . . and Rick [her ex-husband] . . . and my mom . . . and . . . I'm selfish and too ambitious . . . I disappoint everyone I care about." She stopped and slumped back on the couch.

"How long have you felt this way . . . that you have let everyone down?" I asked. Shaking her head, she said, "As long as I can remember. Even as a little girl. I've always felt I was failing people, that I didn't deserve love. So now I run around trying to achieve things, trying to be worthy . . . and I end up failing those I love the most!"

"Take a moment, Marge, and let the feeling of failing people, of being undeserving of love, be as big as it really is." I paused and after a few moments she said, "It's like a sore, tugging feeling in my heart."

"Now," I said, "sense what it's like to know that even as a little girl— for as long as you can remember—you've lived with this pain of not deserving love, lived with this sore tugging in your heart. Sense what that has done to your life." Marge grew very still and then began silently weeping.

Marge was experiencing what I call "soul sadness," the sadness that arises when we are able to sense our temporary, precious existence, and directly face the suffering that has come from losing life. We recognize how our self-aversion has prevented us from being close to others, from expressing and letting love in. We see, sometimes with striking clarity, that we have closed ourselves off from our own creativity and spontaneity, from being fully alive. We remember missed moments when it might have been otherwise, and we begin to grieve our unlived life.

This grief can be so painful that we tend unconsciously to move away from it. Even if we start to touch our sadness, we often bury it by reentering the shame—judging our suffering, assuming that we somehow deserve it, telling ourselves that others have "real suffering" and we shouldn't be filled with self-pity. *Our soul sadness is fully revealed only when we directly, mindfully contact our pain.* It is revealed when we stay on the spot and fully recognize that this human being is having a hard time. In such moments we discover a natural upwelling of compassion—the tenderness of our own forgiving heart.

When Marge's crying subsided, I suggested she ask the place of sorrow what it longed for most. She knew right away: "To trust that I am worthy of love in my life."

I invited her to once again place one hand on her heart and one hand on her belly, letting the gentle pressure of her touch communicate care. "Now sense whatever message most resonates for you, and send it inwardly. Allow the energy of the message to bathe and comfort all the places in your being that need to hear it."

Marge sat very still, her face intent. After a couple of minutes she took a few full breaths and rested her hands in her lap. Her expression was serene, undefended. "This feels right, Tara," she said quietly, "being kind to my own hurting heart." Marge had looked beyond her faults to her needs. She was healing herself with compassion.

Before she left, I suggested that she pause whenever she became aware of guilt or shame, and take a moment to reconnect with self-compassion. If she was in a private place, she could gently touch her heart and belly, and let that contact deepen her communication with her inner life. I also encouraged her to include the metta (lovingkindness) practice for herself and her son in her daily meditation: "You'll find that self-compassion will open you to feeling more loving." Marge's eyes glistened with tears, and I could sense her longing to awaken her heart.

Six weeks later Marge and I met again. "Something happened," she told me, "something I wouldn't have thought possible." At the end of her daily meditation, Marge would do some metta for herself. She'd remind herself of her honesty, her sincerity, her longing to love well. Then she'd offer herself wishes, most often reciting, "May I accept myself just as I am . . . May I be filled with lovingkindness, held in lovingkindness." After a few minutes she'd then bring Micky to mind: "I would see how his eyes light up when he gets animated . . . and how happy he looks when he laughs. Then I'd say, 'May you feel happy . . . May you feel relaxed and at ease . . . May you feel my love now.' With each phrase I'd imagine him . . . happy . . . relaxed . . . feeling held in my love."

Their interactions started to change. She went out early on Saturday mornings to pick up his favorite "everything" bagels before he woke up. He brought out the trash unasked. They watched several episodes of *The Wire* together on TV. They laughed together when their elderly golden retriever had a "puppy moment" at play with a neighbor's dog. "And then," Marge told me, "a few nights ago, he came into my home office, made himself comfortable on the couch, and said nonchalantly, 'What's up, Mom? Just thought I'd check in.'

"It wasn't exactly an extended chat," she said with a smile. "He suddenly sprang up . . . told me he had to meet some friends at the mall. But we're more at ease . . . a door has reopened." Marge was thoughtful for a few moments and then she said, "I understand what happened. By letting go of the blame—most of which I was aiming at myself—I created room for both of us in my heart." Marge gave me a wistful look. "I wish I could have seen this sooner . . . but it's not too late."

WHEN WE'VE CAUSED HARM

Saturday Night Live comedian Jack Handey once wrote: "The first thing was, I learned to forgive myself. Then I told myself, 'Go ahead and do whatever you want, it's okay by me.'" That just about captures our fears about self-forgiveness: Pandora's box will open, unleashing our basest, most destructive instincts. Certainly there are false forms of self-forgiveness—ignoring the hurt we've caused, justifying our grasping and aggression—that indulge ourselves at the expense of others. But self-compassion and forgiveness are healthy when they emerge from an honest engagement with our own suffering.

As Marge was discovering, self-compassion is entirely interdependent with acting responsibly and caringly toward others. Forgiving ourselves clears the way for a loving presence that can appreciate the goodness of others, and respond to their hurts and needs. And, in turn, our way of relating to others affects how we regard ourselves and supports our ongoing self-forgiveness. I watched this process unfold in Sam.

A month after our retreat, Sam met with me for a private session and told me about a recent incident. He had gotten tickets for a concert at the Kennedy Center, and at the time he and his wife had agreed to leave, she still had not returned home. No message, nothing, and she wasn't answering her cell phone. When she rushed in ten minutes later, Sam was, as he put it, "in madman mode." "She apologized, told me her phone was out of juice, traffic . . . all that . . . but I still wanted to go on the attack. I mean, she knew leaving on time was important to me. If I mattered, she would have made it her business to be home on time!"

But Sam had forced himself to keep quiet—a part of him wanted to hurt her, but a deeper place knew otherwise. During their drive into town together, he watched his outrage, and the underlying feelings of being disregarded, of his needs not mattering. "As I said to myself 'forgiven, forgiven,' the feelings turned to powerlessness—I couldn't control her, I couldn't control me—and then to shame. I kept trying to be kind and forgiving toward what was coming up in me. It was like the weather . . . just happening."

At some point during the concert, he glanced at his wife and noticed her rapt attention, open and beautiful. The storm had passed. Back at home, late that evening, she snuggled against him in bed. "I know how hard you're trying," she whispered. "I used to be so afraid of you exploding, but just knowing you're *aware* makes me feel safer." For Sam, Jennie's words, and her understanding, were a healing balm. "I'll still blow it," he told me, "but she trusts me more, and I'm beginning to trust myself. I'm learning to find some space between me and my anger, learning to relate to it . . . and that's when there are choices."

THE URGE TO MAKE AMENDS

We are deeply imprinted by the suffering we have caused others. This imprint is sometimes felt as shame, guilt, or remorse, and it is our heart's sensitivity calling us to attention. In the Buddhist teachings, such sensitivity can be intelligent and healthy—it plays an important role in awakening and freeing our hearts. In contrast to our habit of beating up on ourselves, healthy shame is the signal that we have strayed from our deepest life values—it draws attention to a contracted, diminished sense of self—and it can energize us to realign with our hearts. Similarly, guilt focuses attention on our unskillful actions and can lead us to admitting our mistakes and making amends however we are able.

Self-forgiveness is often not even possible, and certainly cannot be complete, until we have in some way made amends to those we've injured. Making amends is not for the sake of satisfying an external standard of morality. Rather, it is an expression of our belonging to the world and to our own hearts. The urge to make amends arises when we have had the courage to face the reality of our impact on others. It arises when our hearts yearn to relieve their suffering or, like Sam, when we dedicate ourselves to not causing further suffering. Even if someone is no longer alive or an active part of our lives, it is possible to acknowledge the truth of his or her hurt and to offer him or her our wishes, prayers, and remorse. As we intentionally take responsibility for our actions, the harsh grip of self-aversion loosens, and we come home to a sense of connectedness, peace, and ease. This healing is very close to the Christian and Jewish process of atonement. By atoning for our errors, we make possible reconciliation—with God, with the injured other, and with our own heart and being.

I came upon a beautiful illustration of this healing process in the book *Offerings at the Wall*, which includes a selection of some of the ninety thousand letters and mementos that veterans and their loved ones have left at the Vietnam Veterans Memorial in Washington, D.C. In 1989, a worn photograph of a young Vietnamese man and a little girl was placed at the wall, along with the following letter:

Dear Sir,

For twenty-two years I have carried your picture in my wallet. I was only eighteen years old that day that we faced one another on that trail in Chu Lai, Vietnam. Why you did not take my life I'll never know . . . Forgive me for taking your life, I was reacting just the way I was trained . . . So many times over the years I've stared at your picture and your daughter. I suspect each time my heart and guts would burn with the pain of guilt. I have two daughters of my own now. I perceive you as a brave soldier, defending his homeland. Above all else I can now respect the importance life held for you. I suppose that is why I am able to be here today. It is time for me to continue the life process and release the pain and guilt. Forgive me sir.

The man who wrote the letter, Richard Luttrell, had faced the enormity of what it means to take a life, and the reality of how important life is to each of us. By letting himself feel the pain of his guilt, by looking again and again at his own fearful, reactive self—at the person who had been trained to kill—Richard had faced his own human frailty. In acknowledging this and asking for forgiveness, he was seeking to make amends and free his heart.

I shared this story many times with students, and then in 2009 I discovered that Luttrell's journey to forgiveness had not ended with this poignant note. Through a fellow vet, the picture had made its way back to him, and upon receiving it, he made a decision: He was going to find the daughter in the picture, and return the photo to her. Richard traveled to Vietnam, found her and her brother, and introduced himself through an interpreter. "Tell her this is the photo I took from her father's wallet the day I shot and killed him and I'm returning it." With his voice breaking, he asked for her forgiveness. The young woman burst into tears and fell into Richard's arms, sobbing. Later her brother explained that he and his sister believed that their father's spirit lived on in Richard, and that on that day, it had returned to them.

For all of us, the starting place of healing is reconciliation with our own heart. Whether we are unable to forgive ourselves for what seems a major wrongdoing, or we have locked into chronic self-judgment, we are at war, cut off from our own tenderness, our own spirit. If we can see past our faults to our human vulnerability, we are on the path of reconciliation. Our self-compassion will naturally lead to caring about others, and perhaps, as for Richard, to an experience of love and connectedness we never imagined possible.

Guided Reflection: Self-Forgiveness Scan

Even when we are not overtly at war with ourselves, we often move through the day judging ourselves for the ways we feel we are falling short. This practice brings our self-judgments into awareness so they can be seen and released. It's an especially cleansing way to end the day. Try it when you are lying in bed before you go to sleep.

———— ∞ ————

Take some moments to become still and to relax any obvious areas of tension. Then take a few long, slow breaths to help you arrive fully in your body.

Now ask yourself, "Is there anything between me and being at home with myself?" (Feel free to change the wording in any way that helps you identify the presence of self-blame.) Then pause and see what comes up in your body and mind. What stories of wrongdoing have you been telling yourself?—stories of letting others down, of performing poorly at work, of not meeting your standards as a parent, partner, friend, human being.

If something arises, simply acknowledge it and offer it forgiveness. You might gently place your hand on your heart and whisper "forgiven, forgiven" or "it's okay." Recall your intention not to push yourself out of your own heart. Then inquire again—is there anything else you're holding against yourself? Continue in this way until you've identified whatever self-judgments you've been carrying. End the scan by offering yourself a prayer or blessing, a wish for your own peace of heart and mind.

Guided Reflection: Ending the War with Yourself

Often our deepest suffering is the sense that something we have done—something about us—is fundamentally wrong and unacceptable. Finding a way to make peace with our human imperfections is the ground of all healing.

⸙

Find a comfortable sitting position and take a few moments to relax obvious areas of tension in your body. Connect with your intention to open your heart to your own being. Then bring to mind some aspect of yourself that has felt unforgivable. Perhaps you can't forgive yourself for being a judgmental and controlling person, or for how you have hurt others. You might not be able to forgive how you are ruining your life with an addictive behavior. You might feel disgust for your mental obsession. What feels so wrong or bad about your unforgivable behavior, emotion, or way of thinking? Allow yourself to feel the aversion that you have toward yourself.

Now explore more deeply what is driving this unacceptable part of you. If you are addicted to food, nicotine, or alcohol, what needs are you trying to satisfy, what fears are you trying to soothe? When you are judging others, are you feeling fearful yourself? If you have wounded another person, did you act out of hurt and insecurity? Out of the need to feel powerful or safe? Look at yourself and your vulnerability as if through the eyes of the most understanding and loving friend, relative, or deity.

As you become aware of these underlying wants and fears, allow yourself to feel them directly in your body, heart, and mind. Even though you dislike the behaviors, try to hold this underlying vulnerability with compassion. Placing your hand on your heart, send a sincere message of self-compassion directly to the places of fear and unmet needs—to the pain that has given rise to what feels unforgivable. You might mentally whisper, "I see how I've caused myself suffering, and I forgive myself now." Or you might simply offer yourself the words: "forgiven, forgiven."

Meet whatever arises—fear or judgment, shame or grief—with the message of forgiveness. Even resistance to forgiving can be met with "forgiven, forgiven." You might call on the presence of someone you consider to be deeply loving and understanding, and feel his or her compassion flowing into you, supporting you. Discover what happens when you bring an unconditionally forgiving heart to the parts of you that are wounded and vulnerable.

When you feel unable to forgive yourself: *You might believe you don't deserve to be forgiven or fear that if you forgive yourself you'll just do the same thing again. Maybe you're afraid that if you really open yourself to forgiveness, you'll come face-to-face with some intolerable truth. If these doubts and fears arise, acknowledge and accept them with compassion. Then say to yourself, "It is my intention to forgive myself when I am able." Your intention to forgive is the seed of forgiveness—this willingness will gradually relax and open your heart.*

—⊗⊗⊗—

ELEVEN

THE COURAGE TO FORGIVE

Those who are free of resentful thoughts surely find peace.

BUDDHA

Be Ground
Be crumbled, so wildflowers will come up where you are.
You've been stony for too many years.
Try something different.
Surrender.

RUMI

Hakuna, our very "alpha" eighty-five-pound standard poodle, hated the Akitas in our old neighborhood. If we went for a walk on a nearby trail when our neighbor was out with them, I'd have to wrap Hakuna's leash around a tree to hold steady as he lunged and barked ferociously. But after they passed, he would resume his cheerful trot through the woods. He was not ruminating about "those damned Akitas, think they own the hood . . . that stupid curled tail, fancy coat . . . next time I'm going to show them!" He was sniffing and enjoying the day.

When animals like Hakuna get angry, they bristle or bare their teeth, they pounce or slash or bite. After the encounter is over, they go back to homeostasis—a relatively relaxed state. We humans are different. Instead, we replay past outrages and anticipate how others might hurt, impede, or disrespect us in the future. This keeps the hormones of anger and fear circulating in our body, and the related thoughts of blame and vengeance spinning in our mind. The upshot? We become trapped in warrior mode, our heart armored, our mind narrowed. Unlike Hakuna, we are not free to enjoy the day.

Anger arises when someone or something obstructs our needs or desires. If you are on a highway and another car cuts you off, adrenaline pumps into your bloodstream. Your heart rate jumps. Your blood pressure surges. We respond to nonphysical threats the same way. If you find out that your partner has lied to you or your boss tells you you're fired, your body flips into the fight-flight-freeze response—an instantaneous physiological reaction to a perceived threat. You want to regain control, and the "fight" pathway tells you to "get even with" or harm whoever or whatever you perceive is causing you trouble.

Like all emotions, anger is an essential and intelligent part of our survival equipment. We need anger to let us know our boundaries have been violated so that we can respond appropriately. Anger lets us know when something is unfair, unjust, or threatening to our own well-being and that of others. It's essential that we listen to our anger, but we don't need to live with ongoing stories of blame and resentment in order to take good care. Unless we are very mindful, anger does not simply arise and dissipate; rather, it becomes a strongly entrenched habit, always hovering in the background, ready to ignite into aggressive thoughts and behaviors. When anger is a habit of the mind, it invariably causes conflict with even those we most love. It is bad for our health and heart; and as a species, it keeps us at war.

WHICH WOLF WILL YOU FEED?

After the September 11, 2001, attacks, as many people feared an ongoing and vicious spiral of retaliation and global violence, a wonderful Cherokee legend went viral on the Internet:

An old grandfather is speaking to his grandson about what causes the violence and cruelty in the world. "In each human heart," he tells the boy, "there are two wolves battling one another—one is fearful and angry, and the other is understanding and kind." The young boy looks intently into his grandfather's eyes and asks,

"Which one will win?" His grandfather smiles and quietly says, "Whichever one we choose to feed."

It's easy to feed the fearful, angry wolf. Especially if we've experienced great wounding, the anger pathway can become deeply ingrained in our nervous system. When our old sense of injury or fear is triggered, the intolerable heat and pressure of anger instantly surges through us. Our attention gets riveted on the feelings and thoughts of violation and all we want is revenge. Often before we have any sense of choice, the nasty comeback is out of our mouth, we've slammed a door, hit send on an ill-advised e-mail, put someone down behind his back.

Yet we do have a choice. Meditations that train the heart and the mind directly deactivate the anger pathways that propel our habitual behaviors. While the limbic system acts almost instantaneously, we can develop a response from the frontal cortex—which includes the social centers involved with compassion—that interrupts and subdues the reaction. This is where cultivating mindfulness comes in. Mindfulness is the "remembering" that helps us pause and recognize what is happening in the present moment. Once we have paused, we can call on the higher brain centers to open new possibilities. We can soothe ourselves, we can recall another person's difficulties and vulnerability, we can remember our own goodness and strength. No matter how painfully we are triggered by the world's violence and insensitivity, we can direct our attention in ways that carry us home to our intrinsic sanity and good-heartedness. This awakening is our evolutionary potential: For the sake of our own inner freedom and the well-being of others, we can intentionally feed the understanding, kind wolf.

UNDERSTANDING FORGIVENESS

One evening after my Wednesday night meditation class, Amy, a member of our D.C. meditation community whom I've gotten to know quite well over the years, asked me if we might talk for a few minutes. She reminded me that she had been raised by a terrible mother, "a manipulative, narcissistic human." This mother, of whom I'd heard several painful tales in the past, had recently been diagnosed with terminal breast cancer. As the only local offspring, Amy had become her mother's primary caretaker. So there she was, spending hours a day with a person she'd been avoiding for decades. "I've always resented the hell out of my mother," she told me. Then, after a pause, she added more quietly, "Now I can't stand myself for having such a hard heart."

I knew Amy had already worked hard to open her heart. She had spent years bitterly estranged from her ex-spouse, in constant battle with her eldest daughter, and at odds with her business partner. Then, at one of our residential retreats several years earlier, she had discovered how the practice of RAIN could help her bring a clear and kind attention to the conflicts in her life. Gradually, as she became more gentle and present with herself, she found she was more accepting in these important relationships.

But Amy's meditation practice didn't seem to have made a dent in her hostility toward her mother. "When I was a kid, Mom treated me like I was in the way or just there to help her out . . . another puppet in her life," Amy said. "If I'm around her a lot, I'm afraid she'll just trample my adult self too. Even now that she's very sick, it feels impossible to stuff my anger and try to forgive her."

We protect our wounds by armoring ourselves with hatred and blame. Forgiveness, which allows us to let go of this armor, becomes possible as we bring a full, compassionate presence to our underlying vulnerability. Such presence loosens our identification with the thoughts and feelings of anger, and uncovers a heart space that is naturally open, inclusive, and warm. But this seldom happens suddenly or irreversibly. If we are resentful and at odds with someone, it can take many rounds of intentional presence with our own hurt or fear until our self-compassion opens us to more acceptance and understanding. And when our grievance expresses as full-blown hatred, or when we feel deeply violated, as Amy did, forgiveness can seem out of reach or even impossible.

Forgiveness can also seem like a bad idea. Like Amy, we may be afraid that if we let go of blame, we are betraying our own emotions and setting ourselves up for further injury. We may feel that if we forgive, we are condoning a person's hurtful behavior and not honoring our right to be respectfully treated. Maybe we feel that if we forgive someone, we will be stuck feeling that we are the ones to blame. These fears are understandable and need to be recognized, but they are based on a misperception.

Forgiveness means letting go of aversive blame; it means that we stop feeding the fearful, angry wolf. It does *not* mean that we dismiss our intelligence about who might hurt us or that we stop taking actions to protect ourselves and others from harm. Amy did need to practice wise discernment; she did need to recognize her mother's inappropriate demands or hurtful remarks for what they were. We all need to be able to tell who might betray our confidences, take our money, misunderstand our intentions, and abuse us physically or mentally. And when someone threatens our own or others' well-being, we need to find effective ways to communicate our concerns, set boundaries, and determine consequences for harmful actions. We may divorce a spouse, ground a child, make rules for speaking with a friend, vote someone out of office, campaign relentlessly for social change. We can dedicate our lives to preventing harm, while still keeping our hearts free of aversive blame.

Forgiving means not pushing anyone, or any part of our own being, out of our heart. By this I mean that even if we decide it is unhealthy to ever see a certain person again, we still find a way to hold him or her with goodwill. Taking this kind of refuge in unconditional love is courageous and challenging. Choosing to feed the compassionate wolf means stopping the war—the blaming thoughts and punishing actions—and opening directly to the pain of our vulnerability. This was the path in front of Amy. Rather than turning on her mother or herself, she needed to become intimate with the woundedness that fueled her anger. This would require profound self-compassion.

RAIN WITH ANGER

Amy and I agreed to meet privately to explore how she might find more freedom in relating to her mother. At our first session, she talked about her childhood. Now that she was around her mother regularly, early memories were coming back to her. In the most potent of these memories, Amy was three years old. Her mom yelled upstairs that she had prepared a bath for her and she should get in the tub. But when Amy went into the bathroom, what she found waiting for her was a couple of inches of lukewarm water. As she recalled this pivotal moment, she vividly remembered the realization that had flashed through her three-year-old mind: "This is all I'm going to get. No one is taking care of me." And that was close to true.

Her mom had always been preoccupied with her own dramas, perpetually reacting to perceived slights from friends, struggling against weight gain, and berating her husband for his shortcomings as a provider. Little attention was paid to the physical or emotional needs of Amy and her siblings.

After telling me this, Amy slumped back in the chair. "How am I supposed to care about this person who didn't have a maternal bone in her body? How am I supposed to be forgiving and kind? I hate the way she grimaces, her superior tone when she talks about others, the way whatever comes up is about her." I suggested that she didn't need to try to care about her mother right now.

People often tell me stories of great betrayal and wounding and then ask, "How can I possibly forgive her after she had that affair?" "How can I forgive him for physically abusing me as a child?" When we try to forgive someone prematurely we usually succeed only in papering over our anger and underlying hurt. So I encourage a shift in focus: "This isn't the time for forgiving; it wouldn't be possible or real at this point," I might say. "Right now, what needs attention is the place inside you that is hurting, that is afraid. This is the time for offering a compassionate presence to your own heart." In Amy's case, the entry to this presence was through the mindfulness of RAIN.

I guided Amy by asking her what was most disturbing about her situation. She summed it up quickly. "She doesn't care about anyone except herself. She is a self-centered bitch." Then she went on. "It really pisses me off . . . I got gypped out of having a mother, and now I'm here catering to her." Her face hardened and she was barely breathing. I asked her what she was most aware of in this moment. After a long silence she said, "There's so much rage that I can barely contain it."

The beginning of RAIN is to recognize and allow whatever you're feeling, but that isn't always simple or easy. When I asked Amy, "Can you allow rage to be here?" she gave me a wary look. She had spent many years trying to manage her anger by submerging it, doing the opposite of "letting be." She would then have sudden violent outbreaks. Amy looked at me and shook her head. "I'm afraid if I really make space for this rage, it will destroy every relationship I have. I've already hurt people I love."

We usually respond to strong anger in one of two ways. We become possessed by the experience, acting out the emotional energy of our blaming stories. Or we push the anger away by judging it as bad, dissociating from bodily experience and redirecting our attention. Sam (in chapter 10) judged his anger harshly, but it was always lurking beneath the surface, easily triggered. In contrast, many people suppress their anger more fully, perhaps because they fear that it will overwhelm them and/or drive others away. But then, as so often happened for Amy, it builds up and can burst forth with a vengeance.

When anger is buried, the energy gets converted and expressed in different ways. A friend of mine who struggled with a weighty depression took an acting workshop and played the part of a belligerent, angry woman. The role put her in touch with a rage toward men that she had suppressed for decades, a rage that had been masked by a sense of powerlessness and hopelessness. A client with irritable bowel syndrome discovered that he suffers from more stomach pain and indigestion when he's in disagreement with others. Now, if he can acknowledge the unrecognized anger and give the energy permission to be there, his gut relaxes. Anger is a survival energy and it wants our attention.

The "allow" in RAIN does not mean we let ourselves be possessed by anger. Allowing is not acting out. Rather, we allow when we acknowledge the stories of blame without believing them, and when we let the sensations of anger arise, without either acting them out or resisting them.

But Amy had told me that she was afraid to allow her anger to be there, so we started by paying attention to her fear. I encouraged her to check in with it. Was the fear willing to let this rage be here? Could the fear step aside enough so that she could be present with this rage? Amy was quiet for a few moments and then nodded. The fearful part agreed that she could continue "being with" rage.

Now Amy could begin to investigate the emotional energy beneath the blame. But I knew that for her to do so, she'd need to step outside of the seductive sway of her resentful stories. She had spent much of her life consumed by these stories, circling around and around in blaming thoughts. We had talked about the stories, respecting them as windows into her pain. But the anger also lived deeper in her body—in a place beyond thought. The next step was for her to widen and deepen her attention so that she could fully contact these embodied energies.

I asked Amy to notice what she was feeling in her body. She closed her eyes and paused for a moment. "It's like a hot pressured cauldron in my chest." What would happen, I asked, if she said yes to this feeling, if she allowed the heat and pressure to be as intense as it wanted to be? "Tara," she said, shaking her head, "it wants to explode . . ." Again, I encouraged her to let be, to allow her experience just as it was.

Amy was absolutely still for some moments, and then she spoke haltingly. "The rage feels like it is bursting flames . . . like a windstorm spreading in all directions. It's blasting through the windows of this office." She stopped and looked at me. "It's fine," I said. "Let it be as much as it is." She went on in a low voice, "It's spreading through the East Coast. Now it's destroying all life forms . . . ripping through the continent, oceans, earth." She continued telling me about the rage's fury, how it was spreading through space. Then she became very quiet. Speaking in a soft voice she finally said, "It's losing steam." She sat back on the couch and let out a deflated, tired sigh. "Now there's just emptiness. No one is left in the world. I'm utterly alone, lonely." Then in a barely audible whisper, she said, "There's no one who loves me, no one that I love."

Lowering her head and putting her face in her hands, Amy began weeping. Inside the rage, she had found an empty place, a place that felt loveless. Now what was revealing itself was grief: grief for the loss of love in her life.

WIDENING CIRCLES OF COMPASSION

The poet Rumi writes, "Be crumbled, so wildflowers will come up where you are." Amy's armoring of resentment had crumbled, exposing her feelings of being disconnected, cut off from the love that is the very source of feeling at home in life.

When I asked Amy what the grieving part of her most needed from her, she knew right away: "To know that I care about this pain, that I accept and love this grieving place." I guided her in gently placing her hand on her heart, and offering inwardly the message her wounded self most needed to hear. She began repeating a phrase that had resonated for her at retreat a year earlier: "I'm sorry, I love you." "I'm sorry" wasn't an apology. Rather, it was a simple expression of sorrow for her own hurt.

Amy whispered the phrase over and over to herself, and then began rocking side to side. She told me, "I'm seeing the little girl in the bath, and feeling how uncared for she feels, how alone. I'm holding her now, telling her 'I'm sorry, I love you.'"

After a few minutes, Amy sat upright, relaxed her hands in her lap, and took a few full breaths. She looked at me with a fresh openness and brightness in her eyes. "Tara, I think I understand," she said. "I've been angry for so long that I abandoned her—the inner part of me—just like my mom abandoned that three-year-old." She paused, then continued. "I just have to remember that this part of me needs love. I want to love her."

Compassion for oneself is the very essence of a forgiving heart. Yet sometimes it is not possible to hold our own being with kindness because the intensity of our anger, as well as the fear or hurt beneath the anger, is so overwhelming. Those who, like Amy, have experienced deep wounding or trauma are wise to seek the help of a therapist, teacher, or healer to guide them. Because the process of forgiving uncovers deep vulnerability, it requires much patience, whether it is done alone or with support. Especially when we're in an ongoing relationship with someone who has hurt us, we can be wounded over and over again, and it's hard not to feed the angry wolf with thoughts of blame.

Amy anticipated this. When she started talking about seeing her mother later that day, she noticed an anxious tightening in her chest. She told me, "I'm afraid I will close down around her." But then Amy said, "Wait!" and sat back, closing her eyes. She again put her hand on her heart, whispering, "I'm sorry, I love you. I'm sorry, I love you," sending the kind message to her own anxiety. After some moments, she took a few full breaths and smiled. She spoke slowly, as if carefully choosing her words. "When I investigate and catch on to what's happening . . . like this fear . . . and offer it love, I'm no longer hooked." Then she added, "The fear hasn't gone away, it's part of me. But the presence, the loving, lets me know I'm so much larger than that fear."

Offering a compassionate and clear attention to her vulnerability had connected Amy with a vastness of being that could include her pain. This natural awareness, the *N* of RAIN, is the fruition of an intimate attention. When we are resting in this presence, we are inhabiting the refuge of our own awakened heart and mind.

"Amy," I observed, "you've found a beautiful way home to who you really are." She smiled, saying, "Yes, that's just how it feels."

Many people in my classes and workshops have found that when they stop feeding the angry wolf and instead open to their own vulner-ability, it does feel like a homecoming. As one person put it, "Instead of focusing on the person who hurt me, I started down a path of freeing myself." We can either "get back" at someone and let the wound fester, or attend to self-healing. Feeding the angry wolf may come more easily, but learning to stay present with our inner life connects us with our goodness.

Some weeks later, Amy started our meeting by reading me her morn-ing's journal entry: "There is more room in my heart." The night before, after her mother had complained for the third time that her soup still wasn't salty enough, Amy felt the familiar rising tide of irritation and resentment. She sent the message "I'm sorry, I love you" inwardly to herself, giving permission to the annoyance, to the edginess in her own heart. She felt a softening, a relaxing of tension. Looking up, she was struck by her mother's grim, dissatisfied expression. And just as she'd learned to inquire about herself, the thought came: "What is my mom feeling right now?" Almost immediately, she could sense her mother's insecurity and loneliness. Imagining her mother inside her heart, Amy again began offering caring messages. "I'm sorry," she whispered silently, "I love you."

She found herself feeling genuinely warm toward her mom, and evi-dently her feelings were contagious. The evening was surprisingly pleasant for both of them. They joked about her mom doing a "mono diet" of potato chips, not so different from some of the other crazy diets—all fruit, all protein, all liquid—she had tried over the decades. Mother and daughter went online together and ordered a bathrobe and then had fun watching *The Daily Show* on TV.

At our last meeting Amy told me how, several days earlier, her mother had woken up in the morning hot and sweaty. Amy took a cool cloth to her mother's forehead and cheeks, arms and feet. "Nobody's ever washed me," her mom had said with a wistful smile. Amy immediately remembered the little girl in the bathtub, the few inches of water, and felt tears in her eyes. She and her mom had both gone through much of life feeling neglected, as if they didn't matter. And right now, each in her own way, was tasting the intimacy of care. They looked at each other and had a moment of uncomplicated love. It was the first such moment that Amy could remember, one she knew she'd cherish long after her mom was gone.

HOW WOULD A BUDDHA RESPOND?

Amy's anger and armoring softened after a deep and focused process of self-compassion, but sometimes all that's needed for forgiveness to unfold is a new, wider perspective.

Imagine you are walking in the woods and you see a small dog sitting by a tree. As you approach, it suddenly lunges at you, teeth bared. You are frightened and angry. But then you notice that one of its legs is caught in a trap. Immediately your mood shifts from anger to concern: You see that the dog's aggression is coming from a place of vulnerability and pain. This applies to all of us. When we behave in hurtful ways, it is because we are caught in some kind of painful trap. The more we look through the eyes of wisdom at ourselves and one another, the more we cultivate a compassionate heart.

Joshua was inspired by Vietnamese Zen master Thich Nhat Hanh, and particularly by his teachings on forgiveness. He came to me to ask for my help in responding to a situation at work. Joshua was director of marketing for a large computer software firm, and he valued the company's team-centered approach. But he was feeling growing antagonism toward an executive who was part of his unit. "He doesn't play well with others," Joshua said wearily, "and I'm having a hard time being around him." I asked for specifics. "He brags, he reinvents history, makes it sound like he's the driving force behind anything successful in our unit . . . and he's always making snide jokes about other people." As Joshua summed up: "Phil's smart and valuable, but he's addicted to putting himself up and others down . . ." After a pause he added, "And I'm sucked into his game. I want to put him in his place . . . at least a few notches down!"

I asked Joshua to review a recent occasion when he'd felt particularly irate. It was during a team meeting, debriefing a difficult project. "Phil reported on cost overruns and with a scornful smile suggested that the group had, as he put it, caught the virus—'Joshua's overly sunny outlook may have been contagious,' Phil had said. In fact, everyone had agreed this would be a good gamble." Joshua told me that he'd defended himself, reminding Phil of memos he himself had written encouraging investment in the project. "I was probably wasting my breath; he just sat there with that smile, nodding."

I suggested we try a short visualization and Joshua eagerly agreed. "First, remind yourself of his smile and tone of voice as he talked about your sunny outlook, and take a moment to feel what your heart and body is experiencing." I waited as Joshua let his attention go inward. "Got it," he said. "My face is hot."

"Now," I said, "imagine that you could press the pause button and freeze the action. And that you could invite Thay [the familiar name for Thich Nhat Hanh among his followers] to step in and fill your being with his consciousness. You might recall the brightness and kindness of his eyes, remind yourself of the sound of his voice, and then let him take over for you. You can rest on the sidelines and just bear witness to what unfolds." I gave Joshua a few moments to imagine this. Then I asked some questions, pausing a bit after each:

"How does your body feel, with Thay's consciousness filling you? What is it like to witness Phil, and the whole situation, through Thay's eyes? With Thay's heart? How might Thay handle the situation?" Again I paused. I ended the visualization with a final reflection. "Feel yourself back, fully inhabiting your own body and consciousness. Sense that Thay's right by your side and he has an important message for you, something that can guide you in this kind of situation. What is the message? Just listen . . . you might hear it as words . . . you might see a visual image . . . you might just have a felt sense in your body. Whatever you notice can be helpful."

Joshua was quiet for a while and then he opened his eyes. "Well . . ." he said, "that was interesting!"

"Please, what did you notice?"

"I was struck by the shift in my body," Joshua said. "I hadn't even realized how clenched my stomach gets around that guy! When Thay stepped in, everything loosened . . . it was like his consciousness just made space."

Joshua took a few breaths and then went on. "Looking from Thay's perspective, what stood out was that Phil is insecure. Otherwise he wouldn't have to constantly sell himself or make others look diminished. And he doesn't feel likable—that others want to be around him. Just seeing that . . . really letting it into my heart that he's living with that . . . makes a difference."

I nodded and then asked him how Thay had responded to Phil. "He just let that comment about me come and go . . . no defense needed. And as we were walking out of the room, he gave Phil a smile and a friendly pat on the back. The guy looked surprised . . . and confused . . . and . . . touched. He wants me to like him." Joshua paused and then shared the message Thay had given him: "It was to remember that other people want to feel important and loved. Just that."

Joshua could now see that Phil was caught in a painful trap, but he still had some concerns. "I'm worried that by focusing on Phil's insecurity and being more kind, I'll be giving him a message that it's okay to mistreat me and others." I agreed that this question was important, and I asked again, "How do you think Thay would respond?"

After reflecting for a few moments, Joshua said, "Compassion extends to everybody's needs. One person is not free to step all over others. But if we remember that someone is really hurting, we'll give feedback and draw boundaries more kindly."

Joshua left energized, and with a new confidence about challenging situations: "What excites me is that in any moment I can call on Thay—really, on my own heart—to get a bigger take. That feels radical!"

It is radical—cutting through to the root—to call on the wisdom of our hearts. You might try this simple practice the next time you're caught in a reactive pattern. Think of a wise, kind being whom you admire. This could be a person you know, a spiritual figure, a deity. Then imagine that his or her consciousness is within you, that you are looking through that being's eyes, with that being's heart. Let this person or being help you respond. Listen for a message. You may discover that you are really tapping into your own most awake, intelligent, caring self.

FORGIVENESS IS NOT PASSIVITY

My book *Radical Acceptance* came out soon after the United States launched the 2003 invasion of Iraq. As I traveled from city to city, many people asked me whether we were supposed to be radically accepting of our country's militancy. "How can acceptance and activism go together?" they'd say. It's a good question. If we only feed the compassionate wolf, will we ignore the wrongdoing in our world? How will anyone be motivated to stand up against injustice, to speak truth, to stop wars, if they don't feel angry or outraged?

I often responded with my own story. In the weeks before the invasion, I read the newspapers with an increasing sense of agitation. I couldn't stop thinking about the men in our administration who were responsible for what seemed an inevitable next step in the global escalation of violence. Just seeing their pictures in the paper would arouse huge waves of anger and hostility.

Then I became increasingly aware of how creating an enemy in my mind was yet another form of violence. So I decided to start a newspaper meditation. I'd look at the headlines, read a bit, and then stop. In that pause I would witness my thoughts and allow myself to acknowledge my growing outrage. Then I'd investigate, letting the feelings express themselves fully. Almost every day, as I'd open to anger and feel its full force, it would unfold into fear—for our world. And as I stayed in direct contact with the fear, it would unfold into grief—for all the suffering and loss. And the grief would unfold into caring about all those beings who were bound to suffer from our warlike actions. My country was feeding the aggressive wolf, and the pain of that was heartbreaking.

Sitting with the feelings that arose in my newspaper meditation left me raw and tender. It reminded me that under my anger and fear was caring about life. And it motivated me to act, not from an anger that focused on an enemy, but from caring.

I was not alone. A growing interfaith peace movement was committed to feeding the wise wolf. On March 26, 2003, a week after the start of the Iraq war, a large group of us gathered in front of the White House. We carried posters showing Iraqi mothers weeping over bodies of wounded children; young American soldiers whose lives would be endangered; Iraqi orphans; men, women, and children from both societies who would suffer. After the designated speakers were finished, a mike was handed around so that anyone who felt moved could offer a prayer. A young girl perched on her dad's shoulders spoke into the attentive crowd: "The Iraqi kids are just like our kids. *Please, please* . . . don't let them be hurt." We were a nonviolent protest, with poems, songs, and pleas to hold all humans in our hearts. The mood was contagious. When the police arrived to arrest us they were friendly, respectful, and kind. As we were loaded into the paddy wagon, I was given a boost and help with my backpack. In another van sat a bishop and a minister, both in their clerical gear. A policeman poked his head in and said cheerfully, "Ah, white-collar crime."

We can feed the wise wolf if we care about peace and learn to pause. Mattie Stepanek, a thirteen-year-old poet who has since died of muscular dystrophy, wrote about this possibility on the day after September 11:

> We need to stop
> Just stop
> Stop for a moment . . .
> Before anybody says or does anything
> That may hurt anyone else.
> We need to be silent.
> Just silent.

Silent for a moment
Before the future slips away
Into ashes and dust
Stop. Be silent, and notice
In so many ways we are the same.

A SHATTERED HEART

I'm often asked how we can awaken our potential for compassion when we are personally under fire. What if we or our loved ones have been repeatedly threatened, demeaned, or violated? How do we forgive then?

In *Tattoos on the Heart*, Jesuit priest Gregory Boyle writes of the human tragedies and potentials playing out in one of the Los Angeles neighborhoods most torn apart by gang violence. Soledad, a mother of four, was proud when her second oldest son, Ronnie, got his high school diploma—something few in the hood accomplish—and went into the Marines. Back home on leave after serving in Afghanistan, he went out one night to pick up some fast food. Awaiting his return, she could hear the voices in the street challenging Ronnie. Then she heard the shots. It didn't matter that he had never belonged to a gang, that he was minding his own business. Ronnie died in her arms right outside the kitchen door.

Soon afterward, her oldest son, Angel, who had belonged to a gang, also graduated from high school. One day, six months after Ronnie's death, Angel set about helping his mother past her immobilizing grief. He pleaded with her to put on some colorful clothes, have her hair done, and be a mom to her three remaining children. He got through to her, he reached her heart. When she made the effort to dress up, he let her know she looked gorgeous. Later that afternoon, while sitting eating a sandwich on their front porch, Angel was shot dead by kids from a rival gang.

Boyle writes that he found Soledad later that day "sobbing into a huge bath towel . . . the few of us there found our arms too short to wrap around this kind of pain." Soledad was locked in the anguish of separation. Boyle spent many hours with her over the next couple of years. He recalls a meeting when he asked how she was doing. Soledad told him,

"You know, I love the two kids that I have. I hurt for the two that are gone." Then crying from bottomless grief, she admitted, "The hurt wins . . . the hurt wins."

Several months later, Soledad went to the emergency room with chest pains. As she lay there, a kid with multiple gunshot wounds was rushed in on a gurney and put into the spot next to her. No curtain was drawn, and she was witnessing him fighting for his life. Recognizing him as a member of the gang that killed her boys, Soledad knew that her friends might say, "Pray that he dies." But that's not what happened.

As she heard the doctors yelling, "We're losing him!" something in her cracked open. "I began to cry as I have never cried before," she told Boyle, "and started to pray the hardest I've ever prayed. 'Please . . . don't . . . let him die.' I don't want his mom to go through what I have.'" The boy survived, as did Soledad's capacity for loving. She had grieved her way into forgiveness, and she had reconnected with life.

When I read about Soledad, it reminded me of a teaching about forgiveness I often share with students. It's a story told by a character in the film *The Interpreter*:

> Everyone who loses somebody wants revenge on someone, on God if they can't find anyone else. But in Africa, in Matobo, the Ku believe that the only way to end grief is to save a life. If some-one is murdered, a year of mourning ends with a ritual that we call the Drowning Man Trial. There's an all-night party beside a river. At dawn, the killer is put in a boat. He's taken out on the water and he's dropped. He's bound so that he can't swim. The family of the dead then has to make a choice. They can let him drown or they can swim out and save him. The Ku believe that if the family lets the killer drown, they'll have justice but spend the rest of their lives in mourning. But if they save him, if they admit that life isn't always just, that very act can take away their sorrow.

The storyteller then concludes, "Vengeance is a lazy form of grief."

Vengeance *is* a lazy form of grief. It is a lazy form of fear, of shame. Vengeance becomes our false refuge because it is easier to blame and push another out of our heart than to feel our own hurt, loss, and powerlessness. Soledad knew this. She lost both of her boys to vengeance. Grieving was more painful than revenge, yet it was the only pathway to healing, to loving again.

THE FREEDOM OF A FORGIVING HEART

The choice of presence and forgiveness—feeding the wise, compassionate wolf—is the evolutionary current that carries us humans toward peace and full spiritual freedom. True heroes are those who, like Soledad, show us what is possible.

When I was in my teens, Nelson Mandela caught my attention and won my heart. A spiritual activist, Mandela personified the transformative power of a forgiving heart on a national scale. He was imprisoned in 1962 for his antiapartheid activism and spent twenty-seven years of his life in jail. For eighteen of those years Mandela was held on the notorious Robben Island near Cape Town where prisoners were segregated, deprived of food, subjected to countless indignities, and forced to do hard labor. Yet during this time, he managed to befriend a number of his jailers. Mandela believed that people were kind at their core "if you could arouse their inherent goodness," and he did just that: One warden risked his job by sneaking in Mandela's new grandchild, so that, with tears in his eyes, Mandela could hold and kiss the baby.

When Mandela was elected president of South Africa after his release, he riveted the world's attention by inviting one of his white jailers to the inaugural ceremony. His dedication to seeking understanding and reconciliation pulled South Africa back from the brink of civil war and allowed the country to make the transition from the racial tyranny of apartheid to a multiracial democracy. In my eyes, Mandela exemplifies our human potential: He stepped beyond the reactivity of hatred and vengeance, and responded to his world with an inclusive, forgiving heart.

Releasing the armor of anger—stopping the war and opening to vulnerability—takes tremendous courage and dedication. Perhaps it also takes imagination. What makes it possible is our innate longing to be whole and loving and free. As Zen teacher Joko Beck writes, "Our failure to know joy is a direct reflection of our inability to forgive."

Whether we are present with garden-variety blame, the aversion that arises from abuse, or the rage that is a legacy of historic injustice, we have the capacity to step out of trance and come home to our awakened heart. It was possible for Mandela with his tormentors, for Soledad after losing her boys, and for Amy with her mother. It is possible between people of different races after generations of violations, and it is possible between family members who have been painfully estranged. Whatever your situation and history with others, it is possible to decide to no longer push anyone out of your heart. You can't will forgiveness but you can be willing. If it is your sincere intention to forgive, the door is already open.

Guided Meditation: A Forgiving Heart toward Others

This reflection is based on the traditional Buddhist forgiveness practice in which we first ask forgiveness from others, then offer it to ourselves, and finally to those who have caused us injury.

———— ∞ ————

Asking for Forgiveness

Sitting comfortably, close your eyes and allow yourself to become present and still. Rest your attention on the breath for a few moments, relaxing as you breathe in and relaxing as you breathe out.

Bring to mind a situation in which you have caused harm to another person through your words, actions, or neglect. Take some moments to remember the circumstances, and sense the hurt, disappointment, or betrayal that person might have felt. Allow yourself to feel your own sorrow or regret.

Now, holding this person in your awareness, begin asking for forgiveness. Mentally whisper his or her name and say, "I understand the hurt you have felt and I ask your forgiveness now. Please forgive me. Please forgive me." With a sincere heart, repeat your request several times. Then take some moments of silence and let yourself open to the possibility of being forgiven.

Forgiving Ourselves

Just as we have caused injury to others, we have harmed ourselves. Reflect on ways that you have judged or punished yourself, ways you have violated or neglected yourself, ways you have withheld your own care. Remember and visualize the situations, and allow yourself to feel the pain that you continue to carry from harming your body, heart, and mind. As you reflect on this, and on the sorrow and regret you feel for hurting yourself, offer the following words: "I see and feel the ways I have caused myself harm, and I forgive myself now." If you're not yet ready to forgive, say, "It is my intention to forgive myself when I am able." Your intention to forgive is the seed of forgiveness—this willingness will gradually relax and open your heart.

Forgiving Others

In the same way that each of us has hurt ourselves and others, we each have been wounded in our relationships. Bring to mind an experience in which you were deeply disappointed or rejected, abused or betrayed. Without judging yourself, notice if you are still carrying feelings of anger and blame toward the person who hurt you. Have you shut this person out of your heart?

　　Recall with some detail the specific situation that most fully reminds you of how you were wounded. You might remember an angry look on a parent's face, harsh words from a friend, the moment you discovered that a trusted person had deceived you, your partner storming out of the house. Be aware of the grief or shame, anger or fear. With acceptance and gentleness, feel this pain as it expresses itself in your body, heart, and mind. Take some moments to hold the hurt places with compassion. Placing your hand on your heart, offer a tender presence to this woundedness. Take as long as you'd like to rest in self-compassion.

　　When you feel ready, look more closely at this other person and sense the fear or hurt, the guilt or shame, the inner pain that might have caused him or her to behave in a hurtful way. Experience this being as an imperfect human, vulnerable and real. Now, staying connected with the place of your own pain, mentally whisper his or her name and offer the message of forgiveness: "I feel the harm that has been caused and to the extent that I am ready, I forgive you now." Or if you feel unable to offer forgiveness at this moment: "I feel the harm that has been caused, and it is my intention to forgive you." Remain connected with your own feelings of vulnerability, and repeat your message of forgiveness or intention for as long as you like.

　　With such practices, it is common to judge ourselves for how well or fully we are able to do the meditation. Let go of any judgments you are carrying and honor the sincerity of your intention to open and free your heart. End the meditation by releasing all ideas of self and other. Simply rest in the experience of tender awareness. If a thought or feeling arises, sense the capacity to include this entire living dying world in the vast space of a forgiving heart.

> Out beyond ideas of wrongdoing and rightdoing,
> there is a field. I'll meet you there.
> When the soul lies down in that grass,
> the world is too full to talk about.
> Ideas, language, even the phrase "each other"
> doesn't make any sense.
>
> —RUMI

TWELVE

HOLDING HANDS:
LIVING COMPASSION

What I want is so simple I almost can't say it: elementary kindness.

BARBARA KINGSOLVER

*We don't set out to save the world; we set out to wonder how other people
are doing and to reflect on how our actions affect other people's hearts.*

PEMA CHÖDRÖN

*Let those who desire Buddhahood not train in many Dharmas but only one.
Which one? Great compassion.
Those with great compassion possess all the Buddha's teaching as if it
were in the palm of their hand.*

SUTRA THAT PERFECTLY ENCAPSULATES THE DHARMA

As told in her book *Heart Politics,* social activist Fran Peavey was walking
on the Stanford University campus one day when she happened upon a
group of people carrying video equipment. They were crowding around
a male chimp that was running loose and a female chimp that was on a
long chain. The chimpanzees were apparently there for some research
purposes, and the scientists and spectators (most of them men) were trying to get them to mate. The male didn't need much encouragement. He
was grunting and tugging at the smaller chimp's chain, while she was
whimpering and trying to avoid his advances. A feeling of empathy swept
through Peavey. Then something happened that she would never forget:

Suddenly the female chimp yanked her chain out of the male's grasp. To my amazement, she walked through the crowd, straight over to me, and took my hand. Then she led me across the circle to the only other two women in the crowd, and she joined hands with one of them. The three of us stood together in a circle. I remember the feeling of that rough palm against mine. The little chimp had recognized us and reached out across all the years of evolution to form her own support group.

Communion begins in our life before we have any words. Even after we've left the refuge of the womb, our development depends on a profoundly intimate relationship with our earliest caregivers. We immediately enter a dance of attunement: A mother senses her child's discomfort in a whimper or restless movement, and she responds by offering her breast or a soft blanket or a dry diaper. The baby hears the affection in his mother's voice, smells her familiar smell, feels her gentle touch, and relaxes with pleasure. From birth, we are wired to understand other humans' experience and to give and receive care.

This dance of attunement is our birthright. The degree to which our feelings of connectedness are damaged, sustained, or deepened is the most central predictor of our health and happiness throughout life. If our early bonds are severed by death or abandonment, inattention or abuse, we become haunted by our unmet needs to feel safe and loved. Take an infant monkey from its mother and it goes from anguished distress to acute anxiety to depressive collapse and possibly death. In contrast, caring contact is medicine for body and soul. If someone— even a stranger—holds your hand while you're frightened, the fear centers in your brain begin to quiet down. And when we're at the end of our lives, looking back, it's the moments of loving connection that shine most brightly. These are the times that give us meaning; the times when we are fully at home in the wholeness and tenderness of our being.

When I heard the story of the female chimp, I was touched by the sense of her consciousness. She seemed to perceive the empathetic responses of the nearby women, and she instinctively sought a way to affirm her belonging. The men in contrast treated the whole encounter as

a sports event. They were seeking excitement, engagement, and affiliation, yet in a way that reinforced "us" and "them." Seeing the chimps
only as objects of entertainment, they were acting from and reinforcing
the trance of separation.

Finding refuge in relationships begins with recognizing the ways we
distance ourselves from other people. You might pause here and ask
yourself a simple, honest question: "How, in my interactions with others
today, have I created separation?" Take your time and be gentle—it's an
important question.

CREATING SEPARATION: SELF AND OTHER

Cousin Victor was the "strange one" in my extended family. Oxygen-
deprived at birth and disabled throughout life, Victor was supported
financially first by his mother, and then by my grandfather. My parents
included Victor in every one of our big holiday meals, but inevitably my
mother's distaste and embarrassment would leak out before all the other
relatives and friends arrived. "Where should we seat him?" she'd say,
shaking her head. "Whoever's next to him will have to deal with the
spittle when he speaks . . ." As the years passed, Victor lost his teeth.
"He dribbles," she'd mutter. "Those shirts with the stains, it's just
awful." We children didn't mind as much as my mom did, but we knew
Victor wasn't "one of us." We'd give him his yearly Christmas tie and be
polite, but he was "other."

Throughout our evolution, we humans have sought security and advantage by evaluating where we stand in relation to one another. We use
race, sexual orientation, religion, education, looks, intelligence, health,
socioeconomic status, and ethnicity as quick filters for assessment. Like
other animals with pecking orders, we check to see who has more power,
who is likely to meet our needs, who is posing a threat. Whenever we
meet a new person, our genetic, cultural, and personal conditioning instantly generates countless judgments about how this person fits into
our ongoing agenda for feeling secure and fulfilled.

These computations create what I call a trance of "unreal others."
Real humans feel hope and fear; their motives and moods are complex

and shifting; their bodies keep changing. In contrast, "unreal others" are two dimensional. It's fairly easy to recognize our stereotypes—prostitute, crack addict, politician, movie star, dictator. Less obvious is how our insecurities and attachments affect our capacity to accurately "take in" our colleagues, friends, and family. Yet when we are feeling stressed and emotionally reactive, almost everyone becomes an "unreal other."

Here you might pause again and bring to mind someone you want something from: approval, money, help, security, a job promotion. What comes up first? Do you focus on a particular visual image, a recent conversation, a mood? Now take a moment to look closer. Try to imagine this person's life from the inside: What does she love? Where does he fear falling short? What delights him? What makes her anxious? Imagine how this person might be touched by kindness—or hurt by criticism. Has anything shifted in your perspective?

Sometimes it comes as a shock to see the person behind the image we have created. I was reminded of this when I heard the following story at a church service one Christmas Eve.

SEEING PAST THE MASK

A woman was traveling with her husband and two children on Christmas Day. It had been a long, grueling trip, and they finally stopped for lunch at a nearly empty diner.

As they waited for their meal, her one-year-old son began waving from his high chair and calling, "Hi there" to someone sitting across the restaurant. To the mother's dismay, it turned out to be a wreck of a man dressed in tattered, dirty clothes, unkempt and unwashed, obviously a homeless drunk. Now he was waving back at her boy and calling, "Hi there, baby, hi there, big boy . . . I see ya, buster."

She and her husband exchanged looks, and the few other patrons in the restaurant were raising eyebrows, shooting glances at one another. Nobody was amused by what was going on.

As they ate their meal, the disturbance continued. Now the old guy was shouting across the room, "Do ya know patty-cake? Atta boy . . . Do ya know peekaboo? . . . Hey look, he knows peekaboo." The woman and her husband were cringing with embarrassment. Even their six-year-old couldn't understand why the old man was talking so loud.

She tried turning the one-year-old's high chair around, but he screamed and twisted to face his new buddy.

Not even waiting for his family to finish their meal, her husband got up to pay the bill and take their older son to the car. The woman lifted her baby in her arms and prayed to herself that she could pass by the old drunk without further commotion.

Clearly this was not meant to be. As she approached him, her young son reached out to his new friend with both arms—his "pick-me-up" signal—and she could see the man's eyes asking, "Please, would you let me hold your baby?"

There wasn't time to answer. Her boy propelled himself into the old man's arms.

She could see tears beneath the man's lashes as her son laid his head on his shoulder. He gently rocked and cradled the boy, and then he looked straight into her eyes. "You take care of this baby," he said firmly.

When he reluctantly handed the baby back, it was as if he was tearing away his own heart. His final words to her: "God bless you, ma'am. You've given me my Christmas gift."

She mumbled something in return and rushed out to the car, her own tears flowing freely. Her only thought was "My God, my God, forgive me."

After the minister finished telling this story, the entire congregation was absolutely still. In the quiet, I noticed that Paul, the fifteen-year-old seated next to me, was sobbing. His parents were good friends of mine, and I had known him since he was a young child. Over the past two years, Paul had struggled with ADHD, taken on Goth attire, withdrawn into a world of earphones and video games, and started using drugs. When I put my hand on his knee, he leaned over and whispered, "That was me, that was me."

I too was crying. The words "How could I?" played over and over in my mind. How many people had I missed out on, separated myself from? Even this very evening, I had been creating separation. Here was my friends' son sitting by my side, and I had been pitying him from a distance. Yes, I knew he was troubled. Yet my mind had fixed on how that sweet fair-headed child I had read stories to was now dyeing his hair jet black and getting body piercings.

"Please," I prayed during the closing candle-lighting ceremony, "please . . . may we remember the light that shines through each of us. May we love one another."

THE "OTHER" IS PART OF US

After my father's death, my mother became the primary person responsible for Victor's well-being. As he became more infirm, she was the one who found him the best available assisted living facility, visited him weekly, and handled his financial and medical matters. At first she did it out of duty, but Victor's gratitude, innocence, and growing affection began to soften her. She was like Santa Claus with her gifts of pizza and candy, puzzles and magazines, and his eyes would light up when she walked into the room.

Victor's big distress was the assisted-living facility. He had lived in his own small apartment for decades, and this wasn't home. He wanted to leave, yet he had to stay—he was unable to care for himself. After one difficult visit my mother drove to a nearby park, stopped the car, and just sat quietly. She saw Victor in her mind's eye, pacing restlessly up and down in his room, longing for somewhere else, and utterly helpless. A wave of sadness swept through her. He was a trapped child. Then she felt her heart gripped by an even deeper sorrow. He was *her* child—she had to love him. That was it. Realizing this, she told me later, flooded her with tenderness. "In those moments I liked myself better, I was more the person I want to be."

Something fundamental had shifted in their relationship. She would still feel put upon, impatient, short at times. But she loved Victor and he could feel it. At the end of her next visit he reached out and touched her arm, as if to say "I want us together, don't leave." And over the following year, he seemed to relax; he didn't need to complain so much. It was as though he was floating peacefully in her ocean, soothed by their connection.

When we feel compassion, the vulnerability of another person becomes part of us. My mother had stood in the fire of difficult feelings, staying present with Victor's fears and confusion, as well as her own suppressed aversion. In that presence, in paying attention, her heart had opened. Her pity for an "other" had become care for both of them. It was no longer Victor's problems they were dealing with—it was their shared predicament, their shared suffering. He had become part of her heart.

Victor's story ends sadly. Several years ago, when she was eighty-three, my mother decided to move to Virginia and live with Jonathan and me on our property. She found kind people to visit Victor, but she still worried that he'd be bereft. And then, one week after she told him she was moving, Victor died. They had been holding hands, and he didn't want to go on without her.

When my mother called to tell me, she was grieving. "This was a person," she said tearfully. "He had an intelligence, a gentleness, a good heart. But, it was so sad . . . others looked down on him. I did . . . until I got to know him."

COMPASSION CAN BE CULTIVATED

The capacity for compassion is hardwired into our brain and body. Just as we are rigged to perceive differences, to feel separate, and to react with aversion, we are also designed to feel a connection with our fellow humans. Specialized "mirror neurons" attune us to another person's state—to their emotions and the intentions behind their movements—and re-create that state in our own brain. Our experience of them is not just a projection based on visible expressions such as grimaces, narrowed eyes, or furrowed brows. Because of mirror neurons, and other structures in the prefrontal cortex that make up our compassion circuitry, we can actually "feel with" them.

Yet these compassion circuits are easily blocked when we're stressed and out of touch with our emotions and bodies. They can also become blocked when we buy into cultural stereotypes and when we're experiencing unexamined reactivity to the people in our life. Research shows that the less we identify with someone—the less they seem real to us—the less the mirror neuron system gets activated.

The good news is that we can unblock and activate our compassion networks. This happens as we intentionally turn toward the refuges of truth and love. Mindfulness directly engages the parts of our brain (the insula and anterior cingulate cortex) that are key in reading others' emotions. When we mindfully recognize that another is hurt or afraid, we naturally feel the tenderness of compassion. That tenderness blossoms fully as we find ways to express our care. This alchemy of letting ourselves be touched by another's pain and of responding with love is the essence of Buddhist compassion practices.

One such meditation training, the Tibetan practice of *tonglen*, literally means "sending and receiving." (A version of tonglen is on page 159.) The breath is used as a support and guide: Breathing in with deep receptivity, we take in the pain of others. Breathing out, we offer our care and blessings, sending whatever will bring relief and space and happiness. This practice goes counter to our tendency to shut down in the face of suffering. As my mother discovered, the more fully we let ourselves be touched by suffering, the more we soften and awaken our heart. The more we offer our love, the more we discover our belonging to all beings, and to loving awareness itself.

The starting place in tonglen is an intentional relaxing of the armor around our heart. Each of us has been wounded and, in reaction, has erected defenses to protect us from experiencing further harm. We don't want to be vulnerable or available to pain. Yet before we can be tender-hearted, we have to be tender. As poet Mark Nepo writes,

Our challenge each day is not to get dressed to face the world, but to unglove ourselves so that the doorknob feels cold, and the car handle feels wet, and the kiss goodbye feels like the lips of another being, soft and unrepeatable.

BREATHING IN: "EAR OF THE HEART"

Most of us consider listening a great virtue. We love having others listen to us with interest and care, and we hope to be good listeners ourselves. But it's hard. To listen well we must become aware of the mental static that runs interference: aware of our emotional reactivity; aware of all the ways we interpret (and misinterpret) each other; aware of our haste to prepare a response; aware of how we armor ourselves with judgment. Learning to listen involves stepping out of our incessant inner dialogue, and using what St. Benedict called the "ear of the heart." This deep listening, a form of "breathing in," offers a compassionate space for healing and intimacy.

Kate was a meditation student who discovered the power of listening in her relationship with her mother, Audrey, who was a wealthy, successful, brilliant, and narcissistic woman. Those who knew Audrey well kiddingly referred to her as "the center of the known universe." A well-known writer, Audrey treated other people as orbiting satellites, audiences to regale with stories; their role was to let her shine in her own reflected light.

Audrey could be lively and charming when holding forth, but she was exhausting to be around. As soon as they could, both of her daughters settled on the opposite coast. Kate's older sister rarely returned for visits, and while Kate came for holidays, she kept her stays brief. Their stepdad loved his wife, but he and Audrey had drifted into a routine that lacked intimacy. Some of Audrey's friends still tolerated being a captive audience, but as she aged she became increasingly isolated.

Kate came to my Conscious Relationship workshop to focus on her marriage, not on her mother. But by the time she left, she'd become acutely aware of her mother's woundedness, and of the possibility that deep listening might lead to healing. Her inspiration was the image of a fountain.

During the workshop, we envisioned our inner lives and spirits as fountains that become clogged with unprocessed hurts and fears. As we ignore our painful feelings or push them away, they impede our flowing aliveness and obscure the pure awareness that is our source. By not listening to our inner life, we cut ourselves off from reality. What remains is a diminished self, an unreal other.

But when we confide in someone and they listen to us, really listen, the debris naturally begins to dissolve, and the fountain of aliveness is again free to flow. And when we listen, really listen, to another, we help them come home to this same aliveness.

It's important to remember that this process takes time. As we begin to listen, we often come face-to-face with the distasteful tangles, the jealousy or self-consciousness or anger that have been clogging the fountain. The conversation might seem superficial or dull, nervous or self-absorbed. A dedicated listener hangs in there without getting lost in resisting or judging. This unconditional presence is a healing balm. It gradually helps the speaker's tangled defenses relax so that his or her natural vitality and spirit can emerge. Perhaps you've noticed this when someone is really listening to you. You feel calmer, whole, "more like yourself"—more at home. Like an unclogged fountain, the deeper waters of humor, intelligence, creativity, and love begin to flow.

Kate left the workshop with the intention of experimenting, and when an opportunity to attend a professional training session near her mother's home presented itself, she decided it was time to try deep listening with her. She made arrangements to stay for ten days, her longest visit with her mother since she'd left for college.

Now, Kate really listened during their time together. As we had practiced, she listened inwardly to her own tension without judgment when she felt resistance, and then reopened to whatever her mother was saying. In the same way, when she felt unimportant, impatient, bored, or judgmental, she brought mindfulness and kindness to her own experience. Then she was able to bring that same open, clear space of presence to her mother.

At first it was hard. "I had a panicky sensation," Kate told me later. "It was like I would drown if I didn't get away, if I didn't find a way to have some of my own space. She takes up so much room!" But she found that if she kept a sense of humor about it, she could breathe, forgive her own reactions, and keep coming back. Then she would coach herself to deepen presence: "Now . . . what is happening . . . my mother is talking. I am quiet. There is endless time. I hear it, every word . . . and what is beyond the word . . . I hear who she is."

It got easier as Kate listened for what was behind her mother's words. She began to hear desperation, as if her mother was insisting over and over, "I am here, I matter." Taking in her mother's pain, Kate felt her heart soften with care. Through her own quiet, steady presence, she communicated, "You're here, you matter." And her mother started to relax. Kate knew this because there were longer pauses between the stories and commentary—her mother sat back more in her chair, she looked out the window, slowed down, and seemed more reflective.

Several days before Kate was scheduled to leave, her mother began to tell her that she felt alone and unappreciated. Kate responded, sincere, gentle, and honest: "Mom, it's because you don't listen to people." Her mother froze, but she didn't get defensive. Kate had been so truly present, she had offered such uncritical sympathy, that a trust had emerged— this was not an attack, but a caring reflection of truth. Her mother wanted to know more: "Please tell me, I need to know." Kate told her. She explained how it had been for her sister, for their dad, and now, for her stepdad. "When you don't listen, people feel like they don't matter, that they are not known. And it's true—you can't know them if you don't listen. You can't be close."

Audrey looked at her daughter with a sorrow and understanding that pierced Kate's heart. Something changed in that moment. Maybe the pain of alienation had broken through her defenses, maybe this was simply her time. Audrey started to listen. Others noticed. After her sister's next visit, she told Kate, "For the first time in my life I felt like I was a real person to her . . . that I existed!" The change was most poignant with her husband, Kate's stepfather. They began to enjoy the long dinners and evening walks that had been abandoned shortly after their marriage.

Audrey was no longer speaking to demand the world's attention. She was speaking and listening in order to belong with other people, to share their lives. Because Kate had listened and let her heart be touched, her mother's fountain had begun to unclog. Her life could flow again from its source.

SPEAKING AND RECEIVING
DIFFICULT TRUTHS

As part of my wedding vows to Jonathan, I read these lines from Rainer
Maria Rilke:

> I want to unfold. Let no place in me hold itself closed, for where
> I am closed, I am false. I want to stay clear in your sight . . .

In my mind, the path of intimacy meant having the courage to reveal
whatever I didn't want another person to see. This has proven to be no
small task. I'm great at being open and real until I start feeling
vulnerable—ashamed of myself—or critical of Jonathan. At those times
I postpone talking, I get withdrawn, manipulative, or aggressive. It's not
so easy to stay clear in his sight.

Only two years after we married, the extent of my health problems
became clear. Many of the activities we loved doing together—mountain
hiking, biking, skiing, Boogie Boarding—were no longer possible for
me. The future didn't look good. My body would only become less and
less fit and desirable. He, on the other hand, was young for his age and
healthy. I sank into a swamp of shame about my condition, shame about
his being stuck with an aging, sickly woman.

For weeks I felt unable to say this out loud, to have him see my shame
and insecurity. Keeping those feelings to myself was toxic—I was increasingly fearful, distant, and grim.

When I finally told him, he did what good listeners do. He made
sure I said everything I wanted to, and then mirrored back the words I
had used, letting me know he understood. After that, he communicated
a love that was not tied to my being any certain way.

Of course, as he'd readily admit, he's not always that good. He's told
me that when I say, "Honey, we need to talk," his first thought (only
partially a joke) is, "Oh God, I'm going to die!" followed quickly by,
"Okay, what did I do wrong now?" He can start off defensive and tense,
and as I feel his resistance, my criticalness amps up. But we're practicing
open communication. And we keep rediscovering something essential:

No matter how much we don't want to do it, it's worth taking the chance to be vulnerable. It's the only way we can come to trust our love. Poet Adrienne Rich wrote,

> An honorable human relationship, that is, one in which two people have the right to use the word *love*, is a process of deepening the truths they can tell each other. It is important to do this because it breaks down human self-delusion and isolation.

Of course, in some situations it is neither wise nor appropriate to speak your emotional truths. The timing might be off, or the others involved might not have the skill or emotional capacity to listen well. Especially if you are dealing with trauma, finding the right therapist or teacher who can hold the intensity of your experience with you is essential. Even if you are not working with trauma-based feelings, a "container" for truth telling—another person or group of people who are committed to mindful speaking and listening—is necessary. You need to feel a degree of safety. And yet I use the word "degree" on purpose. Embedded in feeling ashamed and vulnerable is the belief that others will not receive you well. You might not feel safe, yet taking the chance may leave you feeling safer and more loved than you did before speaking.

The Buddha described wise speech as speaking what is true and helpful. The simplicity of this description belies its layers of nuance. What is true? Certainly not all our evaluations and commentary about what is happening. The best we can do is become very present to our actual feelings and name them without the second arrow of judgment. And what is helpful? If we sincerely want our words to serve greater mutual understanding and care, that intention will guide us.

There's great power in sharing a difficult truth. Letting your vulnerability be seen by a trusted, attentive other can start unraveling a lifetime of shame. Naming painful feelings without blame can deepen and strengthen mutual attunement and compassion. Relationships become more vibrant. Finding the courage to "take the risk"—to speak what is true—enlarges you. You become more real to yourself, more intimate with others.

BREATHING OUT: OFFERING OUR CARE

The intimacy that arises in listening and speaking truth is only possible if we can open to the vulnerability of our own hearts. Breathing in, contacting the life that is right here, is our first step. Once we have held ourselves with kindness, we can touch others in a vital and healing way.

Richie and I became friends when we were juniors in college. A shy, thoughtful African American man, he was known for carrying his camera everywhere, listening as others poured out their stories to him, and running through the snow wearing gym shorts. Although we lost touch after graduation, I had heard that he was working as a photojournalist in New York. Then, nearly fifteen years later, he called and asked to consult with me on an upcoming visit to Washington, D.C. He explained that he'd recently married Carly, a Caucasian woman he'd met at a meditation class, and he wanted to talk with me about his wife's family. "I knew what I was getting into . . . country club, conservative, the whole nine yards . . . but I had no idea it would be this hard."

"From the start," he told me when we met, "Sharon [his mother-in-law] was dead set against me and Carly getting together." While Carly's father seemed willing to support his daughter's choice, her mother had fought the marriage vehemently. "She warned Carly that we were too different, that we'd end up divorced and miserable. Well . . . ," he said grimly, "we love each other deeply, but she is succeeding in making us miserable."

On their third and most recent visit, Sharon had refused to go to a community theater production with them. She later told Carly that she couldn't bear to encounter her friends from the club: "As soon as I'd turn my back," she complained, "they'd start gossiping about you and Richie." At dinner she ignored Richie's compliments about the salmon, and gave vague, noncommittal responses to his questions about a recent trip to Italy. When Carly confronted her privately upstairs, Sharon acknowledged her behavior. "I admit it, I'm being awful. But I can't help it, Carly. He's a good person, an intelligent person . . . really, he is . . . but you're making a terrible mistake."

Carly wanted to stop visiting—they could just skip Thanksgiving and Christmas, she said—but Richie insisted on hanging in there. "It's not that I'm trying to martyr myself," he told me. "Sharon's a racist, self-centered asshole, and it might do her some good if Carly refused to go home. I'd be gratified . . . I'm way pissed. But something in me feels like she is reachable."

As part of his meditation practice, Richie had recently taken bo-dhisattva vows with his teacher. These express a basic commitment to let whatever arises in our life awaken compassion, and to dedicate ourselves to actively bringing this compassion to all beings. For Richie, these vows had a very specific meaning. "I don't want to give up on anyone, give up on who they can be," he told me. But Richie knew that before he could approach Sharon, he needed to connect with his own anger, and what was behind it.

"That's what I wanted us to focus on, Tara," he said as he sat back in his chair. "I wouldn't be so pissed if I didn't feel insecure. It's that basic issue of being worthy—she's telling me I'm not worthy enough for her daughter."

"Is that feeling familiar?" I asked.

"Oh yeah. This has been the kind of thing I've told myself ever since my dad left. Back then it was that I'm not good enough to make my mom happy." He sat quietly for a few moments and then went on. "I thought I was supposed to fill his shoes and I couldn't. She was always depressed, always anxious."

Richie sat back in the chair, deflated. "It's always this same feel-ing . . . that I'm the kid who can't make the grade, who doesn't deserve good things. And it didn't help going to that vanilla college of ours"—he flashed me a smile—"or working in a white profession. I know this un-worthiness thing's in the culture, Tara . . . but that kid still feels like he's young, and just not cutting it."

"As you pay attention, can you sense what that kid who feels unwor-thy most wants from you?"

He was quiet and then he nodded. "He just wants me to see him, to notice him and to be kind."

"What happens if you offer your kindness inward?"

For a few minutes Richie sat silently, pensive and still. When he opened his eyes, he looked out the window. Then he met my eyes and smiled.

"Thanks," he said softly. "I guess this part of me needs some reassurance, some care. Just now I felt like I was looking through a camera at this kid who was failing at an impossible task. There's no way he could make things okay for his mother."

We talked about their upcoming Thanksgiving visit, and how Sharon might activate his insecurities. Richie came up with a plan: "I'm bringing my camera. I'll keep my eye on the kid inside . . . and on Sharon . . . both of us with kindness." And with that, he swung his legs over the side of my large armchair, visibly more relaxed.

I heard from Richie again right after Thanksgiving weekend. Sharon had treated him with polite formality—everyone else was family, he was a guest. "But I kept imagining I was looking at her through a camera viewfinder," he told me, "and I saw she was in pain. Behind that coldness was a scared, tight heart." He had a freeing realization: "It isn't really me she's afraid of. It's of Carly being unhappy."

A day or so later he e-mailed me two standout photos, both of Sharon. Carly's sister had just had a baby, and he'd caught Sharon cradling her new granddaughter, looking down adoringly at the infant. The other was of a playful moment when her husband had pulled her down to sit with him and she'd toppled over on him. Richie took the shot just as they were looking at each other and laughing.

And then came Christmas. Early on Christmas Eve, Carly's dad (playing Santa) placed two boxes in front of Richie. Sharon had ordered some socks for him online (too large) and had wrapped a box of chocolates (he rarely ate sugar). Sometime later, Sharon opened her gift from Richie. She found the two photos he had taken weeks earlier, simply and elegantly framed. Sharon started trembling and then sobbing. Her husband and Carly came over to see what was wrong. There were the pictures of Sharon with her granddaughter and her husband, looking radiant, loving, and happy. And here she was weeping. When she calmed down, she still couldn't speak and she waved everyone on to continue the gift giving.

Richie had truly "seen" Sharon—her vulnerability and spirit. He had expressed his care by mirroring her goodness. It took another year and a half for her to tell him what those gifts had meant to her and to apologize. But because he hadn't given up on her, a thaw had begun. The following evening Carly's sister asked Richie for a lesson in swing dancing, and he showed her some steps to the jazz music on his iPod. She caught on quickly, and the others applauded as she and Richie spun happily around the living room. Carly glanced over at her mom, who was standing behind the others in the doorway. She was watching with a slight smile, her eyes wet with tears.

OFFERING BLESSINGS

We are blessed whenever someone sees who we are and helps us trust our essential goodness and belonging. One friend felt blessed when her aunt understood what she most needed and paid for her first meditation retreat. A man I know, whose young son had died of brain cancer, felt blessed when his rabbi assured him that he could continue to commune with his son's spirit. As a young boy, my father-in-law felt blessed by his older cousin, who recognized his brightness and gave him a word game.

Physician and author Rachel Naomi Remen tells a beautiful story about how her grandfather's blessings nurtured her:

> My grandfather died when I was seven years old. I had never lived in a world without him in it before, and it was hard for me. He had looked at me as no one else had and called me by a special name, "Neshume-le," which means "little beloved soul." There was no one left to call me this anymore. At first I was afraid that without him to see me and tell God who I was, I might disappear. But slowly over time I came to understand that in some mysterious way, I had learned to see myself through his eyes. And that once blessed, we are blessed forever.
>
> Many years later when, in her extreme old age, my mother surprisingly began to light candles and talk to God herself, I told her about these blessings and what they had meant to me. She had smiled at me sadly. "I have blessed you every day of your life, Rachel," she told me. "I just never had the wisdom to do it out loud."

Most of us need to be reminded that we are good, that we are lovable, that we belong. If we knew just how powerfully our thoughts, words, and actions affected the hearts of those around us, we'd reach out and join hands again and again. Our relationships have the potential to be a sacred refuge, a place of healing and awakening. With each person we meet, we can learn to look behind the mask and see the one who longs to love and be loved. We can remember to say our blessings out loud.

Guided Meditation: Tonglen:
Awakening the Heart of Compassion

The Tibetan practice of tonglen trains us to let in suffering and offer out compassion *(karuna)*. On page 159 I introduced a version of this practice that focused on contacting our own fear and arousing self-compassion. The following trains us to imagine and feel the reality of others. As we include the suffering of others in our heart, we naturally respond with tenderness and care.

Sit in a way that allows you to be relaxed and alert. Let go of any habitual tension and allow your body and mind to settle.

The traditional practice of tonglen begins by taking a moment to sense the stillness or openness that is already here. This is considered a flash of remembrance, a reconnecting with our awakened heart and mind.

Now bring your attention to the natural rhythm and quality of your breath. As the breath flows in, allow your cells to receive this life energy. With each in-breath, open with total receptivity, like a balloon gently expanding with air. Be aware of the experience of no resistance, of allowing yourself to be touched by the sensations of the breath.

With the out-breath, notice the sensations of letting go and releasing into the space that surrounds you. Imagine your total body and consciousness flowing outward with the breath and mingling with the vastness of space. Breathe out into relaxation, ease, and spaciousness.

Continue meditating on the essence of receiving, being touched with the in-breath, and letting go into openness with the out-breath.

Now invite into your awareness someone you know personally who is suffering, someone you want to help. Imagine yourself in this person's circumstances, experiencing this person's fear or hurt or loss. What is it like to look at the world through these eyes? Live inside this particular body? Feel with this heart? What is the most vulnerable, painful part of this person's experience? What does he or she most need?

Now breathing in, invite all this pain into your heart, allowing yourself to feel it fully. Inhale, taking the pain into yourself, so that the other person will have relief. And as you breathe out, respond to his or her needs by sending out relaxation, space, love, or whatever will bring ease and happiness.

Sometimes as you inhale, you will meet your own resistance to pain. If this happens, shift the focus and breathe for yourself and countless others just like you who are feeling this same stuckness, anger, revulsion, or fear. Then as you breathe out, offer whatever helps you and others like you find space and relief.

As your resistance softens, return to breathing for the person you intend to help. As you inhale and let the person's pain touch you, feel how he or she is held in your heart. And as you exhale, send whatever prayer or expression of care feels most sincere or most needed.

Now, enlarge the taking in and sending out to include all those who are in the same situation, experiencing the same suffering. If the person you want to help is grieving a loss, breathe in and out for all those who are experiencing the pain of loss. If this person feels like a failure, breathe in and out for all who feel like failures. Sense, as you breathe in, the unconditional willingness, tenderness, and receptivity of your heart; and as you breathe out, the vastness of loving awareness that is here, holding this world.

Continue breathing, opening to the universal experience of this suffering and letting go into spaciousness with prayer. As your heart opens to the enormity of suffering, you become that openness. As you offer your tenderness, your awareness becomes suffused with compassion.

Flexibility in using the breath: *If at any point you find the breathing instructions interfere with the actual experience of taking in suffering and sending out ease and love, adjust however most serves the meditation. For instance, you might find you need to focus on just the in-breath or just the out-breath for several cycles to more fully contact experience, or to let go. Or you might find that it is easier not to focus on the breath at all.*

Throughout your day: *You can do an abbreviated version of tonglen whenever you encounter suffering. If someone you meet is having a hard time, pause. For several breaths, silently breathe in his or her pain and breathe out relief. If you feel yourself resisting, turned off, or afraid of the pain, do tonglen for yourself and all those like you who are having difficulty opening to pain.*

No matter what comes up, it is an opportunity for practicing compassion. Rather than ignoring pain or judging ourselves, we can train ourselves to open into our full potential to love.

When tonglen may be inappropriate: *If you are struggling with trauma-related fear, unrelenting depression, or severe psychological imbalance, tonglen may cause emotional flooding or a sense of being stuck. In these situations, seek guidance from a spiritual teacher, therapist, or trusted guide in finding what best helps you move toward healing.*

Guided Meditation: Lovingkindness: Seeing Past the Mask

Whenever we recognize goodness, our heart opens with lovingkindness. Starting from the love we feel for those dearest to us, this version of the lovingkindness meditation helps us learn to see goodness in those who are different, distant, or even hurtful.

Sit in a way that allows you to be comfortable and relaxed. Letting go of whatever tension you can, loosen your shoulders, soften your hands, and relax your belly. Feel a smile spread through your eyes, softening the flesh around them. Bring a slight smile to the mouth, and feel the smile on the inside of the mouth. Smile into your heart, and then imagine the smile expanding, creating a receptive, tender space through the whole heart and chest area.

Now bring into your heart someone you love. Take some moments to reflect on the qualities you most appreciate. Recall his or her intelligence, humor, kindness, vitality. Picture this person when he or she is feeling love for you. Be aware of his or her essence as good and wakeful and caring. In your heart feel your appreciation for this dear one and begin offering your prayer. You might draw from four or five phrases below or, if you prefer, create your own.

> *May you be filled with lovingkindness, held in*
> *lovingkindness . . . may you feel my love now.*
> *May you feel safe and at ease.*
> *May you accept yourself just as you are.*
> *May you be happy.*
> *May you touch great and natural peace.*
> *May you know the natural joy of being alive.*
> *May your heart and mind awaken; may you be free.*

As you silently whisper each phrase of lovingkindness, imagine how it might be for this person to experience the fruit of your blessing—the fullness of love, self-acceptance, peace, joy, and freedom.

Now widen your circle of caring by bringing to mind a "neutral" person. (This might be someone you see regularly but don't know well or feel strongly about.) Take some moments to recall how this person looks, moves, and speaks. Now try to imagine him or her gazing at a beloved child . . . or struck by the beauty of a fresh snowfall . . . or laughing, relaxed, and at ease. Remind yourself that he or she wants to be happy and doesn't want to suffer. Then, as this person comes alive for you, use the phrases above, or whatever others you choose, to offer your appreciation and lovingkindness.

Now bring to mind someone with whom you have a difficult relationship—perhaps someone who evokes anger, fear, or hurt. First take a moment to bring a kind, nonjudging attention to your own feelings as you reflect on him or her. Then, turning back to this difficult person, try to see past the mask. Look to see some aspect of his or her basic goodness. It may help to imagine this person as a young child, sleeping peacefully—or at the other end of life, as someone who has just passed away. Can you recall something about this person that you admire, some quality of dedication, caring, or creativity? Even if it's difficult to recognize this person's goodness, remind yourself that all humans want to be happy, want to avoid suffering. Remember that life matters to this person just as it does to you. Holding him or her in a gentle attention, begin offering the phrases of lovingkindness that come most easily for you.

Next imagine that you are bringing together all those you have just prayed for—a dear person, a neutral one, a difficult one. Take a moment to include yourself, honoring the goodness and sincerity you've brought to this meditation. Holding yourself and these others in your heart, sense your shared humanity, your vulnerability and basic goodness. Send prayers of lovingkindness to all at once, recognizing that you are in this together.

Finally, allow your awareness to open out in all directions—in front of you, to either side, behind you, below you, and above you. In this vast space, sense that your loving presence is holding all beings: the wild creatures that fly and swim and run across fields; the dogs and cats that live in our homes; the life forms that are threatened with extinction; the trees and grasses and flowers; children everywhere; humans living in great poverty and those with great riches; those at war and those at peace; those who are dying and those who are newly born. Imagine that you can hold the earth, our mother, in your lap and include all life everywhere in your boundless heart. Aware of the goodness inherent in all living beings, again offer your prayers:

May all beings be filled with lovingkindness.
May all beings know great and natural peace.

May there be peace on earth, peace everywhere.
May all beings awaken; may all be free.

Repeat these phrases several times. Then allow yourself to rest in openness and silence, letting whatever arises in your heart and awareness be touched by loving-kindness.

Throughout your day: *There are many ways to weave the lovingkindness practice into your daily life.*

- *Set an intention to reflect, each morning for a week, on the goodness of the people you live with. Then whenever you remember during the day, silently offer them your prayers.*
- *Whenever a loved one or someone else triggers feelings of irritation or insecurity, pause, recall some specific example of that person's goodness, and mentally whisper, "May you be happy."*
- *Choose a "neutral" person you encounter regularly, and whenever you see them during the following week, remind yourself of their goodness and silently offer your wishes for their well-being. Notice if your feelings for this person change.*
- *Choose a "difficult" person and set a time to reflect daily on his or her goodness. After you've offered prayers of lovingkindness for at least two weeks, do you notice a change in your feelings? Has there been any change in their behavior toward you?*
- *Discover what happens when you let someone know the goodness you are seeing in them.*

Keeping your practice fresh and alive: *Whatever awakens a genuine sense of connectedness and care is a lovingkindness practice. So if your formal practice is feeling somewhat mechanical, experiment with the following:*

- *Use whatever words most resonate in the moment.*
- *Whisper your prayer aloud.*
- *Say the name of the person you're praying for.*

- *Imagine your heart is holding the people you're praying for, or that you're touching their cheeks with care.*
- *Imagine them feeling healed and loved and uplifted by your prayer.*

Even a few moments of reflecting on goodness and offering lovingkindness can reconnect you with the purity of your loving heart.

THIRTEEN

LOSING WHAT WE LOVE: THE PAIN OF SEPARATION

Those we love from the first
can't be put aside or forgotten,
after they die they still must be cried
out of existence . . .
confirming,
the absent will not be present,
ever again. Then the lost one
can fling itself outward, its million
moments of presence can scatter
through consciousness freely, like snow
collected overnight on a spruce bough
that in midmorning bursts
into glittering dust in the sunshine.

GALWAY KINNELL

Cry out! Don't be stolid and silent with your pain. Lament!
And let the milk of loving flow into you.

RUMI

I'll need some Advil if I'm going to get out for a walk . . . but I'll get a stomachache if I
don't eat something first . . . and it's too early. Then the thought *I'm awake,* and as
I dislodge the pillow from under my knees and roll slowly onto my side,
the stabbing in my hip kicks in. It's another morning, another day of
having to live inside a hurting body.

I try not to think of how it used to be. I can let go of the younger me, the one who won a yoga Olympics by holding wheel pose for more than eighteen minutes. I can let go of the woman who ran three miles on most days, who loved to ski and Boogie Board, bike and play tennis. But what about just being able to wander the hills and woods around our home? What about walking along the river?

So much has been taken away. First came an injury to my knees while running. Then knee instability ruled out biking or tennis. I resigned myself to swimming for exercise, only to find that swimming aggravated disks in my neck. Now even walking is often painful. Sweeping the floor, bending over, or picking up anything heavier than a gallon of water can leave me hurting for days. And I'm losing strength on all fronts, because most ways of strengthening the muscles injure my joints.

Losing the freedom to move easily feels like a kind of death, a separation from the experience of aliveness that I love. But the worst part is looking ahead. I imagine being with my future grandchildren, unable to lift them into my arms, splash in the water, horse around on the floor, or play tag on the lawn. I imagine being a prisoner in a body that hurts.

THE COMMUNITY OF LOSS

Because my genetic condition is rare and little known, I felt isolated and separate in my pain for some time after my diagnosis. But my illness has gradually initiated me into what one friend calls the "community of loss." Crossing over into this world has given me an intimate understanding of what it's like for others when something they love is torn away. Clients and students have always told me their stories, but as my own suffering has become more visible, their sharing of vulnerability has become more open and real. One woman told me her loneliness feels like a never-ending death. Another described a fear so great she believes it will cause heart failure.

The Buddha's quest for freedom began when he was confronted with the reality that we will all lose everything we hold dear. As a young prince, Siddhartha Gautama lived a protected life, ensconced in a kingdom that provided him with all earthly comforts and delights. But some inner restlessness moved him to visit the untended outskirts of the kingdom, and there he encountered first a sick man, then an old man, and finally a corpse. Siddhartha was jolted from his trance of complacency. It no longer mattered that he had a beautiful, devoted wife or that he would someday be the king with a great army to defend his people. He became possessed by a single burning question: If suffering and loss can't be avoided, how can we humans find peace and freedom in the midst of our lives?

A friend and longtime Buddhist watched a PBS feature on the Buddha's life while he was recovering from a serious heart attack. After viewing the segment on Siddhartha's three encounters he bolted upright with the thought *There is old age! There is sickness! There is death! Why didn't I know this before?* Of course he'd known it conceptually. But now he really knew. We lose *this* body. *This* loved one. *This* life's continuation into the future.

DEFENDING AGAINST LOSS

The Buddha taught that we spend most of our life like children in a burning house, so entranced by our games that we don't notice the flames, the crumbling walls, the collapsing foundation, the smoke all around us. The games are our false refuges, our unconscious attempts to trick and control life, to sidestep its inevitable pain.

Yet this life is not only burning and falling apart. Zen poems and art revere a natural world that is also flowing, flowering, dancing, emanating, and bursting forth. Sorrow and joy are woven inextricably together. When we distract ourselves from the reality of loss, we also distract ourselves from the beauty, creativity, and mystery of this ever-changing world.

I want to say right here that stepping away from the full pain of loss can be an intelligent and compassionate response—it gives us space and time to regain some energy, perspective, and balance. It may not be a false refuge to keep ourselves occupied after a fresh loss—to bury ourselves in work, books, movies, or to surround ourselves with company. The same is true if we need to withdraw from regular activities and social engagements. But our ways of seeking relief are often neither healthy nor temporary. Instead, they become ongoing attempts to control our experience so that we don't have to open to our grief.

THE ARMOR OF BLAME

Some years ago I worked with a couple that had lost their teenage son, Ron, to leukemia. During the final three years of Ron's life they had desperately pursued and exhausted every medical protocol that the National Institutes of Health offered. Louise, who was my therapy client, quit her job, and her husband, Tony, scaled back to part time. Their life was a roller coaster, with Ron's periodic upsurges of energy and strength fueling their grim determination to "beat the disease." When the boy died, they were crushed by their grief. But soon, without their common enemy, they turned on each other. "Just being around Tony reminds me of what I've lost, of this huge gaping hole," Louise said. "I know intellectually that it's not his fault, but that doesn't make a difference. There's a voice in me screaming, 'You didn't save my baby!'" Tony was at first stunned, and then hurt and angry in return. They separated within eight months.

With Tony gone, Louise redirected her blame. When we met, she'd tell me how one person after another was letting her down in some way—not standing by her in her split with Tony, not really understanding the monstrous loss she was living with. When she finally began dating, her relationships were short-lived. "They just don't know what it's like," she'd say. Louise was stuck—for her, the suffering of feeling wronged and isolated had been piled on top of the suffering of grief.

Blame is a false refuge that armors our hearts and distances us from the felt sense of grief. Our anger or hatred may fixate on the partner who left us for another woman; the ex-spouse who deprived us of visitation; the teens who have lured our son into drugs. Or we might react to loss with a more global anger like my client Justin.

Justin and Donna met in college when they both volunteered at a community service agency, and they married right after graduation. Donna went on to law school and to teaching law; Justin taught history and coached basketball at a small urban college. With their teaching, their passion for tennis, and their shared dedication to advocating for disadvantaged youth, their life together was full and satisfying.

Donna was away at a conference when Justin received the unexpected news of his promotion to full professor. She caught an early flight back to celebrate with him. On her way home from the airport a large truck overturned and crushed her car, killing her instantly.

Almost a year after Donna's death Justin e-mailed me to ask for some phone counseling sessions. "I need to get back to mindfulness," he wrote. "Anger is threatening to take away the rest of my life."

During our first call Justin told me that his initial response to Donna's death was rage at an unjust God. "When I wasn't cursing God, I was shaking my fist at him, demanding answers: 'She was so good, so kind, so needed on this earth . . . why her? And me . . . how could you take her from me? What did I do to deserve this?'" An African American from a working-class family, Justin had put himself through college with the help of a basketball scholarship. He was devoted to his students and team members, putting in extra hours mentoring those who needed personal or academic support. "I loved everything I was doing, but what kept me going, what nourished me most, was Donna. She was my soul mate . . . and . . . she's gone. It doesn't matter that I always tried to do my best, be a good person, a good Christian. God turned his back on me."

In the year after Donna's death, Justin's anger at God morphed into a more general rage at injustice and a desire to confront those in power. He'd always been involved with social causes, but now he became a lightning rod for conflict, aggressively leading the fight for diversity on campus, and publicly attacking the school administration for its lack of commitment to the surrounding community. His department chairman had previously been a staunch ally, but now their communication was badly strained. "It's not your activism, I'm all for it," his chairman had told him. "It's your antagonism . . . your attitude. That's the problem." Justin's older sister, his lifelong confidante, had also confronted him. "Your basic life stance is suspicion and hostility," she'd said. "You're carrying a major chip on your shoulder. It's you against the world." When I asked him whether that rang true, he replied, "When I lost Donna, I lost my faith. I used to think that some basic sanity could prevail in this world. But now . . . well . . . it's hard *not* to feel hostile."

The pain of loss often inspires activism. Mothers have lobbied tire-lessly for laws preventing drunk driving; others struggle for legislation to reduce gun violence; gay rights activists devote themselves to halting hate crimes. Such dedication to change can be a vital and empowering part of healing. But Justin's unprocessed anger had aborted the process of mourning. His anger might have given him some feeling of meaning or purpose, but instead he remained a victim, at war with God and life, unable to truly heal.

THE SECOND ARROW: SELF-BLAME

After suffering great loss, one of the ways we inflict self-pain is by dwell-ing on personal failure. We focus on how we failed others: "I should have been with her when she took her last breath"; or "During those last months I was so busy, I really didn't show up with presence." Or we obsess about our responsibility for our failed marriage, lost job, poor health, or uncontrolled, difficult emotions—adding the second arrow of self-blame to our hurt.

What would make us do this? *We are using self-blame as a way of taking control of our situation.* Loss exposes our essential powerlessness, and we will do whatever is possible to subdue the primal fear that comes with feeling out of control. Much of our daily activity is a vigilant effort to stay on top of things—to feel prepared and to avoid trouble. When this fails, our next line of defense is to whip ourselves into shape: Maybe if we can change, we think, we can protect ourselves from more suffering. Sadly, going to war with ourselves only compounds our pain.

My illness teaches me this over and over. As soon as I realize that I've hurt my knees or back yet again—walking up a steep hill, picking up a heavy bag—a judgment pops up: "I should have known better," "When will I learn not to push so hard?" I can swing the other way when I feel weak and sick: I blame myself for not putting enough time and energy into getting fit.

During a family vacation on Cape Cod, I thought I had found a great way to get the endorphins flowing: speed walking on the beach. I was wrong. By the time I got back to Virginia I was unable to walk upstairs and had an inflammation through my whole body. The sickness dragged on for weeks and my mood tanked. Jonathan had to take care of me and I was a terrible patient—depressed, self-absorbed, and chronically irritated.

One morning I had a pivotal meditation. I asked myself a question I often find helpful: "What is between me and feeling present?" At first, my awareness settled on the familiar heat and ache and queasiness in my body. Next I felt a wave of anger and frustration—here I was day after day, confined and sick. A voice in my head said, "I hate putting up with this . . . I hate my life." Then in the next instance, the voice said scathingly, "I hate myself."

I hadn't heard that voice of self-hatred for a long time, and it opened my eyes. I began to investigate; who exactly was I hating? I hated the self who was full of self-pity, the self who was humiliated by needing help, the self who was so humorless and grim. But worst, it was the self who was spending so much time just thinking about herself—who was selfish and self-centered.

The self-hate unleashed a flood of desperation. I heard myself repeating, "I can't do this any better. I can't do this any better . . ." It was as if the part of me that was supposed to "do it right" was pleading for understanding. I had tried and tried, but when I felt sick, I couldn't make myself into a nicer, less self-centered person. My heart softened and a wave of sorrow swept through me. By turning on myself, I had cut myself off from my loved ones and I was separated from my own heart. "Please," I prayed, "may I hold myself kindly as I go through this sickness."

THE STRUGGLE TO BE GOOD

From earliest childhood, most of us learn that being good is the way to get approval and love. And so we fall back on this lesson in the face of loss. If we are good, maybe we won't be punished; if we are good, maybe we can win back the love or safety we've lost; if we are good, maybe someone will take care of us.

And so we start bargaining with God or with fate. We promise to give up bad foods, to exercise, to be generous with others, to pray regularly. "I'll never again lash out angrily at anyone, if only you'll protect me from another heart attack." "I'll stop drinking for good, if only you'll bring her back to me." And even if none of this works, even in the face of death, we may strive to be seen (by ourselves as well as others) as good, heroic, or enlightened.

You might wonder why this is a false refuge. Is it so bad to try to improve ourselves, or to want others to think well of us? Is it even bad to want to feel good about ourselves? The problem is that in managing life, we aren't living it fully. By expending all our energy on meeting our "good person" standards, we risk missing out on the comfort and intimacy we might have shared.

Julia was a dear friend in our meditation community. When she discovered that her breast cancer had returned, she resolved to bring her spiritual practice to whatever might unfold, and she and I agreed to regular meetings as a way of supporting her through her treatment. Although she took a leave of absence from her social work job, Julia insisted on continuing to volunteer for our community. I remember seeing her one afternoon, leaning against a wall, her bald head covered with a brightly colored scarf. She was giving warm encouragement to one of our newer members. During a break I asked her if it was a good idea for her to be using her energy in this way. "I feel better about myself when I'm helping," she told me. Then with a smile, "God knows, I need a break from thinking about *moi*." Only later did Julia admit that she had arrived home "exhausted beyond words."

Julia lived near the hospital and often walked to her chemo treatments, refusing company or rides. Her friends were concerned about her stubborn independence, her determination not to rely on others. "Her cancer's metastasized, she probably won't get better. When is she going to let us help?" one person wondered.

Julia and I met soon afterward, and she confided, "When I'm hurting, I want everyone to go away so I can just handle it myself."

"How is that for you," I asked, "spending time by yourself in great pain?"

"Well," she said slowly, "I don't want anyone around but . . . as the hours go by, I end up feeling horribly alone. I have this image of the world . . . everything I can imagine . . . receding into a distant blur. And me, locked in a cancerous body."

"What would happen," I asked, "if at those times someone was with you?"

Julia sat silently for a minute. "I don't see why anyone would want to be around me," she said quietly. "It's hard to admit, even to you, but . . . my world has gotten pretty small. Sometimes I'm just trying to sip water without retching. There's not much mindfulness. Mostly I'm feeling sorry for myself and grimly trying to make it through."

She stopped talking, sank back tiredly on the couch, and gazed down at the floor.

"Julia, I'm glad you're telling me," I said. "I want to know what's happening. I want to be in this with you as well as I can."

She took a deep breath and looked at me. "My friends want to see the brave, positive Julia, the spiritual Julia. . . . not the one who feels beaten down . . . who's not sure if there is a reason to keep on living." She paused again and gave me a weary look. "There are times when any trust I ever had—in meditating, in the spiritual path—is gone. I'm just scared and lonely. That's not what I want others to see. That's not how I want to be."

FACE-TO-FACE WITH THE CONTROLLER

At the same time that Julia was struggling with her illness, another friend who was undergoing chemotherapy wrote to me: "I'm discovering that cancer—and perhaps its treatment even more—is a continual stripping away of each part of you that you valued, piece by piece, each part of who you thought you were. Yesterday it was shaving off what remained of my hair. It's an accelerated course in letting go, in humility and humiliation."

Getting sick, getting closer to death, can unravel our identity as a good person, a worthy person, a dignified person, a spiritual person. It also puts us face-to-face with the core identity of the space-suit self that I call "the controller." The controller is the ego's executive director, the self that we believe is responsible for making decisions and directing the course of our lives. It obsessively plans and worries, trying to make things safe and okay, and it can give us at least a temporary sense of self-efficacy and self-trust. But great loss unseats the controller. We couldn't change ourselves (or our partner) enough to keep the marriage together. We couldn't protect our father from feeling the loss of dignity in his illness. We couldn't prevent our daughter from becoming anorexic, our adult son from losing custody of his children. We couldn't make our boss value us enough to keep our job. Or, like Julia, we couldn't go through the darkest phases of our illness and sustain our faith.

When the fabric of our self-protection tears open, we are intensely fragile and vulnerable. Sometimes we scramble to resurrect the controller—getting busy, blaming others, blaming ourselves, trying to fix things. But if we are willing to let there be a gap, if we can live in presence without controlling, healing becomes possible.

DEEPENING SURRENDER

My controller can hold loss at bay for months at a time. If I can keep doing things—teaching, serving our community, counseling others— the ground stays firm under my feet. But some years ago, right before our winter meditation retreat, my body crashed. I landed in the hospital, unable to teach, or for that matter to read, walk around, or go to the bathroom without trailing an IV.

I remember lying on the hospital bed that first night, unable to sleep. At around 3 A.M., an elderly nurse came in to take my vitals and look at my chart. Seeing me watching her, she leaned over and patted me gently on the shoulder. "Oh dear," she whispered kindly, "you're feeling poorly, aren't you?"

As she walked out tears started streaming down my face. Kind-ness had opened the door to how vulnerable I felt. How much worse would it get? What if I wasn't well enough to teach? Should I get off our meditation community's board? Would I even be able to sit in front of a computer to write? There was nothing about the future I could count on.

Then a verse from Rumi came to mind:

Forget the future . . .
I'd worship someone who could do that . . .
If you can say "There's nothing ahead," there will be nothing there.
The cure for the pain is in the pain.

I began to reflect on this, repeating, "There's nothing ahead, there's nothing ahead." All my ideas about the future receded. In their place was the squeeze of raw fear, the clutching in my heart I had been running from. As I allowed the fear—attended to it, breathed with it—I could feel a deep, cutting grief. "Just be here," I told myself. "Open to *this*." The pain was tugging, tearing at my heart. I sobbed silently (not wanting to disturb my roommate), wracked by surge after surge of grief. The house was burning and this human self was face-to-face with its fragility, its temporariness, with the inevitability of loss.

Yet as my crying subsided, a sense of relief set in. It wasn't quite peace—I was still afraid of being sick and sidelined from life—but the burden of being the controller, of thinking I could manage the future or fight against loss, was gone for the moment. It was clear that my life was out of my hands.

Those six days in the hospital were a humbling lesson in surrender. A pulse that wouldn't go above forty-five; doctors who couldn't figure out what was wrong; food I couldn't eat; release date extended. Yet what was most amazing to watch was how the controller struggled to remain in charge.

On the third day I was walking around the perimeter of the cardiac unit, jarred by how weak I felt, how uncertain about my future. Then, for the ten thousandth time, my mind lurched forward, anticipating how I might reconfigure my life, what I'd have to cancel, how I could manage this deteriorating body. When I saw that the controller was back in action I returned to my room and wearily collapsed on the raised hospital bed. As I lay there, the circling thoughts collapsed too, and I sank below the surface, into pain.

Tibetan teacher Chögyam Trungpa taught that the essence of a liberating spiritual practice is to "meet our edge and soften." My edge was right here: the acute loneliness, the despair about the future, the grip of fear. I knew I needed to soften, to open. I tried to keep my attention on where the pain was most acute, but the controller was still there, holding back. It was as if I'd fallen into a black hole of grief and died. Gently, tentatively, I started encouraging myself to feel what was there and soften. The more painful the edge of grief was, the more tender my inner voice became. At some point I placed my hand on my heart and said, "Sweetheart, just soften . . . let go, it's okay." And as I dropped into that aching hole of grief, I entered a space filled with the tenderness of pure love. It surrounded me, held me, suffused my being. Meeting my edge and softening was a dying into timeless loving presence.

In some ways, the hospital was a great place to practice. So little control, so many hours alone, so many rounds of vulnerability. In the remaining days, I repeated to myself again and again: "Sweetheart, just soften." Whenever I recognized that I had tightened in anxious planning and worry, I noted it as "my edge." Then I'd invite myself to soften. I found that kindness made all the difference. When I returned home, the stories and fears about the future were still there. The controller would come and go. But I had deeper trust that I could meet my life with an open and present heart.

UNGRIEVED LOSS

If you have grieved deeply, you know about surrender. Such grieving is healthy, cleansing, and intelligent. It allows us to metabolize the pain of loss and continue living. It lets us open to love. Yet for many people, the controller does not vacate its post sufficiently for full grieving to unfold. And so we may carry a hidden grief for years. The premature loss of childhood, the sexual abuse, the parent lost to divorce, the years lost to addiction, the passing of a close friend—any of these may be still there, sealed away in our body and mind.

There's a price to ungrieved loss: It prevents us from fully engaging with the life we love. The result may be a kind of numbness; we may find ourselves untouched by beauty or by the dearness of others; we may react to events in a mechanical or anxious or angry way. When the next great loss comes along, as it inevitably does, our compulsion to false refuges spikes; we intuit the lurking ocean of grief and resist being swept away. But these fresh losses also present us with a precious opportunity.

A few months after Justin and I had our first phone consultation, his seventy-five-year-old mother had a stroke. His voice filled with agitation as he told me about the wall he had hit when he tried to communicate with her insurance company. They couldn't seem to understand that her recovery depended on more-comprehensive rehab. "There's nothing I can do to reach this goddamned, heartless bureaucracy . . . nothing . . . nothing!"

Justin was once again living in the shadow of loss, and gripped in reactivity. We both agreed that this was an opportunity to bring the mindfulness of RAIN to his immediate experience. He began by quickly identifying what he called "pure, righteous anger" and then pausing, allowing it to be there. Then, after several rounds of investigation, he came upon something else.

"My chest. It's like there is a gripping there, like a big claw that's just frozen in place. And I'm afraid."

"Afraid of what?" I asked gently.

After a long pause, Justin spoke in a low voice. "She'll probably come through this fine, but a part of me is afraid I'm going to lose her too."

We stayed on the phone together as Justin breathed with his fear, feeling its frozen grip on his chest. Then he asked if he could call me back later in the week. "This is a deep pain," he said. "I need to spend time with it."

"Something cracked open, Tara," he told me a few days later. "Being worried about my mom is all mixed up with Donna dying. It's like Donna just died yesterday and I'm all broken up. Something in me is dying all over again . . ." Justin had to wait a few moments before continuing. "I wasn't done grieving. I never let myself feel how part of me died with her." He could barely get out the words, and then he began weeping deeply.

Whenever the controller gets unseated, there's an opening to be with what is. My controller was out of a job when I landed in the hospital. Now Justin's was decommissioned, and this time he was willing to be with the loss he'd never fully grieved. Instead of rushing into a new cause, he spent the next couple of months focused on caring for his mom. He also spent hours alone shooting hoops or hitting tennis balls against a wall. Sometimes he'd walk into his empty house and feel like he had just lost Donna all over again. It was that raw.

But grief has its own timing. As Irish poet and philosopher John O'Donohue tells us:

> All you can depend on now is that
> Sorrow will remain faithful to itself.
> More than you, it knows its way
> And will find the right time
> To pull and pull the rope of grief
> Until that coiled hill of tears
> Has reduced to its last drop.

Justin had opened to the presence that could release his hill of tears. Six months later, during our last consultation, he told me that he was back in action. "I'm in the thick of diversity work again, and probably more effective. Makes sense . . . According to my sister, I'm no longer at war with the world."

Grieving loss consciously is at the center of the spiritual path. In small and great ways, each of our losses links us to what we love. It is natural that we will seek to manage the pain of separation in whatever way we can. Yet as we awaken, we can allow our sorrow to remain faithful to itself. We can willingly surrender into the grieving. By honoring what has passed away, we are free to love the life that is here.

"PLEASE LOVE ME"

Indian teacher Sri Nisargadatta writes, "The mind creates the abyss. The heart crosses over it." Sometimes the abyss of fear and isolation is so wide that we hold back, unable to enter the sanctuary of presence, frozen in our pain. At such times, we need a taste of love from somewhere in order to begin the thaw.

This was true for our community member Julia as her cancer treatments continued. She was uncomplaining about her fatigue and pain, but as her friend Anna commented, "It feels like she's barely there." And despite her determination to "just handle it myself," she was increasingly dependent. Her friends organized themselves to bring her food, and one evening when Anna came with some soup, she found Julia curled up in bed facing the wall. Julia thanked Anna weakly, told her she felt queasy, and asked her to leave the soup on the stove. She heard the door click, and she drifted off for a while. When she woke, she felt the familiar utter aloneness, the sense that she was locked in a dying body. She began crying softly, and then to her surprise she felt a gentle hand on her shoulder. Anna had shut the door, but rather than leaving had been sitting quietly by her side. Now the crying turned into deep sobs. "Go ahead, dear, just let it happen . . . it's okay," Anna whispered. Over and over, she told her, "It's okay, we're here together" as Julia gave in to the agony of held-back fear and grief.

After about twenty minutes, with interludes for tissues and water, Julia quieted. She was still a bit nauseated and felt weak from crying. But for the first time in as long as she could remember, she was profoundly at ease.

"Some shield I had put up between me and the world dissolved," Julia told me the following week. "Even after Anna left, I could feel her care. The aloneness was gone." But then, she went on, several days later the shield hardened again. She had an appointment with her oncologist, and he told her that the cancer had spread. "I guess I feel most isolated when I get scared."

"Is the shield up now?" I asked. "Do you feel scared and isolated?" She nodded. "It's not too intense because we're together. But there's a place inside that feels so afraid . . ."

"You might take some moments and pay attention to that place." Julia sat back on the couch and closed her eyes. "Can you sense what that place in you most needs?"

Julia was quiet for what felt to be a long time. "It wants love. Not just my love, though . . . it wants others to care. It's saying 'Please love me.'"

"Julia, see if you can let that wanting, that longing for love, be as big as it wants to be. Just give it permission, and feel it from the inside out." She nodded and sat quietly, eyebrows drawn, intent.

"Sense who you most want to feel love from . . . and when someone comes to mind, visualize that person right here and ask . . . say the words, 'Please love me.' You might then imagine what it would be like to receive love, just the way you want it."

Julia nodded again and was very still. After a minute or two she whispered a barely audible, "Please love me," and then again a little louder. Tears appeared at the corners of her eyes. I encouraged her to keep going for as long as she wanted—visualizing anyone who came to mind as a possible source of love, saying "Please love me." I also suggested she imagine opening and allowing herself to receive the love. She continued and soon was weeping as she said the words. Gradually her crying subsided, and she was just whispering. Then there were deep spaces of silence between her words. Her face had softened and flushed slightly, and she had a slight smile.

When she opened her eyes, they were shining. "I feel blessed," she told me. "My life is entirely held in love."

We met for the last time three weeks before Julia's death. Anna had taken her to a park early that morning before anyone was around. They put down a blanket to meditate on, and Julia was able to make herself comfortable, leaning against a tree. "I don't know how much more time I'll have," she told me, "so while we were quiet I did an inner ritual. I felt this precious life that I love and that I'm leaving—my friends, the whole meditation community, you . . . swing dancing, singing, the ocean . . . oh, so much beauty, the trees . . ." Tears welled up and Julia paused, feeling the grief as she spoke. Then she went on: "I could feel the solidity of the big oak that was supporting me and sense its presence. I started praying . . . I said, 'Please love me.' Immediately love was here. It flooded me, this knowing of being related, of being the same aliveness, the same one consciousness. Then the grasses and bushes, the birds, the earth and clouds . . . Anna, anyone I thought of . . . each being was loving me and we were united in that consciousness. I *was* love, I was a part of everything." Julia was quiet for a while. Then she said slowly, "Do you know what I'm finding, Tara? When you accept that you are dying . . . and you turn toward love, it's not hard to feel one with God."

We sat silently, savoring each other's company. Then our conversation meandered; we talked about dogs (she loved my poodle and insisted the dog be with us when we met) and wigs and wigs on dogs getting chemo and an upcoming retreat. We were lighthearted and deeply comfortable. We hugged several times before she left. Julia's realization of oneness was embodied as a generous, deeply sweet love. In sharing her wisdom and in expressing that love, she gave me her parting gift.

SEEING PAST THE VEILS

In the Lakota/Sioux tradition, a person who is grieving is considered most *wakan*, most holy. There's a sense that when someone is struck by the sudden lightning of loss, he or she stands on the threshold of the spirit world. The prayers of those who grieve are considered especially strong, and it is proper to ask them for their help.

You might recall what it's like to be with someone who has grieved deeply. The person has no layer of protection, nothing left to defend. The mystery is looking out through that person's eyes. For the time being, he or she has accepted the reality of loss and has stopped clinging to the past or grasping at the future. In the groundless openness of sorrow, there is a wholeness of presence and a deep natural wisdom.

Thich Nhat Hanh expresses this wisdom in a way that has touched me deeply. He experienced his mother's death as one of the great misfortunes of his life. He had grieved for her for more than a year when she appeared to him in a dream. In it, they were having a wonderful talk, and she was young and beautiful. He woke up in the middle of the night and had the distinct impression that he had never lost his mother. She was alive in him.

When he stepped outside his monastery hut and began walking among the tea plants, he still felt her presence by his side. As he says so beautifully, "She was the moonlight caressing me as she had done so often, very tender, very sweet." Continuing to walk, he sensed that his body was a living continuation of all his ancestors, and that together, he and his mother were "leaving footprints in the damp soil."

In my understanding, his year of grieving, of experiencing this great human loss directly, allowed him to find refuge in a timeless loving. We each must surrender into the river of personal loss to discover that which is eternal, that which can never be taken away. As Thich Nhat Hanh expressed this truth, "All I had to do was look at the palm of my hand, feel the breeze on my face or the earth under my feet to remember that my mother is always with me, available at any time."

Whether grieving the loss of our own life, or another's, we each have the capacity to see past the veils of separation. If our hearts are willing, grieving becomes the gateway to loving awareness, the entry into our own awakened nature.

> And when the work of grief is done,
> The wound of loss will heal
> And you will have learned
> To wean your eyes
> From that gap in the air
> And be able to enter the hearth
> In your soul where your loved one
> Has awaited your return
> All the time.

> —JOHN O'DONOHUE

Guided Reflection: Prayer in the Face of Difficulty

Prayer expresses the longing of your heart. When offered with presence and sincerity, it can reveal the source of what you long for—the loving essence of who you are. The following guidelines and reflections are offered as a support in awakening the vitality, depth, and healing power of your prayer.

You may already spontaneously pray at times of great need and distress. Without naming it as prayer, you might say something like, "Oh please, oh please"; and call out for relief of pain, for someone to take care of you, for help for a loved one, for a way to avoid great loss.

If so, begin to investigate your experience. What is the immediate feeling that gives rise to your prayer? What are you praying for? Whom or what are you praying to? Becoming more aware of how you pray spontaneously will open you to a more intentional practice. You might consider prayer as an ongoing experiment, drawing on the guidelines below.

Posture for Prayer:
If you bring your palms together at your heart, do you feel connected with your sincerity and openness? What happens if you close your eyes? If you bow your head? Find out whether these traditional supports for prayer serve you, and if they don't, explore what other positions or gestures are most conducive to openheartedness.

Arriving:
Even when you are in the thick of very strong emotion, it is possible and valuable to pause and establish a sense of prayerful presence. After you have assumed whatever posture most suits you, come into stillness. Take a few long and full breaths to collect your attention. Then as your breath resumes its natural rhythm, take some moments to relax any obvious tension in your body. Feel yourself here, now, with the intention to pray.

Listening:
The strength and purity of your prayer emerges from fully contacting your felt experience. Bring a listening attention to your heart and to whatever in your life feels most

difficult right now. It might be a recent or impending loss or a situation that summons hurt, confusion, doubt, or fear. As if watching a movie, focus on the frame of the film that is most emotionally painful. Be aware of the felt sense in your body—in your throat, chest, belly, and elsewhere. Where are your feelings the strongest? Take your time, allowing yourself to fully contact your vulnerability and pain.

Imagine you could inhabit the most vulnerable place within you, feeling it intimately from the inside. If it could express itself, what would it communicate? Buried inside the pain, what does this part of you want or need most? Is it to be seen and understood? Loved? Accepted? Safe? Is your longing directed toward a certain person or spiritual figure? Do you long to be held by your mother? Recognized and approved of by your father? Healed or protected by God? Whatever the need, let yourself listen to it, feel it, and open to its intensity.

Expressing Your Prayer:

With a silent or whispered prayer, call out for the love, understanding, protection, or acceptance you long for. You might find yourself saying, "Please may I be better, kinder, and more worthy." Or you might direct your prayer to another person or being: "Daddy, please don't leave me." "Mommy, please help me." "God, take care of my daughter, please, please, let her be okay." You might feel separate from someone and call out his or her name, saying, "Please love me, please love me." You might long for your heart to awaken and call out to the bodhisattva of compassion (Kwan-yin), "Please, may this heart open and be free."

Your prayer will continue to deepen if, as you express it in words, you stay in direct contact with your vulnerability and felt sense of longing. Say your prayer several times with all the sincerity of your heart. Find out what happens if you give yourself totally to feeling and expressing your longing.

Embodying Prayer:

Often our particular want or longing isn't the full expression of what we actually desire. Similarly, the object of our longing, the person we call on for love or protection, may not offer what we truly need. Rather these are portals to a deeper experience, an opening to a deeper source.

As you feel your wants and longing, ask yourself, "What is the experience I yearn for? If I got what I wanted, what would it feel like?"

Use your imagination to find out. If you want a particular person to love you, visualize that person hugging you and looking at you with unconditional love. Then let go of any image of that person and feel inwardly that you are being bathed in love. If you want to feel safe, imagine that you are entirely surrounded by a protective presence. Then feel that peace and ease filling your every cell. Whatever you are longing for, explore what it would be like to experience its pure essence as a felt sense in your body, heart, and mind. Finally, discover what happens when you surrender into this experience, when you become the love or peace that you are longing for.

Throughout the Day:

Your formal exploration of prayer creates the grounds for weaving shorter prayers into your life. Remembering to pray in the midst of daily activities will help you become aligned with the kindness and wisdom of your heart.

- At the beginning of the day, set your intention: What situations, emotions, or reactions might be a signal to pray?

- Before praying, take a moment to pause, breathe, and relax. While it is helpful to become still, there is no need to assume a particular posture.

- Pay attention to your body and heart, contacting the felt sense of your emotions. What are you most longing for? What most matters in this moment, and in your life, to open to—to feel and trust?

- Mentally whisper your prayer. The words might come spontaneously, or you might express a prayer you have already discovered that is alive and meaningful to you.

> Ask the friend for love
> Ask him again
> For I have found that every heart
> Will get what it prays for most.

> —HAFIZ

PART IV

THE GATEWAY OF
AWARENESS

FOURTEEN

REFUGE IN AWARENESS

To be intimate is to feel the silence, the space that everything is happening in.

ADYASHANTI

Wisdom tells me I am nothing. Love tells me I am everything.
Between the two my life flows.

SRI NISARGADATTA

Writing and speaking about the nature of awareness is a humbling process; as the third Zen patriarch said, "Words! The way is beyond language." Whatever words are used, whatever thoughts they evoke, that's not it! Just as we can't see our own eyes, we can't see awareness. *What we are looking for is what is looking.* Awareness is not another object or concept that our mind can grasp. We can only *be* awareness.

A friend who is a Unitarian minister told me about an interfaith gathering that she attended. It opened with an inquiry: What is our agreed-upon language for referring to the divine? Shall we call it God?

"No way," responded a feminist Wiccan. "What about Goddess?"

"Ha," remarked a Baptist minister. "Spirit?"

"Nope," declared an atheist.

Discussion went on for a while. Finally a Native American suggested "the great mystery" and they all agreed. Each knew that whatever his or her personal understanding, the sacred was in essence a mystery.

Awareness, true nature, what we are—is a mystery. We encounter the same wordless mystery when someone dies. After his mother passed away, Jonathan looked at me and said, "Where did she go?" I remember sitting with my father as he was dying—he was there, and then he wasn't. His spirit, that animating consciousness, was no longer present in his body. Nothing in this world of experience is more jarring to our view. It takes away all our conceptual props. We can't understand with our minds what has occurred. Love is the same way. We talk endlessly about love, but when we bring to mind someone we love and really investigate "What *is* this love?", we drop into the mystery. What is this existence itself, with all its particularity, its strange life forms, its beauty, its cruelty? We can't understand. When we ask "Who am I?" or "Who is aware?" and really pause to examine, we can't find an answer.

Tibetan teacher Sogyal Rinpoche writes,

> If everything . . . changes, then what is really true? Is there something behind the appearances, something boundless and infinitely spacious, in which the dance of change and impermanence takes place? Is there something in fact we can depend on, that does survive what we call death?

This inquiry turns us toward the timeless refuge of pure awareness. When we ask ourselves, "Is awareness here?" most of us probably pause, sense the presence of awareness, and say yes. Yet every day we restlessly pull away from this open awareness and immerse ourselves in busyness and planning. Our conditioning prevents us from discovering the peace and happiness that are intrinsic in taking refuge in awareness. Seeing how we paper over the mystery of who we are is an essential part of finding freedom.

THROUGH THE REDUCING VALVE

In *The Doors of Perception*, Aldous Huxley called awareness "Mind at Large." He reminds us:

> Each one of us is potentially Mind at Large. But in so far as we are animals, our business is at all costs to survive. To make bio-

logical survival possible, Mind at Large has to be funneled through the reducing valve of the brain and nervous system. What comes out at the other end is a measly trickle of the kind of consciousness which will help us to stay alive on the surface of this Particular planet.

Our brain's primary function is to block out too much information, and to select and organize the information that will allow us to thrive. The more stress we feel, the smaller the aperture of our attention. If we're hungry, we obsess about food. If we're threatened, we fixate on defending ourselves or striking first to remove the threat. Our narrowly focused attention is the key navigational instrument of the ego-identified self.

I saw a cartoon once in which a guy at a bar is telling the bartender: "I'm nothing, yet I'm all I can think about." If you reflect on how often you are moving through your day trying to "figure something out," you'll get a sense of how the reducing valve is shaping your experience. And if you notice how many thoughts are about yourself, you'll see how the valve creates a completely self-centered universe. It's true for all of us!

This incessant spinning of thoughts continually resurrects our space-suit identity. Our stories keep reminding us that we need to improve our circumstances, get more security or pleasure, avoid mistakes and trouble. Even when there are no real problems, we have the sense that we should be doing something different from whatever we are doing in the moment. "Why are you unhappy?" asks writer Wei Wu Wei. "Because 99.9% of everything you do is for yourself . . . and there isn't one."

While we might grasp this conceptually, the self-sense can seem very gritty and real. Even single-cell creatures have a rudimentary sense of "self in here, world out there." As Huxley acknowledges, developing a functional self was basic to evolution on our particular planet. But this does not mean the space-suit self marks the end of our evolutionary journey. We have the capacity to realize our true belonging to something infinitely larger.

If we fail to wake up to who we are beyond the story of self, our system will register a "stuckness." It's a developmental arrest that shows up as dissatisfaction, endless stress, loneliness, fear, and joylessness. This emotional pain is not a sign that we need to discard our functional self. It is a sign that the timeless dimension of our being is awaiting realization. As executive coach and author Stephen Josephs teaches, "We can still function as an apparent separate entity, while enjoying the parallel reality of our infinite vast presence. We need both realms. When the cop pulls us over we still need to show him our license, not simply point to the sky."

Most of us are too quick to reach for our license. If our sense of identity is bound to the egoic self, we will spend our lives tensing against the certainty of loss and death. We will not be able to open fully to the aliveness and love that are here in the present moment. Sri Nisargadatta writes,

> As long as you imagine yourself to be something tangible and solid, a thing among things, you seem short-lived and vulnerable, and of course you will feel anxious to survive. But when you know yourself to be beyond space and time you will be afraid no longer.

A brief reflection: Imagine you are looking through a photo album of your life. There you are in kindergarten, in senior year of high school, when you started your first job, fell in love, had your first child (if you have one). There are photos celebrating your achievements, but perhaps there are also photos of times of great insecurity and loss. Then you look in the mirror. Who are you? Consider how your body has changed, your worldview, your sense of what is important in life, your pleasures, your moods. Now ask yourself, in every time and place, through all these years and moments, what about me has been unchanging? What has always been here?

Can you sense that there has always been, and is right now, a consciousness, a presence that knows, a space of awareness that perceives what's happening? If we can begin to realize this mystery within our own existence, our relationship to this changing world shifts. We can hold the personal sense of self more lightly. We don't react so strongly to things not going our way.

Again, the words of Sri Nisargadatta:

The real world is beyond our thoughts and ideas; we see it through the net of our desires divided into pleasure and pain, right and wrong, inner and outer. To see the universe as it is, you must step beyond the net. It is not hard to do so, *for the net is full of holes.*

TRUSTING WHO WE ARE

When I first joined the Boston ashram at age twenty-two, I assumed that it would take me about eight years of dedicated effort to realize freedom beyond the net. Stories of spiritual seekers like the Buddha caught my imagination. They had experienced a sudden, distinctive moment of awakening—a liberating moment of realizing their true nature as changeless, luminous awareness. This awakening was irreversible, they were no longer bound by the identity of self. Afterward, their hearts were wide open, their minds clear and free.

While I've been eagerly drawn to "liberated forever after," this has not been my path. Awakening has been gradual, and the trance of self can still feel sticky and painful. Since I'm public about my foibles, students are often curious about what has changed over the decades. The difference between now and some years back is this: I trust awareness— and the felt experience of living, loving presence—as the most familiar and real and true sense of what I am. Even when I'm most miserable, that trust, the sense of loving presence as refuge, is still in the background, guiding me home.

Some years ago I became increasingly aware of getting caught in a mindset I named "special person." Feelings of self-importance and specialness had been with me for as long as I could remember. The oldest child of four, I was used to being the boss, being the one who deserved the largest portion and the most attention. As I shared in *Radical Acceptance*, I knew the flip side of "special person" intimately—the sense of being flawed and inadequate. But with my growing role as spiritual teacher and guide, I found myself periodically caught in a form of self-inflation that caused suffering. Whenever I assumed I was in some way better than others—wiser, more spiritually evolved, smarter—I was creating separation. Not only from those I was with, but from my own heart.

I wanted to get rid of "special person." When I noticed I was in "busy mode," assuming that others would accommodate me, I'd mentally whisper "special person" and mindfully pause. When students would compliment me or I'd get flattering e-mails, I'd pause, sense the swelling of pride, and deepen my attention. "This isn't about 'me,'" I'd remind myself. "No need to take this personally." When I caught myself about to ask Jonathan if he could go to the post office because I had too many important things to do, I'd keep quiet. But often I didn't notice special person until after the fact. I'd come home from teaching a day-long workshop and then wonder how much of the time I'd been caught in a role that separated me from full presence and connectedness.

One Sunday evening I sat down to meditate and immediately started reviewing the lineup of the coming week's activities. Then, as I quieted, an image appeared in my mind. It was radiant light all around me, beckoning. But I was caught inside a sticky bubble—special person. I wanted to release the bubble, pop out of it, merge with the light of awareness that felt so close. But the cherished experience of oneness felt painfully out of reach: my space-suit self was too constricting, too entrenched. "What else can I do?" said a despairing voice in my mind. "I'm trying as hard as I can to wake up from this. I don't know what else I can do."

A wave of understanding swept through me. This was so familiar. Of course "I" can't do this—a self can't undo itself, a self can't free itself. And the self isn't a problem. How many times had I struggled and struggled to be different, feeling myself to be flawed, only to realize the answer was to stop struggling? It didn't matter whether the self felt inflated or deflated, the pain was in being at war. A gentle voice inside me said, "Stop. Just stop."

I wanted to, I knew the wisdom of letting go. But my body was holding on, distressed, wanting things to be different, afraid something was wrong. Again I heard the voice. "Sweetheart, please, stop." And once again, as I had experienced so many times, the presence of lovingkindness allowed me to open to truth. I found myself bowing my head and cupping my hands in a gesture of prayer. In some way I was offering the

whole tight sense of a controlling self into loving awareness. I wasn't trying to get rid of anything. I was simply acknowledging that all this belonged to something larger. The struggle stopped. The words in my
mind, the ideas about what was wrong, all dropped away. At that, the
bubble of self dissolved. My world opened into a space of quietness, with
currents of warmth and tenderness moving through. When thoughts
and feelings began popping up, I noticed some hints of special person. "Look what I did, I surrendered and am free of this," and then of
course, "Oh no—she's back!" and then an inner smile. Again, the words
"Stop . . . just stop," followed by bowing my head and letting go. Then
letting go of letting go. When the struggle stopped, a quiet presence
opened up that I knew was home. And with that I had a sense of peace,
of trusting who I really am.

REMEMBERING TO STOP

Most of us are working so hard. It's like we're in a motorboat noisily
zipping around, trying to find a place that is quiet, peaceful, and still.
We're solving a problem, responding to demands, preparing for what's
next, improving ourselves. But we're just making more waves and noise
wherever we go. It counters all our ambitious conditioning, but true
freedom comes when we throttle back the motor and come naturally
into stillness. What we are seeking is not "out there," not an improved
self that just requires more vigilant effort or control. It is the silent
awareness that is always right *here*, discovered in the background of whatever we experience.

The most liberating meditation practice is to stop controlling and to
let things be as they are. When I teach my students this, many of them
are concerned that if they stop actively directing their attention, they'll
spend the entire time in a mental trance. I let them know that there
are many wise practices—quieting the mind by following the breath,
noting what is happening, offering self-compassion, bowing the head in
prayer—that help incline us toward noncontrolling. But if our tendency
is to latch on to these practices, we reinforce the sense of a self who is in
charge of the show. The art is to direct the attention with a light touch,

and then let go of all directing. We can't trust a state of mind that is manipulated into being. Only by truly allowing life to be as it is do we come to realize and trust our natural state of awareness. We need to stop.

Ananda, the Buddha's most devoted disciple, served and accompanied the Buddha for many years. Through all this time, he worked strenuously at becoming enlightened. He practiced meditation, was impeccable in his generosity, wise in speech, good in heart. Yet after the Buddha's death, when a great council of enlightened monks was planned, Ananda was not entitled to attend. While honored as deeply kind and wise, he had not yet attained inner freedom.

On the eve of the council meeting, Ananda vowed to practice vigorously all night and not stop until he attained his goal. But in spite of his heroic efforts, he made no progress. Toward dawn, exhausted and discouraged, he decided to let go of striving and simply relax. In that state, attentive yet with no clinging to attainment, he rested his head on the pillow—and became liberated.

Of course, the recipe for freedom is not simply lying back and resting. It's important to remember that Ananda had devoted decades to serving others and to cultivating a lucid, mindful awareness. He was dedicated to realizing truth. Yet, like many of us, he had hooked his mind and heart to a goal. He had to unhook, to stop "doing" entirely, to realize the freedom of his true nature.

LEARNING TO UNHOOK: TRAINING IN OPEN AWARENESS

Tibetan teacher Chögyam Trungpa once opened a class by drawing a *V* on a large white sheet of poster paper. He then asked those present what he had drawn. Most responded that it was a bird. "No," he told them. "It's the sky with a bird flying through it."

How we pay attention determines our experience. When we are in doing or controlling mode, our attention narrows and we perceive objects in the foreground—the bird, a thought, a strong feeling. In these moments we don't perceive the sky—the background of experience, the ocean of awareness. The good news is that we can intentionally incline our minds toward not controlling and toward an open attention.

My formal introduction to open awareness was through *dzogchen*—a Tibetan Buddhist practice. Until then, I had trained in concentration and mindfulness, always focusing on an object (or changing objects) of attention. In dzogchen, as taught by my teacher Tsoknyi Rinpoche, we repeatedly let go of whatever our attention fixates on and turn toward the awareness that is attending. The invitation is to recognize the skylike quality of the mind—the empty, open wakefulness of awareness—and *be* that.

My first retreat with Tsoknyi Rinpoche loosened my moorings in a wonderful way. The more I became familiar with the presence of awareness, the weaker the foothold was for the feelings and stories that sustained my sense of self. Tensions in my body and mind untangled themselves, and my heart responded tenderly to whoever or whatever came to mind. I left that retreat, and later dzogchen retreats, feeling quite spacious and free.

I recently learned of the work of Les Fehmi, a psychologist and researcher who for decades has been clinically documenting the profound healing that arises from resting in open awareness. In the 1960s researchers began to correlate synchronous alpha brain waves with profound states of well-being, peace, and happiness. Fehmi, an early and groundbreaking leader in this research, sought strategies that might deepen and amplify alpha waves. Experimenting with student volunteers, he tracked their EEG readings as they visualized peaceful landscapes, listened to music, watched colored lights, or inhaled various scents. But it was only after he posed the question "Can you imagine the space between your eyes?" that their alpha wave levels truly soared. He posed another: "Can you imagine the space between your ears?" The subjects' alpha waves spiked again. Further experimentation confirmed the effects of what Fehmi termed "open focused attention." The key was inviting attention to space (or stillness or silence or timelessness) and shifting to a nonobjective focus.

Narrowly focused attention affects our entire body-mind. Whenever we fixate on making plans, on our next meal, on judgments, on a looming deadline, our narrowed focus produces faster (beta) waves in the brain. Our muscles tense, and the stress hormones cortisol and adrenaline are released. While necessary for certain tasks, as an ongoing state this stress constellation keeps us from full health, openheartedness, and mental clarity.

In contrast, open-focused attention rests the brain. With a sustained pause from processing information—from memories, plans, thoughts about self—brain waves slow down into synchronous alpha. Our muscles relax, stress hormone levels are lowered, blood flow is redistributed. No longer in fight-or-flight reactivity, our body and mind become wakeful, sensitive, open, and at ease.

You may have noticed the effect of open awareness when looking at the night sky and sensing its immensity. Or during the silence in the early morning before sunrise. Or when the world is still after a snowfall. We resonate with such moments because they connect us with the most intimate sense of what we are. We sense the depth of our being in the night sky, the mystery of what we are in the silence, the stillness. In these moments of objectless awareness there's a wordless homecoming, a realization of pure being.

EXPLORING INNER SPACE

My awareness of inner space came alive when I took my son, Narayan, to an IMAX film called *Cosmic Voyage*. We were catapulted out into space, first through our solar system and the Milky Way, and then in stages to the outer edges of the observable universe.

To get a sense of scale, light from Andromeda, the galaxy closest to our own, takes 2.4 million years to reach us. When we see it, the light has been rushing toward us at 186,000 miles a second for 2.4 million years. And beyond our galactic neighborhood lie an estimated 80 billion more galaxies, unimaginably far away.

Then the film took us back to earth, and through a drop of water, the cosmic zoom was reversed. We descended through ever diminishing realms to the tiniest known particle, a quark.

We know outer space is vast and mostly empty, but we usually consider our familiar world as more solid. Yet the atoms that make up our own bodies are actually 99.99 percent empty space. The distance between atoms, and the space within atoms, compared with their mass makes us as spacious internally as the universe we live in.

I was struck by the reality that inner space is a microcosmic version of outer space. Since then, I've found that becoming mindful of the body, and then intentionally sensing inner space, collapses our habitual orientations. Self and other, here and there, now and then, all recede. So does inside and outside. As we sense the infinite reaches of the universe and the infinite depth within us, we experience ourselves dissolving into continuous awake space—into a vast undivided awareness.

THE BACKWARD STEP

I've found it helpful to think of existence—the entire play of sounds and thoughts and bodies and trees—as the foreground of life, and awareness as the background. In the Zen tradition, the shift from focusing on the foreground of experience to resting in pure being is called "the backward step." Whenever we step out of thought or emotional reactivity and remember the presence that is here, we are taking the backward step. If we wake from a confining story of who we are and reconnect with our essential awareness, we are taking the backward step. When our attention shifts from a narrow fixation on any object—sound, sensation, thought—and recognizes the awake space that holds everything, we are taking the backward step. We come to this realization when there is nowhere else to step. No anything. We have relaxed back into the immensity and silence of awareness itself.

You might pause for a moment and receive this living world. Let your senses be awake and wide open, taking everything in evenly, allowing life to be just as it is. As you notice the changing sounds and sensations, also notice the undercurrent of awareness—*be conscious of your own presence.* Allow the experience of life to continue to unfold in the foreground as you sense this alert inner stillness in the background. Then simply *be* this space of awareness, this wakeful openness. Can you sense how the experiences of this world continue to play through you, without in any way capturing or confining the inherent spaciousness of awareness? You are the sky with the bird flying through. A short Tibetan teaching evokes this boundless presence:

> Utterly awake, senses wide open.
> Utterly open, nonfixating awareness.

THE THREE QUALITIES OF AWARENESS

When Siddhartha Gautama sat down under the bodhi tree, his resolve was to realize his true nature. Siddhartha had a profound interest in truth. The questions "Who am I?" and "What is reality?" impelled him to look deeply within and shine a light on his own awareness.

As a Zen story reminds us, this kind of inquiry is not an analytic or theoretical exploration. One day a novice asks the abbot of the monastery, "What happens after we die?" The venerable old monk responds, "I don't know." Disappointed, the novice says, "But I thought you were a Zen monk." "I am, but not a dead one!" The most powerful questions direct our attention to this very moment.

To practice self-inquiry, we quiet the mind and ask "Who am I?" or "Who is aware right now?" or "Who is listening?" Then we look gently back into awareness to see what is true. Ultimately, we find that there is no way for the mind to answer these questions—there is no thing to actually see or feel. The point is simply to look, and then let go into the no-thing-ness that is here. The question "Who am I?" is meant to dissolve the sense of a searcher.

But this is not what happens right away. First we find all sorts of things we think we are, all our patterns of emotions and thoughts, our memories, the stories about who we take ourselves to be. Our attention keeps fixating on elements of the foreground. Maybe we have contacted a feeling. But we keep inquiring. "Who is feeling that?" we ask, or "Who is aware of this?" And the more we ask, the less we find to land on. Eventually the questions bring us into silence—there are no more backward steps. We can't answer.

The discovery of no-thing, according to Tibetan Buddhist teachings, is "the supreme seeing." It reveals *the first basic quality of awareness:*

emptiness or openness. Awareness is devoid of any form, of any center or boundary, of any owner or inherent self, of any solidity.

Yet our investigation also reveals that while empty of "thingness," awareness is alive with wakefulness—a luminosity of continual knowing. Rumi puts it this way: "You are gazing at the light with its own ageless eyes." Sounds, shapes and colors, sensations are spontaneously recognized. The entire river of experience is received and known by awareness. This is *the second basic quality of awareness: awakeness or cognizance.*

If we let go and rest in this wakeful openness, we discover how awareness relates to form: When anything comes to mind—a person, situation, emotion—the spontaneous response is warmth or tenderness. This is *the third quality of awareness: the expression of unconditional love or compassion.* Tibetan Buddhists call this the unconfined capacity of awareness, and it includes joy, appreciation, and the many other qualities of heart.

When Siddhartha looked into his own mind, he realized the beauty and goodness of his essential nature and was free. The three fundamental qualities of our being—openness/emptiness, wakefulness, and love—are always here. Much of the path of true refuge is becoming familiar with them and living from them. Gradually we realize that this wakeful, tender awareness is more truly who we are than any story we've been generating about ourselves. *Rather than a human on a spiritual path, we are spirit discovering itself through a human incarnation.* As we come to understand and trust this, our life fills with increasing grace.

BECOMING A CHILD OF WONDER

One of the reflections I most love is drawn from a Tibetan Buddhist teaching that offers a beautiful reassurance. It tells us that the refuge of awareness is:

> Closer than we can imagine.
> More profound than we can imagine.
> Easier than we can imagine.
> More wondrous than we can imagine.

Closer than we can imagine.

What if today, just right now, is all you have? Can you allow yourself to arrive in the center of now and experience the alert inner stillness within you? Can you sense the consciousness that is looking through your eyes, listening to sounds, perceiving sensation? What is it like to recognize that awareness is closer than you can imagine?

More profound than we can imagine.

Ask yourself, "Am I dreaming?" and look to see if your mind is occupied in a story of reality that is veiling the mystery. What happens if you stop for just a moment, step out of your thoughts, and sense the space between and around them? Can you let yourself rest in the space of not-knowing? Can you sense the measureless depth and wakefulness of inner space? What is it like to recognize that awareness is more profound than you can imagine?

Easier than we can imagine.

Sufi poet Hafiz says that we are different from the saints because we still think we have "a thousand serious moves." But just as we fall asleep and get lost in doing, we can fall awake. Invite yourself to be at ease, to give up any planning or attempts to control. Relax your body and mind, and allow everything to happen—sounds, sensations, feelings. Explore what it means to fall back into presence, to truly rest in presence. Can you sense the wakeful openness that is always and already here? What is it like to realize that coming home to awareness is easier than you can imagine?

More wondrous than we can imagine.

Awareness experiences its own essence through the sensitivity of our body, heart, and mind. Can you sense that right now, awareness is perceiving its own dynamism, aliveness, and creativity in your body? Can you sense that it is realizing its capacity for boundless love through your heart? Can you sense that it is awakening to its vastness and luminosity through your mind? What is it like to realize that living with this awakened body, mind, and heart is more wondrous than you can imagine?

———— ∞ ————

When we understand that this mysterious awareness is creating and shining through everything, including ourselves, we become a "child of wonder." We remain wholeheartedly engaged in life. We give ourselves to work and play, to creativity and passion, to our family and friends. We feel emotions, pleasure, and pain. And throughout it all, we remember our timeless nature. This allows us to move through the world with receptivity, awe, and unconditional love.

Until a few years ago, being "a child of wonder" was a beautiful idea, something I aspired to, but had not lived in any ongoing way. Then, in the midst of my illness something shifted, bringing fresh air into my life. In the brief final chapter that follows, I'll try to share this experience of true refuge.

Guided Reflection: Exploring Inner Space

As we move through life we need a flexible attention, one that is capable of a narrow focus on objects or experiences (like images, sensations, or sounds), as well as an open focus that perceives the presence of space. Learning to attend to inner space cultivates this flexibility: We become familiar with the formless, impersonal ground of all experience. Even at times when the lens narrows, we are less inclined to fixate and react with grasping or resisting.

Because most people find it less effective to follow a written meditation, the full audio version of this meditation can be found on my website (see page 291). To get a simple taste you might read the following questions, and after each, close your eyes and reflect for about fifteen seconds. Notice whatever spontaneously arises. There's no need to make an effort—simply be receptive to your experience.

—∞—

Can you imagine the space between your eyes?

Can you imagine the space between your ears?

Can you imagine that the region between your forehead and the back of your skull is filled with space?

Can you imagine that your hands are filled with space?

Can you imagine that your chest is filled with space?

Can you imagine that your belly is filled with space?

Can you imagine that your whole body is filled with space?

Can you imagine that the space inside your body, and the space that extends out infinitely, is continuous?

Can you imagine that this continuous space is wakeful—filled with awareness?

Can you imagine resting in this wakeful, continuous space?

Guided Reflection: Who Am I?

The fundamental question in most spiritual traditions is "Who am I?" The formal practice of self-inquiry is a powerful way of seeing beyond our stories of self and revealing the mystery of our true nature.

Before exploring the following meditation, take some time relaxing and quieting the mind. You might practice "A Pause for Presence" (see page 15) or "Exploring Inner Space," on the previous page. While thoughts and emotions will naturally continue to arise during this meditation, it is best initiated when emotions are not intense.

If you would like to explore practicing with your eyes open, try to find a setting where you can look directly at the open sky or at a view that is not distracting. It is also fine to look out a window, at a blank wall, or at the open space of a room.

———— ∾ ————

Sit comfortably in a way that allows you to feel both alert and relaxed. If your eyes are open, rest your gaze on a point slightly above your line of sight. Soften your eyes so that your gaze is unfocused and you are also receiving images on the periphery of your vision. Relax the flesh around your eyes and let your brow be smooth.

Looking at the sky or imagining a clear blue sky, let your awareness mingle with that boundless space. Allow your mind to be wide open—relaxed and spacious. Take some moments to listen to sounds, noticing how they are happening on their own. Rest in the awareness that includes even the most distant sounds.

In the same way that sounds are appearing and disappearing, allow sensations and emotions to arise and dissolve. Let your breath move easily, like a gentle breeze. Be aware of thoughts drifting through like passing clouds. Rest in an open and undistracted awareness, and with a receptive attention, notice the changing display of sounds, sensations, feelings, thoughts.

As the mind rests in this listening attention, inquire "Who is aware right now?" or "Who is listening?" You might instead ask "What is aware right now?" or "What is listening?" Glance back into awareness with interest and a light touch—simply taking a look to see what is true.

What do you notice? Is there any "thing" or "self" you perceive that is static, solid, or enduring? Is there an entity that exists apart from the changing stream of feelings, sensations, or thoughts? What actually do you see when you look into awareness? Is there any boundary or center to your experience? Are you aware of being aware?

After you have looked back into awareness, let go and relax fully into the sea of wakefulness. Let go and let be, allowing life to unfold naturally in awareness. Rest in nondoing, in undistracted awareness.

Continue to rest in awareness until the mind again focuses on a sound or sensation or some other experience. When you realize your mind has fixated on a particular thought—on a judgment or mental comment, an image or story—gently look into awareness to recognize the source of thinking. Inquire: "Who is thinking?" Or you might ask "What is thinking?" or "Who is aware right now?" Glance back into awareness with a light touch, simply taking a look to see who is thinking.

Then let go and relax fully into whatever you see. Let go and let be, allowing life to unfold naturally in awareness. Rest in nondoing, in undistracted awareness. With each instance of releasing the grip of thoughts, be sure to relax completely. Discover the freedom of wakefully relaxing, of letting life be as it is. Look and see, let go and be free.

If sensations or emotions call your attention, look back into awareness in the same way, asking who is feeling hot or tired or afraid. However, if they are in any way strong or compelling, instead of turning toward awareness, bring an accepting and kind attention directly to the experience. You might feel the grip of fear, for instance, and use the breath to reconnect with openness and tenderness. (See tonglen instructions on page 159.) When you are able to relate to your experience with equanimity and compassion again, resume the practice of resting in awareness and inquiry.

If at any point you find the mind has become distracted, reopen your attention to the senses—listening to sounds, feeling sensations. Then as you settle into mindful presence, continue to inquire into the awareness that is behind all experience.

As you choose, you might weave in a similar practice to active inquiry: Say or think "I am" and add nothing to it. Be aware of the silence and stillness that follows the words. Sense your presence, your pure uncontrived beingness. Let go and be that presence.

❧

It is important that we practice self-inquiry in an easy and effortless way, not contracting the mind by striving to do it right. To avoid creating stress, it is best to limit practice to five- to ten-minute intervals. You might do short periods of formal practice a number of times a day.

As an informal practice take a few moments, whenever you remember, to look into awareness and see what is true. Then let go and let be. In time, the trance of a separate self will become increasingly apparent, and you'll begin to realize the empty radiance of awareness that is your true home.

Guided Reflection: Taking the Backward Step

Our natural awareness is revealed when we stop struggling to control or manipulate our attention. This meditation offers a seeming paradox: We intentionally let go of any purposeful doing. While this itself is a subtle kind of doing, with continued practice, letting go begins to occur spontaneously whenever we recognize the tension of controlling.

Before beginning, you might practice "Exploring Inner Space," or some other meditation that helps you settle, quiet your mind, and relax.

———— ∞ ————

Find a posture that is upright and comfortable and come into stillness. If possible, let go of any seeking, any struggle, any goals. Now allow yourself to enter the receptive state of listening. Listen in all directions, near and far, not fixing on any particular sound, taking everything in evenly. Explore listening not just with your ears, but with your whole awareness—listening to sounds, to sensations, to breathing.

In this receptive state, let life be, just as it is. Check in with your body, and if you find tension, recognize it as a sign of resistance to letting go. Simply note the tension, and allow it to be as it is. If there is restlessness, allow it to be as it is.

Awareness is fluid; it recognizes different experiences without directing or resisting. Imagine yourself as a passenger in a car, aware of experience as it arises and passes, like the view out your window. You are not in control. You have no idea of what should happen, of where you are going. You are just noticing and allowing. You are being *awareness.*

If thoughts arise, simply note "This is just a thought." Let go, return to now, to presence. If you find the mind trying to interpret or direct the meditation, let go. Sometimes mentally whispering "drop" can help the mind release what it's holding on to. Once you have opened out of a thought, take some moments to notice the difference between any thought and the vividness and mystery of the here and now.

You may find that you've let go of thoughts and are focusing on the sounds, feelings, or sensations in the foreground of your experience. Explore what happens when you let go yet again, and sense the background *of experience, your own presence. You can't see or hear or locate this presence, yet you can relax back into this formless dimension of being.*

When you take the backward step and surrender into presence, a silent spaciousness enters awareness. The silence is listening to sounds, to thoughts. A great stillness receives the experience of aliveness. Everything is happening in wakeful openness. Simply rest in this open space of awareness, continuing to allow the sounds and feelings of life to flow through.

As your meditation practice deepens, it is valuable to spend at least part of your practice time letting go of all controlling, relaxing back and resting in an open, allowing awareness.

FIFTEEN

A HEART THAT IS READY
FOR ANYTHING

There is a place in the heart where everything meets.
Go there if you want to find me.
Mind, senses, soul, eternity, all are there.
Are you there?
Enter the bowl of vastness that is the heart.
Give yourself to it with total abandon . . .
Once you know the way
  the nature of attention will call you
  to return, again and again,
  and be saturated with knowing,
"I belong here, I am at home here."

RADIANCE SUTRAS, TRANSLATED BY LORIN ROCHE

My teacher at the retreat was guiding us: "Send chi to the places that are in pain." I visualized flowing streams of light bathing my hurting knees. He continued: "Imagine what these parts of you would be like if they were totally vital and strong, energetically flowing with the rest of your body."

This was not a Buddhist practice. I was doing a ten-day qigong healing retreat, based on a Chinese system of still and moving meditation. At the heart of qigong is the understanding that this world is made of *chi*, an invisible field of energy, the dynamic expression of pure awareness.

For years I had heard that qigong was an ideal meditation for physical healing. When I first experimented with the practices, I found they helped me feel more embodied and energetically attuned. Then, after my health took a downturn I decided to explore qigong more deeply. But by the third day of the retreat, I'd run into doubts. Some of the instructions seemed distinctly "un-Buddhist"! Here I was trying to manipulate my experience and create a happy, healthy body. Whatever happened to letting go of control and accepting life as it is? Wouldn't all this directing of energy and visualization just make me more attached to being healthy? Given the realities of my illness, this seemed like a losing proposition.

Still, I had paid my tuition and I kept on following the teachers' instructions. The next morning I got up before dawn and did the practice on my own—connecting to the ocean of chi, bringing attention and energy to various parts of my body. After about half an hour, I went outside and started walking along a winding path through the Northern California countryside. Each step hurt. My knees ached, and there was stabbing in one of my hips.

"Now what?" I muttered grimly. "Am I supposed to send more chi to my body?"

Then I paused—the resentment toward my body caught my attention. As I looked more closely, the resentment quickly gave way to a familiar grief. Why couldn't I just walk on this earth without feeling pain? Tears started flowing as I contacted the enormity of my frustration and longing. "I want to feel alive. I want to feel alive. Please. Please. May I feel fully alive." Naming it opened me to what was behind the longing. "I love life." Embedded in the grief, as always, was love. A voice inside me was repeating the words over and over, as a delicate, tingling warmth filled my heart.

PERMISSION TO LOVE LIFE

I had been holding back this love, holding back from fully engaging with life. It was a reaction to feeling betrayed by my body, a defense against more loss. But in my fear of being attached to health, I had not allowed myself to feel the truth—I love life. Qigong wasn't about fueling attachment, it was about fully embracing aliveness. At that moment I decided to stop holding back my love.

As I allowed the "I love life" feeling to be as full as it wanted to be, the "I" fell away. Even the notion of life fell away. What was left was an open radiant heart—as wide as the world.

This tender presence was loving everything: the soft streaks of pinks and grays in the sky, the smell of eucalyptus, the soaring vultures, the songbirds. It was loving the woman who was standing silently about two hundred feet away, also gazing at the colors of dawn. It was loving the changing painful and pleasurable sensations in this body. Now, sending chi to my knees made intuitive sense. It was awareness's natural and caring response to its creation. "I" wasn't loving life—awareness was loving life.

This experience led me to see and release a limiting unconscious belief that I had held for some time—a belief that the realm of formless awareness was more spiritual and valuable than the living forms of this world. This bias against the living world can be seen in many religious traditions. It emerges in some interpretations of the Buddha's teachings as an insistence on guarding ourselves against the pleasures of the senses—beauty, lovemaking, music, play. It emerges in the superior status of monks over nuns, in valuing monastic life over family and lay life and in the warnings against attachment in close personal relationships. I now believe this bias comes from fear and mistrust of life itself. For me, recognizing this in my own psyche was a gift.

We do not need to transcend the real world to realize our true nature and to live in freedom. In fact, we can't. We are aliveness *and* we are the formless presence that is its source; we are embodied emptiness. The more we love the world of form, the more we discover an undivided presence, empty of any sense of self or other. And the more we realize the open, formless space of awareness, the more unconditionally we love the changing shapes of creation. Refuge in awareness and refuge in aliveness (the truth of present moment) are ultimately inseparable. For me, the three refuges become one when I sense that I am awareness, loving its expression as aliveness.

The Heart Sutra from the Buddhist Mahayana texts tells us: "Form is emptiness, emptiness is also form. Emptiness is not other than form,

form is not other than emptiness." We can't separate the ocean from the waves. Our path is to realize the vast oceanness of our being, and to cherish the waves that appear on the surface.

HAPPY FOR NO REASON

During the final days of the retreat, my willingness to love life unfolded into a very deep, stable happiness. The happiness wasn't reliant on things being a certain way—my moods and physical comfort went up and down. I was happy for no reason. This unconditioned happiness or well-being is a flavor of awakening. It arises when we trust our essence as awareness, and know that this entire living world is part of our heart. Being happy for no reason gave me a kind of confidence or faith that no matter what happened, everything would be fine.

I returned home and jumped into a delicious daily ritual of meditation and qigong. During those first weeks I'd go to the river and scramble down through rocks and bushes to a secluded beach. Nourished by the sounds of rushing water, the firm sand and early morning air, I practiced presence in movement and stillness. You can probably imagine what came next. After I hurt my knee on the small incline down to the beach, I moved my practice to our deck. Some of the arm movements strained my neck so I had to minimize them. Then standing up started to strain my legs, so I began to practice in a chair. Then it rained for a week straight.

And yet it was all really okay. More than okay. One of those wet mornings as I was sitting, my mind became very quiet. My attention opened gently and fully to the changing flow of experience—aching, waves of tiredness, fleeting thoughts, sounds of rain. Continuing to pay attention, I felt the subtle sense of aliveness (chi energy) that pervades my whole body. This aliveness was not solid, it was spacious, a dance of light. The more I opened to this aliveness, the more I could sense an alert inner stillness, the background inner space of pure being. And the more I rested in that stillness, the more vividly alive the world became.

After about thirty minutes I opened my eyes and looked at the lush fern that hangs in our bedroom, at its delicacy and grace. I was in love with the fern, with the particularity of its form (how did this universe come up with ferns?), and with the vibrancy and light of its being. In that moment, the fern was as wondrous as any glorious scene by the river. I was awareness loving my creation. And I was happy for no reason. I didn't need to have things go my way. I was grateful for the capacity to enjoy life, just as it is.

When I guide meditations on saying yes to life, I sometimes invite students to sense just how deep this yes can go. We can decide to love life. We can consciously intend to love without holding back. Although we will continue to shut down, we can always start with exactly what we are experiencing and bring kindness to our resistance. We can say yes to our no. As we intentionally deepen our yes, we discover an unconditional acceptance—an open allowing awareness—that frees us. We are not dependent on life being a certain way; the openness of our presence itself gives rise to deep contentment.

Our habit is to think there is a particular cause for our happiness— the new green in early spring, the sound of a child's laugh, or the sensations of playing in the ocean waves. But what actually allows us to be happy is the background space of silent, allowing presence. Each time we meet aliveness with presence, presence intensifies, and *awareness senses itself.* The living green awakens us to this inner space of presence, the laugh to presence, the sparkle and splash to presence. We are inhabiting our wholeness and are happy being who we are.

The next time you are aware of well-being—of feeling happy or peaceful—see if you can sense the space of presence that has made room for the experience. As philosopher Friedrich Nietzsche wrote,

> For happiness, how little suffices for happiness! . . . The least thing precisely, the gentle thing, the lightest thing, a lizard's rustling, a breath, a whisk, an eye glance . . .

EMPTINESS DANCING

This world of form is empty awareness in its dynamic display. Trees, worms, buildings, computers, rockets, humans. Forms have no inherent abiding self. Like waves arising from the ocean, forms are a temporary constellation, and they are inherently connected to all other forms. We are each the activity of awareness—emptiness dancing.

I love this Zen phrase because it recognizes the inseparability of formlessness and form, of the emptiness of awareness and its expression in aliveness. Remembering that moods and actions all arise from empty awareness—that they are not owned by a self—frees us from reactivity. This makes us more responsible and better able to respond to our inner weather. As we become aware of awareness and awake in our senses, we enter the flow of life and can respond to whatever happens with care and grace.

When I talk about the selflessness and freedom of emptiness dancing, students sometimes wonder if this means turning away from personal growth and service. Is this just another way to devalue the life we are living here and now? If we find inner freedom, will we still be interested in healing ourselves and our world?

If this question comes up, I usually recall Mari, who started coming to meditation classes when she realized she was burning out. For more than a decade, Mari had worked as a fund-raiser for a large human rights group. But the political environment was increasingly nasty, rival factions were vying for control of the organization, donors were scarce, and she questioned the ethics of some of her colleagues. Mari had given notice and wanted nothing to do with politics or activism. She was done.

Over the next four years, Mari worked at a sporting-goods store, attended meditation classes and retreats, and found the time to reconnect with a former passion—bird-watching. After a meditation class she told me, "It's during those walks, during the early morning hours of watching and listening, that I come home to silence, to my own presence." In that attentive silence, Mari's love affair with birds deepened. "They are not something outside of me," she told me, "they are part of my inner landscape." As she grew more alarmed about habitat loss, Mari realized her activist life was not over.

We explored this together in a counseling session, and Mari began to trust that this time around things would be different. She agreed to fund-raise for an environmental group, knowing that there would

be conflicting egos within this organization too. She would inevitably have bouts of discouragement, but Mari had found refuge.
She could reconnect with the awareness that gives rise to birds and
trees, to egos and discouragement, to the entire play of life. She could
remember the wisdom of emptiness dancing and serve this imperfect
world.

Spiritual teacher Adyashanti, who wrote a book called *Emptiness Dancing*, suggests that as we move through the day, we ask: "How is emptiness
or awareness experiencing this (eating, walking outside, showering, talking)?" I also like to ask myself, "How is this empty, awake heart experiencing what's happening?" It is illuminating to step out of our story of
self and receive sensations and feelings and sounds from the perspective
of heart and awareness. We are not in opposition to anything, not resisting or evaluating anything. Life flows through us.

When I pay attention like this, I'm not at all removed from life.
Rather, without the self-focus I become part of the flow of aliveness. Just
as the river knows how to flow around rocks, I can respond intuitively to
life's unfolding. I'm more spontaneous in the moment, more naturally
clear and caring in my response to what's around me. I've seen this with
others too. Whether we are serving or savoring, when there's an awareness of emptiness dancing, we become wholehearted in how we live.
This is true even in the face of inevitable loss.

A few years ago, I read a memorable story about violinist Itzhak
Perlman. Perlman had polio when he was a young child, and at each
of his performances he makes a slow entrance on crutches, sits down,
unclasps the braces on his legs, and then prepares to play. He did this
as usual at a 1995 performance at Lincoln Center in New York. On
this occasion, however, he'd only played the first few bars when one
of the strings on his violin broke. The whole audience could hear the
crack when it snapped. What will happen next? they wondered. Will he
have to put on his braces, make his way across the stage, find another
violin?

He sat still, closed his eyes, and paused. Then he signaled for the
conductor to begin again. Perlman reentered the concerto, playing with
an unimaginable passion, power, and purity. Perhaps some of those
watching could sense him modulating, changing, reconfiguring the piece

in his head, so deep was his immersion in creating. When he finished there was an awed silence. Then came the outburst of applause, as people rose and cheered from every corner of the hall.

Perlman smiled, wiped the sweat from his brow, and raised his bow to quiet the crowd. Then he spoke, not boastfully, but in a quiet, pensive, reverent tone. "You know, sometimes it is the artist's task to find out how much music you can still make with what you have left."

Recently I was disappointed to learn that this story has been called into question. But the message stays with me. We weigh down our lives with memories of how it used to be and fears of what we have yet to lose. But when we surrender into the living moment, we, like Perlman, become emptiness dancing—a part of the creative flow. We respond with a tender heart to our world's pain and beauty. We make music with what we have left.

A HEART THAT IS READY FOR ANYTHING

When the Buddha was dying, he gave a final message to his beloved attendant Ananda, and to generations to come: *"Be a lamp unto yourself, be a refuge to yourself. Take yourself to no external refuge."*

What did he mean? Our ultimate refuge is none other than our own being. There is a light of awareness that shines through each of us and guides us home. We are never separated from this luminous awareness, any more than waves are separated from ocean. Even when we feel most ashamed or lonely, reactive or confused, we are never actually apart from the awakened state of our heart-mind.

This is a powerful and beautiful teaching. All of us ordinary humans have this essential wakefulness; this open, loving awareness is our deepest nature. We don't need to get somewhere or change ourselves—our true refuge is what we are. Trusting this opens us to the blessings of freedom.

Buddhist monk Sayadaw U Pandita describes these blessings in a wonderful way: *a heart that is ready for anything.* When we trust we are the ocean, we are not afraid of the waves. We have confidence that whatever arises is workable. We don't have to lose our life in preparation. We don't have to defend against what is next. We are free to live fully what is here, and to respond wisely.

You might ask yourself: "Can I imagine what it would be like, in this moment, to have a heart that is ready for anything?"

If our hearts are ready for anything, we can open to our inevitable losses, and to the depths of our sorrow. We can grieve our lost loves, our lost youth, our lost health, our lost capacities. This is part of our humanness, part of the expression of our love for life. As we bring a courageous presence to the truth of loss, we stay available to the immeasurable ways love springs forth in our life.

If our hearts are ready for anything, we will spontaneously reach out when others are hurting. Living in an ethical way can attune us to the pain and needs of others, but when our hearts are open and awake, we care instinctively. This caring is unconditional—it extends outward and inward wherever there is fear and suffering.

If our hearts are ready for anything, we are free to be ourselves. There's room for the wildness of our animal selves, for passion and play. There's room for our human selves, for intimacy and understanding, creativity and productivity. There's room for spirit, for the light of awareness to suffuse our moments. The Tibetans describe this confidence to be who we are as "the lion's roar."

If our hearts are ready for anything, we are touched by the beauty and poetry and mystery that fill our world. When Munindra Ji, a vipassana meditation teacher, was asked why he practiced, his response was, "So I will see the tiny purple flowers by the side of the road as I walk to town each day." Our undefended heart can fall in love with life over and over every day. We become children of wonder, grateful to be walking on earth, grateful to belong with one another and to all of creation. We find our true refuge in every moment, in every breath. We are happy for no reason.

⸺∞⸺

My prayer is that we trust the beauty of our hearts and awareness. Holding hands, may we help to bring healing and freedom to our world.

May all beings realize their essence as loving awareness.
May all beings live their lives from this awakened heart.
May all beings be happy.
May all beings touch great, natural peace.
May there be peace on earth, peace everywhere.
May all beings awaken and be free.

Guided Reflection: Prayer of Aspiration

The key to spiritual awakening is remembering—being in touch with what your heart most cares about. There are two classical prayers of aspiration in the Buddhist tradition that help us remember.

———— ∞ ————

- May whatever circumstances arise in my life—the great difficulties, the good fortune and joy—serve to awaken my heart and mind.

Bring to mind whatever you are encountering right now in your life. As you deepen your attention to this situation, can you imagine how it might help call forth your natural love and wisdom?

- May this life be of benefit to all beings everywhere.

Consider how your life is inextricably woven with the entire natural world. Can you sense that as you become increasingly open and kind, the ripples extend endlessly in all directions?

Guided Reflection: Finding True Refuge

The three facets of true refuge—awareness, truth, and love—come alive as we dedicate our presence to them. This simple reflection will give you increasing access to both the outer and inner refuges first introduced in chapter 4. Ultimately, it is an invitation to rest your heart in what is true, the purity and radiance of your own essence. I've placed this meditation at the end of this book, as you have now journeyed through each of the gateways. Taken together, they reveal the one taste of freedom inherent to all paths of awakening.

You will be mentally reciting the three phrases—I take refuge in awareness; I take refuge in truth; I take refuge in love—and after each, reflecting on what is vital and meaningful about the particular refuge. Instead of awareness-truth-love, you might use the Sanskrit words *Buddha* (or Buddha nature)-*dharma-sangha*.

In my own practice I use the classic Buddhist order (above) for the refuges. Feel free to adapt this reflection—the sequence and language—in whatever way most resonates for you. Let this practice be a fresh and creative ritual, one that aligns your life with what most matters.

———∞———

Now begin the first recitation, mentally whispering I take refuge in awareness.

As you offer these words, you might feel a resonance with a human being or spiritual figure who expresses the qualities of enlightened awareness—of luminosity, openness, love. Can you imagine that same presence illuminating your being? Or perhaps it is more natural to directly sense the awakened presence that lives within you. You might simply ask yourself, "Is awareness (or consciousness) here?" What is it like to notice the presence of awareness? How does your mind experience the space of awareness? Your body? Your heart? What happens as you let go into this refuge of awareness? What happens as you rest your heart in what is true?

Now begin mentally repeating the phrase I take refuge in truth.

As you offer these words, take a moment to recall what is precious to you about the spiritual path—about meditation practice and teachings, about living a compassionate life. This is the outer expression of a path of truth. With this in your awareness, open without resistance to the changing flow of your moment-to-moment experience. Coming into the center of now, be aware of the sounds, feelings, and sensations that are arising and passing. What is the experience of opening to life, just as it is? What happens as you let go into this refuge of truth? What happens as you rest your heart in what is true?

Now turn to the phrase I take refuge in love.

As you offer these words, notice what they mean to you. Do you feel a sense of treasuring and valuing your family and friends? Does it bring up a yearning for more belonging? Allow a particular friend or loved one to come to mind, and as you sense that person's goodness and dearness, notice the response of your heart. Is there warmth? Tenderness? Openness? Now let go of any idea of "other," and open directly to the loving itself. Notice what happens as you relax and be that *loving. What happens as you fully inhabit this refuge of love? What happens as you rest your heart in what is true?*

—◦◦◦—

You can "take refuge" in this way as part of your regular meditation practice, or at any time on its own. If you approach this practice each time with freshness and curiosity, it will continue to reveal the profound depths of your being. Sometimes you may spend many minutes reflecting on each refuge, and at other times, just a brief contact will awaken you to an open and tender presence.

—ooo—

In the name of daybreak
And the eyelids of morning
And the wayfaring moon
And the night when it departs,

I swear I will not dishonor
My soul with hatred,
But offer myself humbly
As a guardian of nature,
As a healer of misery,
As a messenger of wonder,
As an architect of peace.

In the name of the sun and its mirrors . . .
And the uttermost night . . .
And the crowning seasons
Of the firefly and the apple,

I will honor all life
—wherever and in whatever form
It may dwell—on Earth my home,
and in the mansions of the stars.

—DIANE ACKERMAN, "SCHOOL PRAYER"

ACKNOWLEDGMENTS

My extended community has been a cherished source of refuge through this journey of writing:

It has been my great good fortune to have Toni Burbank—editor par excellence and now dear friend—keeping me company in the unfolding of this book. Her understanding of the human heart and brilliance in the writer's craft lent invaluable editing and mentoring throughout.

I benefited from the bright talent of Barbara Gates in the initial shaping and drafting of the first chapters, and then, still the early days, the astute commentary of Beth Rashbaum, my first editor at Random House. Angela Polidoro, again from Random House, offered her great attentiveness, clarity, and care to bring *True Refuge* to near readiness, and, in the final hour, executive editor Marnie Cochran stepped in with her wonderful intelligence, know-how, and energy to help deliver the book to the world.

A deep thanks to my agent, Anne Edelstein, for the warmth, enthusiasm, and sage guidance that has made her such a trusted, wonderful ally and friend through the years.

I've been blessed with a circle of dear ones who reviewed the manuscript, offering encouragement that refreshed my spirits and suggestions that helped simplify and refine my writing. Much gratitude to Jack Kornfield, Barbara Graham, Stephen Josephs, Darshan Brach, and Nancy Brach.

Supporting me throughout, my assistant, Janet Merrick, has taken care of every loose end, from making copies to responding to e-mails to seeking permissions. I have great appreciation for her generous and loving service. More recently, Cindy Frei has joined the team, bringing her extraordinary energy, brightness, and competency in media, marketing, and video production. And, in the final months, Tim Kenney offered his abundant creative talents to designing *True Refuge*'s jacket and website page.

To my sangha in the D.C. area and beyond—fellow teachers, students, and friends on the spiritual path—my deep appreciation for sharing your stories and your hearts, for teaching me, and for bringing your sincerity and dedication to the practices of presence.

A great bow of love and gratitude to my teachers, past and present. These bodhisattvas have inspired me with their dedication to realizing truth, embodying love, and serving the awakening of all beings.

To Cheylah, Hakuna (now deceased), and Dandy (also gone)—who took me for walks, cheered me with wagging tails, and showered me with unbounded affection—you have my wishes for ample strokes and treats and play, here and hereafter.

PERMISSIONS

———— ⦵⦵⦵ ————

RESOURCES

—⬤⬤⬤—

For information about Tara Brach's teaching schedule please go to her website: www.tarabrach.com.

For information about the Insight Meditation Community of Washington: www.imcw.org.

Book: *Radical Acceptance: Embracing Your Life with the Heart of a Buddha* (Bantam, 2003)

Audio Talks: http://www.tarabrach.com/audiodharma.html

Video Talks: http://www.tarabrach.com/video.html

Audio CDs and Downloads: http://www.tarabrach.com/products.html

Finding True Refuge (web series): Stories of intimate journeys into meditation: www.tarabrach.com/findingtruerefuge/

YouTube Channel: http://www.youtube.com/tarabrach

Facebook Page: http://www.facebook.com/tarabrach

Twitter Page: http://www.twitter.com/tarabrach

Blog: http://blog.tarabrach.com/

Pinterest: http://pinterest.com/tarabrach

ABOUT THE AUTHOR

————⟨∞⟩————

TARA BRACH, PH.D., is a clinical psychologist, lecturer, and popular teacher of Buddhist mindfulness (vipassana) meditation.

She is the founder and senior teacher of the Insight Meditation Community of Washington, D.C., and teaches meditation at centers throughout the United States including Spirit Rock, Omega Institute, Kripalu Center, and the Smithsonian Institute. Dr. Brach has offered speeches and workshops for mental health practitioners at numerous professional conferences. These, along with more than five hundred audio talks and ninety videos, address the value of meditation in relieving emotional suffering and serving spiritual awakening. Dr. Brach is the author of *Radical Acceptance: Embracing Your Life with the Heart of a Buddha* (Bantam, 2003). She lives in Great Falls, Virginia, with her husband, Jonathan, her mother, Nancy, and their three dogs.

ABOUT THE TYPE

This book was set in Centaur, a typeface designed by the American typographer Bruce Rogers in 1929. Centaur was a typeface that Rogers adapted from the fifteenth-century type of Nicolas Jenson and modified in 1948 for a cutting by the Monotype Corporation.